PHONOLOGICAL VARIATION AND CHANGE IN THE DIALECT OF CHARLESTON, SOUTH CAROLINA

PHONOLOGICAL VARIATION AND CHANGE IN THE DIALECT OF CHARLESTON, SOUTH CAROLINA

MACIEJ BARANOWSKI

University of Manchester

Publication of the
American Dialect Society

•

Number 92

•

*Published by Duke University Press
for the American Dialect Society*

Supplement to American Speech, *Volume 82*

PUBLICATION OF THE AMERICAN DIALECT SOCIETY

Editor: ROBERT BAYLEY, *University of California, Davis*
Managing Editor: CHARLES E. CARSON, *Duke University*

Number 92
Copyright 2007
American Dialect Society
ISBN: 978-0-8223-6692-8

Library of Congress Cataloging-in-Publication Data

Baranowski, Maciej.
   Phonological variation and change in the dialect of Charleston, South
Carolina / Maciej Baranowski
       p. cm. — (Publication of the American Dialect Society ; no. 92)
   Includes bibliographical references.
   ISBN-13: 978-0-8223-6692-8 (cloth : alk. paper)
       1. English language—Dialects—South Carolina—Charleston.
   2. Americanisms—South Carolina—Charleston. 3. English language—
   Variation—South Carolina—Charleston. 4. Charleston (S.C.)—Lan-
   guages. I. American Dialect Society. II. Title.
PE2927.C53B37 2007
427'.973–dc22   2007024379

British Library Cataloguing-in-Publication Data available

CONTENTS

v

FOREWORD

WILLIAM LABOV, *University of Pennsylvania*

Maciej Baranowski's splendid study of the Charleston dialect is the first of what I hope will be a long series of explorations that build upon *The Atlas of North American English* (*ANAE* 2006). He was himself a major contributor to the atlas; a good number of the 439 acoustic analyses of vowel systems were his doing. The speed and accuracy he developed undoubtedly played a role in developing the rich and revealing displays of Charleston vowel systems found throughout this monograph. More importantly, Baranowski uses the analytic framework of the *ANAE* to discover new and striking findings on the transformation of Charleston English in the second half of the twentieth century.

The *ANAE* is not a study of community variation, since the fundamental plan of the telephone survey was to accept the speech of the first two native speakers encountered as representative of the community (up to six for the biggest cities). This allowed us to view the geographic dispersion of the various phonological systems that defined American dialects and set the stage for more detailed studies. *ANAE*'s view of Charleston's population of 97,000 is based on five speakers (with acoustic analyses of the second, third, and fifth):

1. Evan D., 54, a general manager in communication;
2. Peggy C., 40, who worked from home as a babysitter, word processor, cleaner, and fund-raiser;
3. Vickie D., 38, a data processor at a bank;
4. Maxine D., 34, an operating room nurse; and
5. Nora D., 12, a junior high school student whose father was a teacher.

The age range is concentrated in the 30–40 group (our policy was to obtain at least one interview with a woman in the 20–24 range), and the social class range in the lower-middle class, with one upper-middle-class speaker. The results of our study showed no trace of the traditional Charleston dialect described by O'Cain (1972) or the Beaufort, South Carolina, dialect I had recorded in an exploratory study in 1965. At the same time, these five speakers showed Charleston to be outside the general Southern dialect area on a number of phonological criteria. Since there were no other major cities in our sample like Charleston, we could not reinforce our findings by a general areal configuration. When Baranowski began his wide-ranging sociolinguistic study of Charleston, I was particularly interested in finding out whether our small sample had led us astray or whether we had actually succeeded in capturing the unique status of this city.

The fieldwork for Baranowski's study is an extraordinary accomplishment. The 100 speakers interviewed include a social class sample that ranges from 24 working-class to 20 upper-class speakers, with an age range from 8 to 90. The systematic way in which the sample was constructed, as described in chapter 3, provides a model that I hope can be followed in future studies of major cities. After a careful study of U.S. Census data and other sources, four areas of the city were selected and within each area, residents were randomly selected. Refusal rates were less than 10%. The resulting sample yielded a dramatic view of linguistic change and variation on a large scale.

First of all, I was pleased to see that our small sample of five had not misled us. No monophthongization of /ay/, the defining feature of the South, appeared in this larger study of Charleston, and no trace of the complex rotations of the Southern Shift that followed this initial sound change. The *ANAE* did find the merger of /i/ and /e/ before nasals, as in *pin* and *pen*, which had expanded elsewhere beyond the South, and Baranowski confirmed that this was typical of the age and class of the *ANAE* sample.

A confirmation of the *ANAE* findings plays only a small part in the rich and exciting discoveries to be found in this book. It is a study of a linguistic revolution, in which the traditional dialect of the city was entirely overthrown in favor of a very different type of linguistic system. I do not know of any other linguistic study which shows such rapid and thorough reorganization. The importation of constricted /r/ to New York City affected only careful speech for the largest part of the population and has since advanced only slowly, with only slight effects on the rest of the vowel system. At about the same time—directly after World War II—Charleston shifted from complete *r*-lessness to consistent *r*-fulness. The *ANAE* shows that this happened throughout the South, but only in Charleston was it accompanied by the radical readjustment of the vowel system as a whole.

A striking exemplar of this change was the shift from monoph-thongal and ingliding [oːə] in *go* and *boat* to a centralized nucleus with a back upglide [əʊ], along with the loss of ingliding [eːə] for the long mid front vowel. The ingliding of the long mid front and back vowels in *say* and *go* was the most distinctive part of the tra-ditional Charleston dialect, but also the most confusing and most open to misunderstanding. American English in general makes a close association between ingliding and short vowels, so that when such a phonetic pattern appears in a long vowel, it is frequently misunderstood. This has been reported occasionally in the North Central states, but in Charleston ingliding was the norm. Chap-ter 12 reports some revealing accounts of the misunderstanding of Charleston speech. The most remarkable incident concerns a Charlestonian aviator in World War II who panicked the ground forces in his approach: his pronunciation of *eighty-eight* was mistak-en for a Japanese accent.

The most extraordinary fact about this reorganization is that it was led by the same speakers who were the chief exponents of the earlier system—the upper class. It seems most likely that this aspect of Baranowski's analysis will draw the lion's share of attention from readers of this volume. Until now, the only systematic study of up-per-class speech has been the interviews that Kroch carried out in the late 1970s, incorporated into the study of linguistic change and variation in Philadelphia (Kroch 1996; Labov 2001). Baranowski provides a study of this group, their speech, their social attitudes, and their social connections outside of Charleston (reported in some detail in the final chapter).

Baranowski's portrait of the upper class is insightful and thor-ough. He makes a convincing case for Gullah influence on the for-mation of the traditional dialect, through the early effect of Gullah caretakers on upper-class children. He also argues that the shift away from the local dialect to a non-Southern phonology is motivated by the dense web of social connections of Charlestonians to other areas outside of the South. A major focus of his discussion is the fact that the linguistic changes in Charleston are not led by a centrally located group, the upper working class or lower middle class, but plainly initiated by a group whose status is recognized by everyone as the highest in the community. Thus, the Charleston events do not conform to the general argument for the curvilinear pattern of linguistic change. At the end, Baranowski interprets this as a case of "change from above," in which the linguistic pattern is imported from outside the community system.

Among the innovations of the upper class, the most striking is the reversal of the traditional merger of /ihr/ and /ehr/, as in *fear* and *fair*. The ongoing merger of these two classes in New Zealand has been a major focus of attention recently (Gordon and Maclaglan 1989; Holmes and Bell 1992; Maclagan and Gordon 1996; Gordon et al. 2004; Hay, Warren, and Drager 2006). Baranowski's clear account of the reversal of the merger is startling, given the strong arguments for the irreversibility of mergers (Garde 1961; Labov 1994). He connects this phenomenon with the introduction of constricted [r] in these words, as well as the unusual degree of public awareness of the merger.

Baranowski makes a strong case for the systematicity and connectedness of the language changes in Charleston. The correlations between linguistic variables displayed in chapter 12 are very high, and the relation between the development of *r*-pronunciation and vowel changes is a recurrent theme. This is made even more evident in the superposition of S-shaped curves in the series of diagrams in that chapter, along with linear transformations by logistic regression. If all of the linguistic changes followed the same pattern in age and social class, this would be less indicative of connections dictated by internal linguistic relations and more motivated by external forces like those generated during World War II. However, it appears that there are a pair of changes that spread through the community at a later time. One of these, the low back merger of /o/ and /oh/, as in *cot* and *caught*, is not connected with the importation of /r/ (figure 12.8). On the other hand, the merger of *merry* and *marry* is. Therefore, the development of *r*-pronunciation only partially motivates the organization of Charleston changes, and there is still more to be done in explaining the sequence of sound changes that we observe here and the interaction of linguistic and social forces.

Charlestonians think that they have lost their Southern accent and speak like "Northerners." But Baranowski points out that they have not acquired anything resembling the dialects of the North. Instead, they have acquired the paradigmatic pattern of the Southeastern super-region, with strong fronting of /ow/ and /aw/, the nasal short-*a* pattern, and an incipient low back merger. Thus, the modern Charleston dialect is close to that of the Midland city of Columbus, Ohio. This is not due to any direct connection between Charleston and Columbus. Rather, the reorganization of North American regional dialects in the Midland has a linguistic logic which leads to the nasal short-*a* pattern as a default system and a generalized fronting of the nuclei of back upgliding vowels. Since Charleston /oh/ has never had the back upglide which protects it from merger with /o/, the collapse of these categories follows the pattern found throughout the marginal areas of the South.

The array of linguistic and social events in this monograph are truly extraordinary. Though studies of small groups in face-to-face interaction may add to our understanding of how change and variation is effected, we need this overview across gender, class, and age to understand the larger forces that are operating on linguistic systems.

ACKNOWLEDGMENTS

I would first like to thank my parents for their continued and unconditional support, without which this book would not have been possible.

I am greatly indebted to William Labov, who has guided me throughout this project and who has been a constant source of inspiration, enthusiasm, and encouragement since the day I arrived at Penn; working with him has been the greatest adventure of my life. I would also like to thank Gene Buckley and Gillian Sankoff for being extraordinary teachers and for their many insights. I have benefited immensely from working with them in various capacities during my linguistics career. Tony Kroch has been another important influence on my thinking about language change that I would like to acknowledge.

A special thanks goes to my friend Sherry Ash for her unflinching support over the years; without her this book would never have been written. Sherry has kindly read and commented on large parts of it. I would also like to express my gratitude to Corky Feagin for her advice and many insightful comments and to Walt Wolfram for his support during my fieldwork travels.

I am also grateful to my friends at Penn and elsewhere for their useful comments, advice, and support: Jeff Conn, Kathy Dean, Aaron Dinkin, Suzanne Evans Wagner, Damien Hall, Uri Horesh, Alan Lee, Christine Mallinson, Kimiko Nakanishi, Bill Poser, JC Smith, Erik Thomas, Tracey Weldon, and Tonya Wolford. I would like to express my thanks to the two anonymous reviewers for their thorough comments and many helpful suggestions; to the editor of the series, Robert Bayley, for steering me through this project; and to Charles Carson of Duke University Press for his editorial assistance. I would also like to thank my colleagues at the School

of Languages, Linguistics, and Cultures at the University of Manchester for their support during the final stages of the writing of
this book.

Finally, I wish to thank the people of Charleston for making it
the great city that it is, for their hospitality, and for their fascinating
speech patterns.

PHONETIC SYMBOLS

The vowel notation used in this book follows the conventions of *The Atlas of North American English* (*ANAE* 2006, chap. 2). It is essentially a phonemic notation representing the historical vowel classes of English at a point after the Great Vowel Shift. It represents an initial position from which all dialects of American English can be derived through a series of sound changes such as mergers and chain shifts. Short vowels are represented by a single symbol, whereas long vowels are represented by two symbols, corresponding to the three subsystems of long vowels in American English: front upgliding, back upgliding, and ingliding vowels. The second element in this binary notation represents the direction of the glide: /y/, as in /ay/ (*bite*), for front upglides; /w/, as in /aw/ (*bout*), for back up-

	SHORT		LONG					
			Upgliding				Ingliding	
	front	back	Front upgliding		Back upgliding			
Nucleus	front	back	front	back	front	back	unrounded	rounded
High	/i/ *bit*	/u/ *put*	/iy/ *beat*		/iw/ *suit*	/uw/ *boot*		
Mid	/e/ *bet*	/ʌ/ *but*	/ey/ *bait*	/oy/ *boy*		/ow/ *boat*		/oh/ *bought*
Low	/æ/ *bat*	/o/ *cot*		/ay/ *bite*		/aw/ *bout*	/ah/ *balm*	

| | V + /r/ | |
Nucleus	front	back
High	/ihr/ *fear*	
Mid	/ehr/ *fair*	/ohr/ *four*
Low		/ɔhr/ *for*

glides; and /h/, as in /oh/ (*bought*), for inglides. This is not merely another way of identifying vowel phonemes akin to a system of key words, such as the one proposed by Wells (1982). The system of notation used in the *ANAE* emphasizes the structural connectedness of vowels belonging to the same subsystem and identifies them as such. This helps us see more easily the different patterns of change involving vowels belonging to different subsystems, such as front upgliding versus back upgliding.

While a system of key words is sometimes said to be easier for students to understand and use, it is arguably quite the opposite. It is much easier, for instance, to see the connection between the three front upgliding vowels involved in the Southern Shift when they are represented as /iy/, /ey/, and /ay/, rather than as FLEECE, FACE, and PRICE. Similarly, students are less likely to be surprised to see the vowels of GOOSE, GOAT, and MOUTH behaving in the same way when the parallelism among them is made explicit in their representation as /uw/, /ow/, and /aw/. Consequently, the *ANAE* notational system not only identifies the phonemes, but can also remind us of the structural relations between sounds. In this way, it can aid us in our analysis of the changes involving these sounds.

1. CHARLESTON:
A HISTORICAL OVERVIEW

THE HISTORY OF ENGLISH in Charleston begins in 1670, with the landing of the first English and Irish settlers on the western bank of the Ashley River, five miles from the ocean. They called the area Albemarle Point, now known as Charles Towne Landing, and named the settlement Charles Town in honor of King Charles II of England. Ten years later the settlement was moved to the peninsula between the Cooper and Ashley rivers and formed what is now the historic part of Charleston.

The first settlers were predominantly English, and while most of them probably came from the south of England (McDavid 1948), their exact origins in Britain are not entirely clear. Some of the very first settlers were Irish, and from the very beginning the Irish played an important role in the new community; some of the oldest Charleston names, such as the Lynches and the Rutledges, were originally Irish. Two of the early governors were Irish, one in 1684 and another one in 1700.

Another very influential group were the settlers who had come from the West Indies, most of them from Barbados. Some historians argue that Charleston, and South Carolina in general, was in a way a colony of Barbados, also a colony, which had become overpopulated. The Barbadian heritage can be seen in the city's architecture—Charleston's single house with piazzas was very similar to a typical Barbadian house—as well as in the original judicial system adopted from a Barbadian act, and early forms of government, military organization, and election methods (Fraser 1989, 5; Rosen 1992, 15). In addition, some features of Charleston's traditional dialect, such as the ingliding long mid vowels, as in *take* and *goat*, closely resemble those found in West Indian English.

French Huguenots were another sizable group of early settlers in Charleston. They first arrived in the 1680s and were quickly assimilated into Charleston society; by the late 1690s they were granted full citizenship rights and were allowed to own land provided they pledged allegiance to the King (Rosen 1992, 14). Well-known

1

Charleston names of Huguenot origin include the Legares, the Laurens, and the Ravenels.

Other European ethnic groups which settled in Charleston in the eighteenth century included the Dutch, Sephardic Jews, and the Scots, who poured into Charleston after the union of England and Scotland in 1707 (Rogers 1969, 5).

African slaves did not start coming in large numbers until the 1690s (although some of the very first slaves actually came from the West Indies), but by 1720 they formed the majority of the population. This was the case for the whole of South Carolina: in 1708 there were 4,080 whites and 4,100 African slaves in the colony (O'Cain 1972, 11). Their numbers continued to grow, and eighteenth-century Charleston became a major American slave port. The number of African slaves in the city continued to be equal to or slightly higher than that of whites until 1850 (Rogers 1969, 141).

The economy of early Charles Town was based on trade, mainly with England and the West Indies. It began with deerskins and furs from the local Indians, shipped to England, and often Indians themselves, traded in the West Indies for rum, sugar, and trinkets (Fraser 1989, 6). Then by the 1730s the cultivation of rice had gained importance, soon followed by indigo, introduced in the 1740s. The two crops quickly become the basis of Charleston's economy. This led to the transition from a merchant to a planter economy for South Carolina, with some of the merchants becoming great planters, "for the ideal both in the 18th century England and America was the English country gentleman" (Rosen 1992, 23). Rice and indigo planting was so successful that the planters of South Carolina became the wealthiest people in the American colonies. The crops were shipped through Charleston, which developed into a great colonial port.

By the time of the Revolutionary War, South Carolina was one of the richest colonies, with a strong governing class of merchants and planters leading the fight for independence from England. There were four Charlestonians in Philadelphia in 1787 helping to draft the Constitution of the United States: Pierce Butler, Charles Pinckney, Charles Cotesworth Pinckney, and John Rutledge. The end of the eighteenth century saw the culmination of Charleston's growth in wealth: the 1790s were the city's high point in prosperity and luxury, and at the beginning of the nineteenth century Charleston was among the five largest cities in the United States. At the same time, the region had an extensive underclass of slaves who had been brought in large numbers to provide labor for the plantations and who constituted the workforce of its economic base.

Eighteen-century Charleston was an outward-looking and cosmopolitan city, with religious tolerance and strong contacts with other cultural and economic centers of the Atlantic coast, particularly New York, and with England: it was customary for the wealthiest Charlestonians to send their children to schools in England before the Revolutionary War. Those connections with the outside world were in fact stronger than those with the rest of South Carolina, a region termed "the Upcountry," which had grown resentful of the influence of Charleston's ruling elite. The opposition came "from the lesser folks within the city or from the backcountry, particularly that part above the fall line" (Rogers 1969, 118). The growing tensions between Charleston and the Upcountry resulted in the decision by South Carolina legislators to move the capital inland in 1786, to a place which was to be named Columbia. Some Charlestonians, however, refused to acknowledge the new capital for years (Fraser 1989, 176).

Toward the end of the eighteenth century, the price of rice had fallen low enough to make it unprofitable, though it was soon replaced by cotton, which contributed to the city's growth in the early nineteenth century. The 1820s mark the beginning of the economic decline of South Carolina and Charleston, precipitated by a worldwide collapse of cotton prices in 1819 but also caused in part by the growing prosperity of the North, which no longer needed to rely on economic support from the South. In addition, the opening of the Erie Canal in 1825 resulted in the growing importance of New York City as a commercial port. This coincided with the rise of Alabama and Mississippi as the main providers of cotton, undermining Charleston's position further. As Rogers (1969, 139) comments, "She had been *the* rice port but she had never been *the* cotton port."

Though slaves were bought and sold in South Carolina until the Civil War, foreign slave trade ended in 1808, which essentially cut the supply of labor for the economic base of the region. Slavery was becoming a source of growing tension between the South and the North. In the 1820s free blacks were no longer allowed to enter South Carolina, not even on ships from New England or Britain, which resulted in a further decline of commerce in Charleston (Rogers 1969, 145). In contrast to the heyday of the late eighteenth century, pre–Civil War Charleston was becoming an increasingly inward-looking and closed society.

Unhappy with restrictions over free trade and the call for the abolition of slavery that led to the Civil War, South Carolina became the first Southern state to secede from the Union. The Civil War began with the firing on Fort Sumter in Charleston Harbor on April 12, 1861. The city was devastated during the Civil War, and its economy suffered for many years afterward. There were some signs of recovery by the 1870s, with phosphate becoming an important commodity and cotton picking up, though that was not enough to stop the city's decline, exacerbated further by a dramatic slump in port business after the Civil War. A series of natural disasters at the end of the nineteenth century did not help matters: a cyclone in 1885, an earthquake in 1886, and a major hurricane in 1893 all contributed to the economic woes of the populace. As a result, poverty was rife in Charleston until World War II.

The Reconstruction years were a period of dramatic social change in Charleston and in the rest of the South, marked by violence and corruption. There were some 400,000 freed blacks in South Carolina, some of whom moved to Charleston immediately after the end of the war. As a result, in 1870 there were 4,000 more blacks than whites in the city (Rosen 1992, 123). The blacks were intent on taking over the government, whereas the whites still believed that slavery was essentially right. This led to increased tensions between the two groups and resulted in race riots in 1865, 1866, and 1876.

Blacks were allowed to vote for the first time in 1867 as part of the Reconstruction reforms, enacted in the South Carolina constitution of 1868, which outlawed segregation, provided for universal male suffrage, and called for a free public school system. The Reconstruction government lasted only until 1876, which marks the beginning of less violent times for South Carolina and for Charleston under Governor Wade Hampton.

The end of the Reconstruction era also marks the start of racial segregation in Charleston, which intensified at the beginning the twentieth century. In the nineteenth century there was little residential segregation, with many blacks continuing to live in the back quarters of whites' houses in the historic downtown section south of Broad Street up to the 1930s (Rogers 1969, 71; Rosen 1992, 149). There was religious segregation, however, as many black Charlestonians left white churches and formed their own congregations, which have since served as central social institutions for the black community. Segregation became institutionalized in South Carolina in 1889 with the repeal of the state civil rights law passed during Reconstruction. It could thereafter be seen in schools, hotels, restaurants, railroads, streetcars, ferries, and playgrounds, as well as in politics. This was followed by the move of black Charlestonians north, beginning in the 1940s, out of the area south of Broad, and north out of Charleston and South Carolina toward the industrial cities of the North.

The turn of the twentieth century saw growing tensions between Charleston and the rest of the state, the Upcountry, which was resentful of the disproportionate political influence of prominent Charlestonians in state affairs. The backlash resulted in no Charlestonian being elected governor of South Carolina between 1865 and 1938 (Rosen 1992, 138). The disagreements also manifested themselves in Charleston's failure to enforce fully the state monopoly on the sale of alcoholic beverages imposed by South Carolina in 1893. Charlestonians continued to purchase alcohol at private establishments, referred to as "blind tigers," and to enjoy gambling despite the vice laws enacted by the state. This no doubt helped Charleston earn its reputation for hedonism, which Charlestonians have never made an effort to repudiate.

The end of the nineteenth century was a period of further decline for Charleston as a trading post. The volume of trade through the port was at $29.5 million in 1900, representing less than 1% of the total U.S. export trade, as compared with $98.5 million a decade earlier. Charleston's population was also declining in comparison with other American cities: it was the 26th largest urban center in 1870, 53rd in 1890, and 91st by 1910 (Fraser 1989, 327–28).

The creation of a U.S. Naval Station in Charleston in 1901 marked the beginning of the opening of Charleston to the outside world, resulting in significant changes to its character. Rosen (1992, 138) describes the opening of the navy yard as "the most important economic decision in the history of Charleston." The yard became the largest employer in the city, and its opening was followed by an influx of people into the area from both the Upcountry and other areas of the South. World War I provided an additional economic stimulus: while the navy yard was employing 1,240 workers at the outset of the war in 1914, the number jumped to 5,000 when the United States entered the war in 1917 (Fraser 1989, 359–61).

This coincided with the long-awaited construction of railroads into Charleston during the first term of Governor John P. Grace between 1911 and 1915. Grace was also instrumental in modernizing the docks and substantially expanding the port of Charleston during his second term between 1919 and 1923 (Rosen 1992, 140). Around the same time, Charleston's connections with the surrounding areas improved greatly with the construction of a bridge across the Ashley River in 1926 and another one across the Cooper River in 1929, for the first time connecting Charleston with Mount Pleasant, Sullivan's Island, and Isle of Palms, which eventually became part of the same metropolitan area. In addition, the opening of a municipal airport in 1929 made travel into and out of Charleston even easier. In the 1920s tourism became an important industry: by the end of the decade over 47,000 tourists were visiting the city every year (Fraser 1989, 374); that number grew to more than 300,000 in 1939 (Fraser 1989, 386).

The population of Charleston County rose from 101,000 to around 165,000 between 1930 and 1950 (Rosen 1992, 55), largely as a result of the economic stimulus provided by World War II, with construction workers, sailors, bookkeepers, and secretaries moving into the area. The old peninsula city reached 71,000 inhabitants in 1940 and continued to grow for the next few years (Fraser 1989,

388). Most of the increase in population, however, occurred in the area of North Charleston, where the navy yard and the Charleston Shipyard were located. As a result of the U.S. involvement in World War II, the two grew in importance in the 1940s, leading to a substantial influx of migrant workers from South Carolina and the rest of the South. Rosen (1992, 156) reports that while there were 1,632 workers in the navy yard in 1938, there were over 25,000 by the mid-1940s—or 28,000, according to Fraser (1989, 388), who comments that "by late 1941 the Charleston Navy Yard had supplanted tourism as the lowcountry's largest industry." As a consequence, the population of metropolitan Charleston rose dramatically during World War II, reaching 225,000 by 1944 (Fraser 1989, 388). In 1945 the navy yard, renamed the U.S. Naval Shipyard, became part of the newly created U.S. Naval Base, Charleston, which was to grow into a sprawling military-industrial complex over the next few decades.

The 1950s saw a decline in the population of the historic peninsula section of the city, with more and more Charlestonians moving to the suburbs, many of them to St. Andrew's parish, also known as "West of the Ashley," across the Ashley River. This trend continued in the 1960s, facilitated by the opening of the Interstate 26 expressway and the construction of the second Cooper River bridge. In consequence, in 1980 the old peninsula area had 40,000 inhabitants, the same number as in 1850 (Rosen 1992, 163).

The city as a whole, however, has grown in size and population in the last few decades, partly as a result of the incorporation of former suburbs and partly through a steady wave of migrants moving into the area from the rest of the South, the Midland, and the North: Charleston County had some 310,000 inhabitants according to the 2000 U.S. Census. The city's economic revival began in the 1960s and was strengthened through the cleaning and restoration of the historic houses in the downtown area in the 1970s and 1980s, as part of the very successful preservation movement initiated in Charleston as early as the 1920s and later emulated in other U.S. cities.

Following the revitalization of the downtown area, Charleston became rediscovered as a major tourist attraction, beginning in the 1970s: the number of visitors rose by 60% between 1970 and 1976, reaching 2.1 million in 1980 and 4.7 million in 1990 (Rosen 1992, 164). Charleston has also become an increasingly desirable place to live, appreciated not only by other Southerners but also by people from the Midland and the North. As a consequence, the average house value in downtown Charleston has increased dramatically in the last few decades. This has resulted in drastically higher property taxes, causing many native Charlestonians to leave the peninsula area for the suburbs. The exodus is reflected in the 2000 U.S. Census, which reports that fewer than half of the inhabitants of the historic peninsula area were born in South Carolina. The demographic changes of the twentieth century may have contributed to the dramatic reshaping of the dialect's sound system discussed in the chapters to follow.

2. THE TRADITIONAL DIALECT

2.1. THE TRADITIONAL DIALECT

THE DIALECT OF CHARLESTON, South Carolina, has long been known for the distinctiveness of its sound system. It was first noted in 1888 in an article by Sylvester Primer entitled "Charleston Provincialisms." The features first presented by Primer can also be found in later descriptions of the dialect, such as McDavid's (1955) article "The Position of the Charleston Dialect," in which he summarizes the findings of the analysis of the field records for the Linguistic Atlas of the United States and Canada, and presents Charleston and its dialect as a focal point exerting great influence over the Lower South, both along the coast and in the inland areas. Kurath and McDavid present features of the Charleston dialect in the first half of the twentieth century in *The Pronunciation of English in the Atlantic States* (*PEAS* 1961). They discuss phonological features found throughout the region, as well as those restricted to Charleston and a few neighboring cities. It appears that the dialect of Charleston, South Carolina, includes not only the city of Charleston but also the surrounding areas in the 50-mile radius, including the city of Beaufort (*PEAS* 1961, maps 19–21). Finally, O'Cain (1972) provides a detailed account of the city's sound system and its more recent changes.

The accent that emerges from these descriptions, as well as from tape recordings of speakers from the Charleston dialect area born at the turn of the twentieth century, is indeed distinct not only from most other dialects of American English but also from the rest of the South. The special position that it occupies among the dialects of North America is not necessarily due to the uniqueness of any single feature, as each one can be found in some dialects of English at some point in their development (though admittedly some are very rare), but rather to the unique combination of these features and to their sources.

9

The most distinctive feature of the traditional Charleston accent is the quality of the long mid vowels, as in *day* and *made* on the one hand, and *go* and *boat* on the other—they are monophthongal and often ingliding in checked position, and not upgliding as is the case for the vast majority of North American English dialects. Up to the seventeenth century there was a distinction in English between words such as *ale-ail* and *toe-tow*—the first in each pair was monophthongal and the other had an upglide, front and back, respectively. In Middle English the monophthongal vowels were probably pronounced as [aː] and [ɔː], and the diphthongized ones as [ɛi] and [ɔu]. The front monophthongal vowel moved to [ɛː] by around 1600, and the back monophthong was raised to [oː] by around the same time. At the same time the diphthongs were losing their glides and in the seventeenth century became monophthongal, to finally merge with the existing mid monophthongs in what is now referred to as the Long Mid Mergers (Wells 1982, 1: 192–94), although the merger probably happened only in London and in the area around it. This way pairs such as *pane-pain* and *nose-knows* became identical, that is, monophthongal.[1] Later the front vowel was raised to [eː] and, around the beginning of the nineteenth century, developed a front upglide. Similarly, around the same time the back vowel developed a back upglide, and this diphthongization of the long mid vowels is referred to as Long Mid Diphthonging. The two processes are schematized in table 2.1.

According to Wells (1982), Long Mid Diphthonging has not occurred in all dialects of English or has occurred only variably.

TABLE 2.1
Long Mid Diphthonging
(from Wells 1982, 1: 193)

	pane, raze, daze	*pain, raise, days*	*toe, sole, nose*	*tow, soul, knows*
Middle English	aː	ɛi	ɔː	ou
Great Vowel Shift	ɛː	–	oː	–
Long Mid Mergers	ɛː		oː	
Eighteenth-Century Raising	eː		–	
Long Mid Diphthonging	ei		ɔʊ	

Monophthongs are found today in conservative accents of northern England, in Wales, Ireland, and Scotland, in cultivated West Indies speech (Wells 1982), and in the United States in Wisconsin and Minnesota (Wells 1982, 1: 211; Labov, pers. comm., April 10, 2000). However, the North Central monophthongization is believed to have been the result of substrate influence from Scandinavian and German immigrants. Similarly, monophthongization is found in eastern Pennsylvania (*PEAS* 1961, maps 18 and 20), in German-influenced English. Charleston was yet another dialect area with monophthongal long mid vowels. According to Kurath and McDavid (*PEAS* 1961), the vowels in words such as *take, day* and *goat, go* are monophthongal or ingliding in checked position. As shown in maps 18 and 21 of *PEAS*, the ingliding checked vowels are found only in the Charleston area—in eastern Pennsylvania the vowels are monophthongal in both environments, that is, free and checked, which points to a different nature and different sources of the monophthongization. It appears that Charleston up to the first half of the twentieth century was the only dialect of American English with ingliding long mid vowels. In addition, the high long vowels in such words as *beet* and *boot* are also described as monophthongal in the Charleston dialect, and this is in parallel to the monophthongal nature of the long mid vowels.

Another marked feature of the dialect in its traditional form is Canadian Raising, the raising of the nuclei of /ay/ and /aw/ before voiceless consonants, as in *tight* and *house*, respectively. The phenomenon first described by Joos (1942) is a noticeable feature of Canadian accents, but as Chambers (1973) points out, it is by no means limited geographically to Canada and occurs in Martha's Vineyard (Labov 1963) and Virginia. Vance (1987) reports that while /ay/-raising is the norm in the Inland Northern region, extending from Minneapolis to Chicago to Rochester, /aw/-raising does not usually occur there, except for some lexical items. Kurath and McDavid (*PEAS* 1961) report that the raising of /ay/ before voiceless consonants occurs in the Charleston area in South Carolina, in scattered points in North Carolina, in Virginia and in Maryland, and in New York and New England (map 27). /aw/-raising occurs primarily in the Charleston area, Virginia, and coastal Maryland (map 29; Keyser 1963).

Another prominent Charleston feature is a lack of distinction between /ihr/, as in *dear* and *peer,* and /ehr/, as in *pair* and *care,* leading to the homophony of words such as *ear-air, hear-hair, beer-bear, fear-fair,* and so on. Charleston is one of the few dialects of English characterized by a merger of these two vowels. In *r*-less dialects the vowel is normally a centering diphthong, the first element of which is usually [i] in /ihr/, as in *near* [niə], and [e~ɛ] in /ehr/, as in *square* [skwɛə]. There are some accents, however, in which the vowel is identical in both word-classes—the nucleus of the resulting vowel is usually realized as [e~ɛ], as in the dialects of West Indies, such as Trinidad, the Bahamas, Barbados and Jamaica (Wells 1982), East Anglia (Trudgill 1974), though it can also be [i], as reported for New Zealand by Holmes and Bell (1992), Maclagan and Gordon (1996), and Gordon and Maclagan (2001). The merger occurs in both nonrhotic and rhotic accents; examples of the latter are Barbados and Jamaica, which are variably rhotic (Wells 1982), and Newfoundland (Paddock 1981; Thomas 2001). In addition, the two vowels merge in high position in extreme forms of the New York City dialect (Labov 1966). Charleston in the first half of the twentieth century was yet another area where the two vowels before /r/ were merged, with the resulting homophony of words such as *fear-fair* and *ear-air*—the vowels were merged in low position, that is, the nucleus of the merged vowel was realized as [e].

Charleston appears to have been characterized by the fronting of /ah/ to /ə/, evident in words such as *pa, ma, palm,* and *calm.* At the same time, the dialect had palatalized /k/ and /g/ before /ah/ in words such as *car* and *garden,* pronounced as [kʲa:] and [gʲa:dn]. Yet another peculiarity of Charleston's traditional dialect is the use of /ʌ/, as in *buck,* in *book, put, pull,* and *pudding,* and a lack of contrast between /v/ and /w/ in words such as *veil* and *wail.*

In addition, it is worth noting that the short vowels /i/, /u/, /e/, and /ʌ/, as in *bit, put, bet,* and *but,* are described as monophthongal and short in the region of Charleston, Beaufort, and Savannah, as opposed to ingliding and often prolonged elsewhere in the Lower South and in the South in general. /oh/, as in *saw* and *talk,* is also quite monophthongal with no back upglide common in the South.

Finally, Charleston was an *r*-less dialect, in which postvocalic /r/ was realized as /ə/ or contributed to the length of the preceding vowel, unless followed by a vowel in the same word—linking *r*, as in *your aunt*, is said to have been vocalized as well.

In addition to these rather distinctive features, Charleston's traditional accent contained elements common in many dialects of American English at the beginning of the twentieth century. One is the fronting and centralization of /u/ and /uw/. Another is a distinction between the nucleus of /o/ and /oh/, as in *cot-caught*, the latter not being based on a back upglide. There are also distinctions between /ɔhr/ and /ohr/, as in *horse-hoarse* and *morning-mourning*, and between /uw/ and /iw/, as in *do-dew*, both features being present in most dialects of English at the turn of the twentieth century (see Pitts 1986 and Phillips 1981, 1994 for discussions of the disappearance of the palatal glide in the South).

2.2. THE SPEECH OF WILLIAM MCTEER AS AN ILLUSTRATION OF THE TRADITIONAL DIALECT

The traditional accent of Charleston as described above can be illustrated with the speech of William McTeer from Beaufort, interviewed by William Labov in 1965. McTeer had lived in Beaufort all his life (his date of birth is unknown), working as the local sheriff for 37 years, as his father had before him. His speech can be expected to be representative of Charleston in the first half of the twentieth century, as the *PEAS* maps show Beaufort to be within the Charleston dialect area.

The most striking feature in McTeer's speech is the position and quality of the long mid vowels, /ey/, as in *gate*, and /ow/, as in *goat*. Both the checked and the free allophones of /ey/ are very high and front (figure 2.1). The vowel sounds very high and front and the acoustic analysis shows that it is slightly higher and considerably fronter than /i/. Equally striking is the glide that follows that nucleus: the front upglide is very short and often there is no glide at all—the vowel is monophthongal, and it is sometimes has a back-glide or inglide, rather than the upglide found in most other dia-

FIGURE 2.1

William McTeer (1965), Beaufort, S.C., Middle Class: /ey/ and /e/

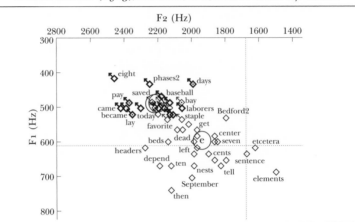

| | /ey/ in free position, as in *pay*   /ey/ in checked position, as in *eight* |
| ◇ /e/, as in *pet*   monophthongal and ingliding tokens are highlighted |

lects in words such as *day* and *take*. All three types occur in both checked and free tokens, though it is possible that checked vowels are more likely to be ingliding and free vowels are more likely to be monophthongal. The front upglides, when they do occur, tend to be short.

The realization of /ey/ in McTeer's speech conforms to the descriptions of the Charleston dialect cited above, where /ey/ is described as having a "decidedly close beginning" (*PEAS* 1961, 22) and being monophthongal, with ingliding allophones in checked position. It is indeed very close and usually monophthongal or ingliding. Figure 2.2 presents the nuclei and glide targets of /ey/ in McTeer's speech—the words in the graph are next to the nuclei, while the vowels without a connected target are monophthongal. It can be seen that many of the vowels glide toward the back and center of the vowel space, rather than toward the upper-front corner. Figure 2.3 shows a spectrogram of a monophthongal /ey/ in the word *lay*, and figures 2.4 and 2.5 show ingliding vowels in the words *pay* and *came*, respectively.

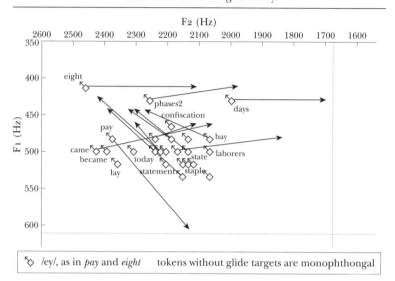

FIGURE 2.2

William McTeer (1965), Beaufort, S.C., Middle Class:
Nuclei and Glide Targets of /ey/

FIGURE 2.3

William McTeer (1965), Beaufort, S.C., Middle Class: *lay*

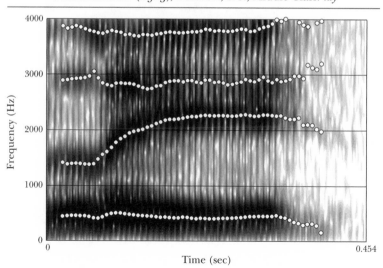

FIGURE 2.4
William McTeer (1965), Beaufort, S.C., Middle Class: *pay*

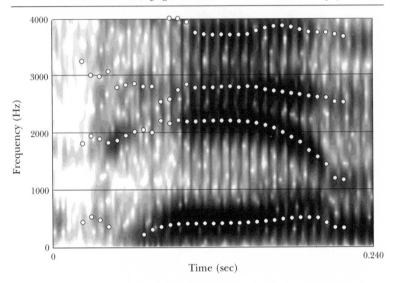

FIGURE 2.5
William McTeer (1965), Beaufort, S.C., Middle Class: *came*

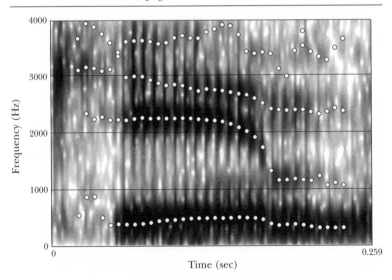

Similarly, the back long mid vowel, /ow/, as in *so* and *boat*, is rather high and quite back with little fronting, and most important, it is often monophthongal (figures 2.6 and 2.7). It sounds very distinctive and, along with long mid /ey/, is the most striking feature of the Charleston dialect as it sounded in the first half of the twentieth century.

The other front vowels also conform to the descriptions of the dialect found in the sources cited above. /iy/, as in *see* and *feet*, is at the front periphery of the system and is largely monophthongal. /i/, as in *sit*, is monophthongal (and not ingliding either), but it is somewhat farther back than usual—a few tokens are in fact central, and the mean for this vowel is slightly farther back than the mean for /e/, as in *pet*. It is interesting to note that there is no PIN-PEN merger—two tokens of /iN/ are as low as the mean of /e/, but the mean of /iN/ is considerably higher than the mean of /eN/ (figure 2.8). This is rather different from the general pattern found in the South, where /i/ and /e/ are merged before nasals (Brown 1991; *ANAE* 2006). /e/, as in *pet*, is right above the F1 mean for the whole system and is monophthongal.

FIGURE 2.6
William McTeer (1965), Beaufort, S.C., Middle Class: /ow/

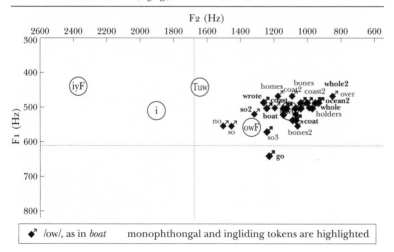

FIGURE 2.7
William McTeer (1965), Beaufort, S.C., Middle Class: *so*

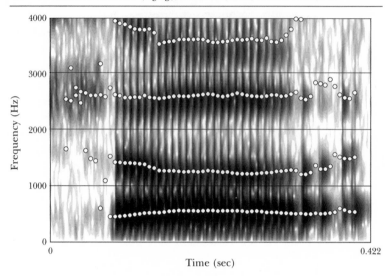

FIGURE 2.8
William McTeer (1965), Beaufort, S.C., Middle Class: /iN/ and /eN/

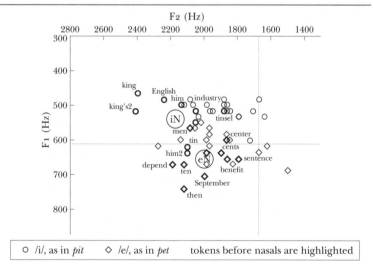

/æ/ is a low front vowel and is monophthongal. It is quite striking that there is not a separate allophone before nasals (figure 2.9). Today in most dialects of American English there is a marked allophonic distinction between /æ/, as in *pat*, and /æN/, as in *pan*, the latter being higher and fronter, and sometimes there is even a division into two distinct phonetic targets. It seems, however, that this was not the case for those in Charleston and the surrounding areas born at the beginning of the twentieth century.

/ay/, as in *high* and *height*, is back of center and back of /aw/, as in *how* and *house*, and thus conforms to the general pattern found today in the Midland and the South (*ANAE* 2006). /ay/ conforms to the early descriptions of this vowel in the Charleston dialect in that there is a centralized allophone before a voiceless consonant (figure 2.10). In effect the *rice* tokens sound very much like *race*. This is contrary to Chambers's (1989, 77) suggestion that Canadian Raising in the southeastern states is represented only by /aw/-raising. At the time of William McTeer, /ay/-raising appears to have been

FIGURE 2.9

William McTeer (1965), Beaufort, S.C., Middle Class: /æ/ and /æN/

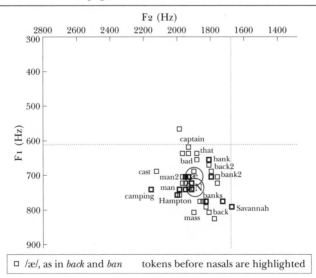

FIGURE 2.10
William McTeer (1965), Beaufort, S.C., Middle Class: /ay/

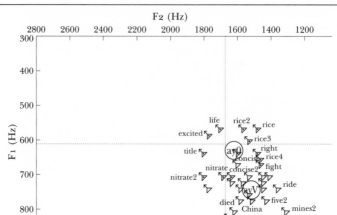

> ▽ /ay/ before voiceless consonants, as in *height*
> ▽ /ay/ before voiced consonants and word finally, as in *hide* and *high*

rather strong in the Charleston area, in accordance with *PEAS* and Keyser (1963).

The nucleus of the back upgliding vowel /aw/, as in *how*, is slightly front of center and rather low. The vowels before nasals are more fronted, but they are no higher (the mean is actually lower) than the overall mean for the vowel, contrary to what might be expected in Southern American English dialects today (*ANAE* 2006). In accordance with the sources cited above, /aw/ is raised and centralized before voiceless consonants (figure 2.11). Thus, Canadian Raising can be said to have been characteristic of Charleston with both /ay/ and /aw/ being raised, conforming to the pattern found throughout the southeastern states, as described in *PEAS* (1961, maps 27 and 29) and Keyser (1963).

Regarding McTeer's back vowels, in accordance with the sources cited above, /uw/ with coronal onset, as in *two* and *do*, shows considerable fronting and is largely monophthongal. It is located in the center of the vowel space. However, /uw/ with noncoronal

FIGURE 2.11

William McTeer (1965), Beaufort, S.C., Middle Class: /aw/

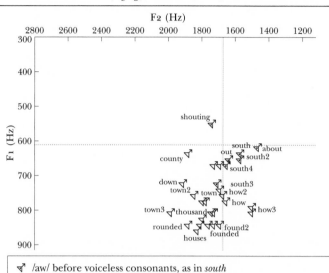

/aw/ before voiceless consonants, as in *south*

/aw/ before voiced consonants and word finally, as in *town* and *how*

onset, such as *coon*, and /uwl/, as in *school*, are quite back. There is a distinction between /uw/, as in *do*, and /iw/, as in *dew* (see Phillips 1981, 1994)—the second is extremely fronted and identified by the speaker as distinct from /uw/ in a minimal-pair test of *do* and *dew* (figure 2.12). /u/, as in *book*, is considerably fronted and centralized and is monophthongal, as described above. /ʌ/, as in *cut*, is rather low and back and also monophthongal.

There is a distinction between /o/, as in *cot*, and /oh/, as in *caught*. Although some tokens overlap, most do not and the means are clearly separated (figure 2.13).[2] Both vowels are rounded and monophthongal, without any discernible glides, as opposed to the general pattern of back upglide /oh/, which is generally realized as /aw/ in the Inland South (*ANAE* 2006).

Postvocalic /r/ is usually not pronounced as a consonant unless followed by a vowel in the same word. Linking /r/, that is, word-final /r/ followed by a vowel belonging to the following word, does not occur; nor does intrusive /r/. Postvocalic /r/ is realized as [ə] word

FIGURE 2.12

William McTeer (1965), Beaufort, S.C., Middle Class: /iw/ and /uw/

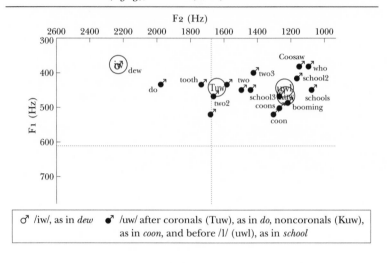

♂ /iw/, as in *dew*   ♂ /uw/ after coronals (Tuw), as in *do*, noncoronals (Kuw), as in *coon*, and before /l/ (uwl), as in *school*

FIGURE 2.13

William McTeer (1965), Beaufort, S.C., Middle Class: /o/ and /oh/

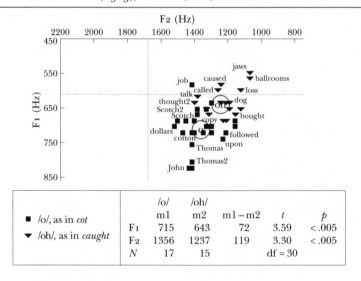

		/o/	/oh/			
■ /o/, as in *cot*		m1	m2	m1 – m2	t	p
	F1	715	643	72	3.59	< .005
▼ /oh/, as in *caught*	F2	1356	1237	119	3.30	< .005
	N	17	15		df = 30	

finally. Stressed syllabic /r/ in closed syllables, as in *hurt* and *shirt*, is with constriction. It does not show a front upglide ([ʌɪ]), found in some other Southern dialects, such as rural Louisiana.

As mentioned above, the Charleston area is reported to have had no contrast of high-mid front vowels before tautosyllabic /r/, as in *near* and *square*. This merger is found in McTeer's speech (figure 2.14). /ihr/, as in *ear*, has lowered to an intermediate position between /i/, as in *sit*, and /e/, as in *pet*, though closer to /e/, while the vowel of /ehr/, as in *air*, is raised slightly—the resulting merged vowel begins in a position slightly higher than /e/ and is followed by an inglide. The speaker confirms the existence of the merger in a minimal-pair test, pronouncing *beer-bear* and *here-hair* as the same (realizing the vowel as [e]) and describing the words as sounding identical.

As described in the sources cited above, the class of /ɔhr/, as in *horse*, is distinct from /ohr/, as in *hoarse* (figure 2.15). /ɔhr/ is a back open-mid to mid vowel that is monophthongal and merges

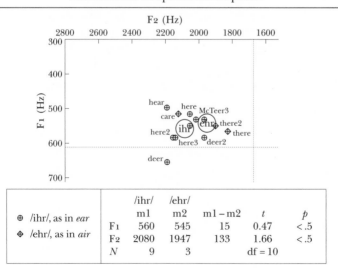

FIGURE 2.14
William McTeer (1965), Beaufort, S.C., Middle Class:
/ihr/ and /ehr/ in Spontaneous Speech

		/ihr/	/ehr/			
		m1	m2	m1−m2	*t*	*p*
⊕ /ihr/, as in *ear*	F1	560	545	15	0.47	< .5
⊕ /ehr/, as in *air*	F2	2080	1947	133	1.66	< .5
	N	9	3		df = 10	

FIGURE 2.15

William McTeer (1965), Beaufort, S.C., Middle Class: /ɔhr/ and /ohr/

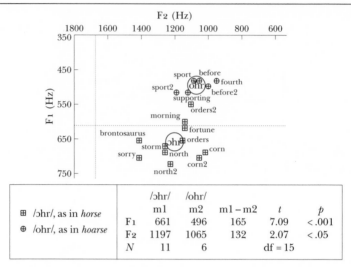

		/ɔhr/	/ohr/			
⊞ /ɔhr/, as in *horse*		m1	m2	m1 – m2	*t*	*p*
	F1	661	496	165	7.09	< .001
⊕ /ohr/, as in *hoarse*	F2	1197	1065	132	2.07	< .05
	N	11	6		df = 15	

with /oh/. /ohr/ is also a back vowel but is much higher; it is rough-ly the same as /ow/, as in *so*, but slightly farther back; it sounds more rounded than /ɔhr/ and has a slight inglide in both free and checked positions. The distinction between /ɔhr/ and /ohr/ found in McTeer's speech, showing considerable phonetic separation, is very rare in today's dialects of English (*ANAE* 2006).

Summing up, McTeer's speech appears to be an accurate illus-tration of the Charleston dialect as it was spoken in the first half of this century. Although he was from Beaufort, there is good reason to believe that Beaufort was under a strong linguistic influence of Charleston and that it shared many of this focal city's features. This is confirmed by the analysis of McTeer's speech, which conforms to the descriptions of the Charleston dialect cited above.

2.3. THE TRADITIONAL DIALECT
AND THE SOUTHERN SHIFT

Overall, the Charleston dialect as represented by William McTeer's speech differs considerably from the pattern found throughout the South in that it does not seem to be engaged in the Southern Shift (figure 2.16). Not only is there no laxing and lowering of /ey/—it is a monophthong—as might be expected in a Pattern 4 shift (Labov 1994), but /e:/ shows some dramatic tensing and is in fact more front and higher than /i/ (figure 2.17). Similarly, there is no lowering and laxing of /iy/. At the same time, /i/ and /e/ remain lax in a nonperipheral position. There is no /ay/ monophthongization, and generally no raising of back vowels before /r/. Two features that are commonly found in the South and are found in Charleston are the considerable fronting of /uw/ and the front-back alignment of /ay/ and /aw/. They are not, however, specific to the South, as the /ay/-/aw/ alignment is also characteristic of the Midland and the fronting of /uw/ is found in many American dialects (*ANAE* 2006).

FIGURE 2.16
The Southern Shift (after *ANAE*)

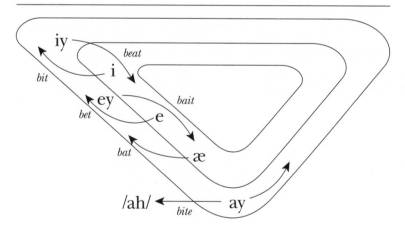

FIGURE 2.17

William McTeer (1965), Beaufort, S.C., Middle Class: Front Vowels

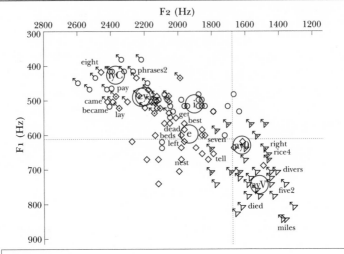

3. METHODS

ACCORDING TO THE 2000 U.S. Census, the city of Charleston has 97,000 inhabitants, and Charleston County has a population of approximately 310,000 people. In the center of the city is the peninsula area, which includes the Historic District at its southern tip. The other major metropolitan areas surrounding the peninsula are Johns Island and James Island south of the peninsula; North Charleston, Daniel Island, and Mount Pleasant to the north; and Sullivan's Island and Isle of Palms on the east (figure 3.1).

In order to obtain an accurate picture of the sound changes in progress in the dialect, I designed a study that would be representative of the community and that would also allow me to trace change within families. The method achieves a stratified random sample by first making a judgment sample of neighborhoods, then selects randomly within that judgment sample, and, importantly, allows us to trace change across generations. Based on the data from the 2000 U.S. Census, four major areas of the city were identified as representing a range of socioeconomic classes, on the basis of occupation, education, and income (figures 3.2–3.7). As the study is concerned with the phonological features of the European American population of Charleston, areas identified by the 2000 U.S. Census as inhabited predominantly by African Americans were not included in the sampling (figure 3.8).

The areas selected for sampling are the following:

1. Two neighborhoods that represent the upper and upper-middle class: (1) the southern tip of the downtown peninsula, the historic part of the city, including City Hall and the Battery; and (2) Sullivan's Island, to complement the historic downtown section, as it is very similar to it socioeconomically;
2. Mount Pleasant, a middle- to upper-middle-class neighborhood;
3. James Island, a lower-middle- to middle-class neighborhood;
4. West Ashley and North Charleston, working- to lower-middle-class neighborhoods.

27

FIGURE 3.1

Map of Charleston and the Surrounding Areas

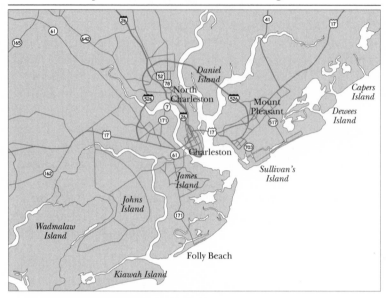

FIGURE 3.2

Percentage of Residents Age 25+ with Less Than Nine Years of School

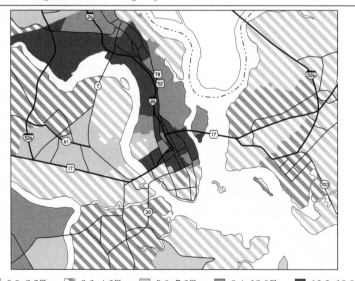

0.0–2.3%   2.6–4.6%   5.0–7.6%   8.4–12.0%   13.3–19.8%

FIGURE 3.3

Percentage of Households with Income Less Than $10,000

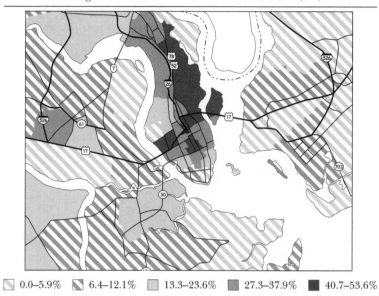

0.0–5.9%   6.4–12.1%   13.3–23.6%   27.3–37.9%   40.7–53.6%

FIGURE 3.4

Percentage of Residents Age 25+ with a Bachelor's Degree or Higher

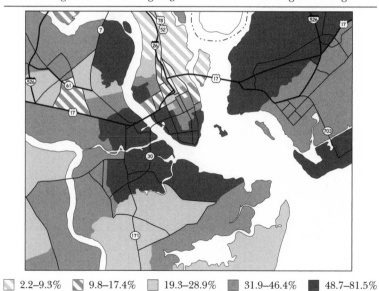

2.2–9.3%   9.8–17.4%   19.3–28.9%   31.9–46.4%   48.7–81.5%

FIGURE 3.5

Percentage with Jobs Such as Professionals, Managers, Etc.

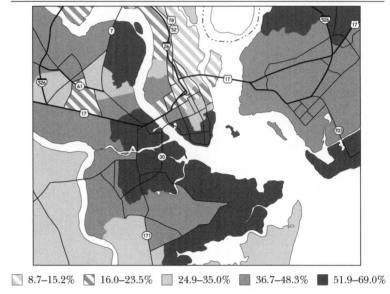

◩ 8.7–15.2%   ◩ 16.0–23.5%   ▢ 24.9–35.0%   ▨ 36.7–48.3%   ■ 51.9–69.0%

FIGURE 3.6

Median Household Income

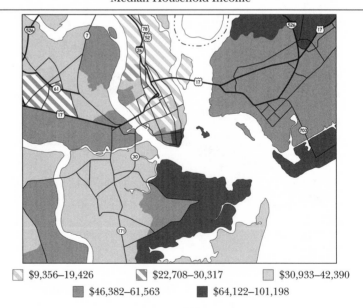

◩ $9,356–19,426   ◩ $22,708–30,317   ▢ $30,933–42,390

◪ $46,382–61,563   ■ $64,122–101,198

FIGURE 3.7
Per Capita Income

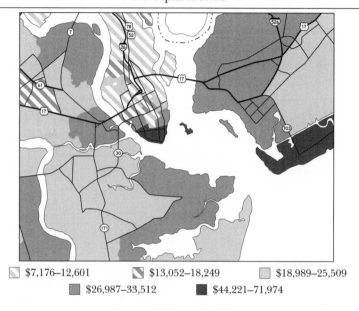

� $7,176–12,601   � $13,052–18,249   � $18,989–25,509
� $26,987–33,512   � $44,221–71,974

FIGURE 3.8
Percentage of African American Residents

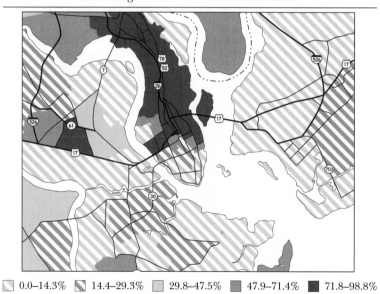

� 0.0–14.3%   � 14.4–29.3%   � 29.8–47.5%   � 47.9–71.4%   � 71.8–98.8%

Figure 3.9 shows the four major areas. All the streets contained in each area were enumerated and five were randomly selected in each. On each of the selected streets, a house was randomly chosen and approached, with a view to interviewing all inhabitants who had grown up in Charleston. The goal was to obtain data from three age groups (18–30, 31–55, 56+) in each of the four areas (representing a range of socioeconomic classes), with two men and two women in each of the age brackets, as well as any children available for interviews.

While the refusal rate was low, less than 10 percent, finding native Charlestonians proved to be rather difficult, as a great many people currently living in the city moved there in the last few decades from either elsewhere in the South or from the North. Fig-

FIGURE 3.9
Major Samping Areas

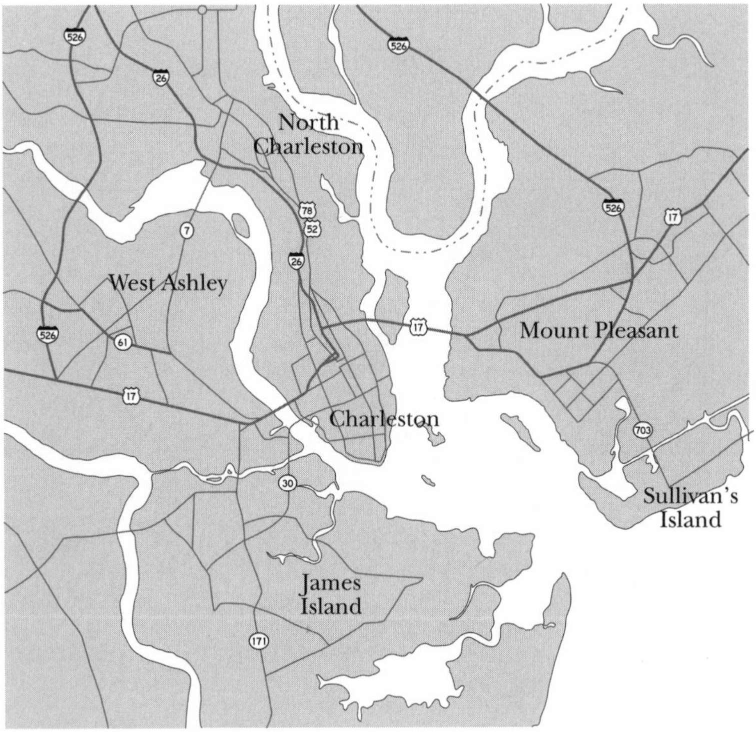

ure 3.10 shows that in some of the areas sampled, the proportion of people born in South Carolina is less than 50%. If no one in the household was a native Charlestonian willing to be interviewed, the house next door was approached. If there were no Charlestonians in that house either, the person present was asked which houses on the block were inhabited by native Charlestonians, and one of those houses was then approached. Each of the 32 informants found in this way and interviewed for the project was then asked if he or she had relatives or friends who might be willing to be interviewed as well, which led to 33 more informants. In addition, five fire stations in the Charleston area were approached, resulting in interviews with 6 male firefighters and 1 female dispatcher. As a result, a total of 72 Charlestonians from the working, lower-middle, middle-middle, and upper-middle classes were located.

The upper class was approached differently, because, as Kroch (1996) suggests, the upper class is best accessed through an initial contact, who then introduces the interviewer to other members of this rather exclusive social group. There were three initial contacts,

FIGURE 3.10
Percentage of Residents Born in South Carolina

3.1–17.1%	31.7–48.4%	50.1–60.1%	61.9–75.3%	77.4–94.2%

which led to further interviews. One was Brian R., 55, a lawyer practicing in downtown Charleston, who provided contact information resulting in 7 interviews. Another was Elizabeth O., 82, living in the historical downtown section of Charleston at the tip of the peninsula, who arranged for 5 more interviews with members of her family spanning three generations. An interview with another upper-class Charlestonian, Richard A., 77, resulted in further interviews with his daughter and two grandchildren. In addition, five other informants were located randomly in the downtown section of Charleston. A total of 19 upper-class Charlestonians were interviewed for the project.

The sample of 91 Charlestonians discussed above was supplemented by 9 informants interviewed for a pilot study in 2002, resulting in a total of 100 speakers, aged 8 to 90, representing five social classes, with 52 women and 48 men. Table 3.1 presents the distribution of the sample in terms of age and social class.

The assignment of particular speakers to a social class was based primarily on occupation, which has been shown by Labov (2001) to be the best single indicator of social standing as related to linguistic variation, better than, for example, education or house value; children were assigned the social class of their parents. The only exception was the upper class. Occupation was not the primary factor in the assignment of informants to this group, as the types of professions held by members of this group might not in themselves reflect accurately the degree of social prestige they enjoy. While 5 out of the 20 in the sample are lawyers, one is a teenage daughter of a lawyer, and one is a medical doctor; some of the

TABLE 3.1

Charleston Sample by Age and Social Class

Age	WC		LMC		MC		UMC		UC		Total
	M	F	M	F	M	F	M	F	M	F	
8–18	0	1	1	0	5	5	0	3	1	1	17
19–30	2	5	0	3	1	2	1	2	2	0	18
31–55	7	1	3	5	3	7	2	2	2	3	35
56–90	3	5	1	1	4	1	3	1	7	4	30
TOTAL	12	12	5	9	13	15	6	8	12	8	100

other occupations are travel agent, company proprietor, politician, tour guide, and Boy Scouts activist. As McDavid (1955) writes, the upper class of Charleston was based primarily on ancestry and connections, to an extent on education, and to a much lesser degree on wealth. That wealth did not seem to play a primary role in social class differentiation is seen in the comments made by some of the Charlestonians in the sample, including upper-class Charlestonians such as Richard A., 77. He says that when he was a child, his family was poor, and he stresses that during the Depression everybody in Charleston was poor. At the same time, however, some families, such as Richard A's, owned plantations, while others did not.

The upper-class Charlestonians interviewed for this project share the following characteristics:

1. They usually live or were brought up in the historic downtown section of Charleston below Broad Street, usually referred to as "south of Broad," or on a plantation outside the city owned by their family.
2. They had full-time maids or nannies when they were growing up.
3. They went to private schools, often boarding schools for secondary school, often single-sex schools.
4. They go back at least seven generations in the United States, often as many in Charleston itself. For example, the ancestors of Elizabeth O., 82, whose family's three generations are represented in the sample, arrived in Charleston right after the city was founded in 1670. The family of Richard A., 77, whose daughter and two grandchildren are also in the sample, has been in Charleston since 1686. The family of Christopher B., 79, and his son Robert has been in Charleston for 250 years, and Charles C., 71, described his ancestry as going "all the way back to the Mayflower."
5. Finally, they usually know each other; hence, they recommended contacting other members of this group when asked to suggest Charlestonians of similar social standing.

The distinction between the upper-middle and the upper class can be rather subtle, as on the economic level there may often be no difference at all. Again, what seems to play the most important role is the heritage and connections, rather than financial success. This is reflected in the comment made by Steve M., 24, an upper-middle-class Charlestonian, who went to the same private school as his upper-class friends and who now lives in downtown Charleston:

There were a number of families at the time whom– I think a lot of people would refer to as sort of your old Charleston families, who were– even though we lived amongst them, my parents were what I would call sort of transplants to the area, who would own properties aside from the peninsula and other places, say around the Edisto.

The term social class is viewed here as a matter of prestige which different social groups are accorded within the community. It is a subjective dimension which has certain objective indicators, such as education, occupation, residence value, and income. Ultimately, however, these indicators cannot be used unreflectively, as they may mean different things in different communities. Their role has to be confirmed by the local values of the community. There has been some question in sociolinguistics recently as to whether social class should be used at all as a factor, because supposedly such categorization no longer accurately reflects people's perceptions and thus cannot be successfully used to account for sociolinguistic variation. While this may be true to an extent of some communities in the United States, it is definitely not true of Charleston. The comments made by the informants in this project suggest that Charlestonians are sensitive to the differentiation between various social groups and their locations in the city, especially to the contrast between the upper class and the other groups. This is how William V., 37, a middle-class Charlestonian, responds to the question of whether there are any differences between different parts of the city:

Yeah, absolutely. James Island is probably more upper-middle class. You've got some rich folks but– upper-middle class, and some middle class, even lower class, and you can see the neighborhoods; very friendly, and very– uh. More people who live here are from here, from Charleston. Mount Pleasant is very upscale, for the most part. You still have your areas, but it's the– more upscale people, more snobbish people. You won't get as friendly as response, but you'll get more of the I'm-better-than-you attitude. You know, all, they would much rather, in my opinion, drive uh $80-thousand car and have a hundred dollars in the checking account and look the part than than [*sic*] actually be OK. And they're very– they seem to be—and there's more Northern folks that had moved in, and they hear about Mount Pleasant and the real estate value is going crazy over there. And then, of course, you have downtown Charleston, which is, as they say, the true bluebloods, who are CONVINCED they are better than everybody [laughter] and are still very friendly, but they're friendly to someone like you, an outsider, only if you understand that they're better than you. As long as you understand that ground rule there then they're very friendly to you. If you question any of their standards or styles or how they do things, well, then you're wrong and they're right, and you should have known that from the beginning.

Sherry D., 63, a lower-middle-class speaker, offered the following characterization of the highest-status social group:

Now you did have some class differences. You had your elitists, that were those that had the most money, and they lived like near or below Broad. We used to call them, what was it, snobs? What was it? S.O.B.s, south of Broad.

She further notes a distinctive character of their speech:

And they had a little, their language was a little bit different. I don't wanna say unnatural. It was uh, more, more, you know, *hello, how are you today?*, that type of thing; but uh, very prissy, almost sound to uh, the ladies. And uh, I don't know. I was in place downtown and that was, you know, a different sounding group of people.

The speech of the 100 informants was recorded during sociolinguistic interviews: 91 with individual informants, 2 with married couples, 1 with a father and son, and 1 interview with three children of the same family. The general topic of the interview as introduced to the informants was growing up in Charleston and recent changes in the city. Each interview began with the informant counting to ten, which was used for both the setting of the recording level and for the elicitation of the numbers 1–10. The informants were then asked if they had been born in Charleston and were asked to list all the places they had lived; all other questionnaire-type demographic questions were asked at the end of the interview, unless a topic came up naturally during the conversation. The first topic of the interview was usually the games the informant used to play during his or her childhood in Charleston, which was found to be fairly effective in getting the informants to feel relaxed. This led to other topics which were likely to elicit personal narratives, such as memorable childhood experiences, relations with parents, dating, or meeting the future spouse. This was followed by a series of questions about if and how Charleston had changed in recent times, which also led to a number of narratives and to the question of how Southern Charleston was.

The final part of the interview introduced the issue of language in the context of the changes that Charleston was undergoing. The informants were asked about the difference in meaning between three pairs of words and expressions: to *fear* something versus to *be scared* of something; *fair* versus *just*; and *deck* versus *porch*. They were then asked to read a word list consisting of 140 items representing all the vowel classes of American English in different environments (listed in the appendix).

Finally, each informant was asked to perform a minimal-pair test with the words in table 3.2. They were asked to read each pair and decide whether the two words sounded different, close, or the same. Each reply was scored on a scale from 0 to 2: 2 for different, 1 for close, and 0 for the same. I scored the informants' productions, that is, the degree of phonetic similarity between the two words in each pair, impressionistically in the same way.

The speech of the informants was recorded with a Marantz PMD-670 Compact Flash digital recorder at a sampling rate of 32 kHz in mono, with a battery-powered external Sony ECM55B

TABLE 3.2
Minimal Pairs

fear-fair	dew-do	him-hem
saw-sore	merry-Mary	full-fool
morning-mourning	merry-marry	pill-peel
cot-caught	horse-hoarse	beer-bear
here-hair	dawn-Don	fell-fail
feel-fill	card-cord	born-barn
pull-pool	pin-pen	sell-sail

microphone. The recordings were then transferred digitally from the Compact Flash card to a PC laptop and the vowel systems of 43 of the informants were analyzed acoustically with Praat 4.1.2 (Boersma and Weenink 2004).

The acoustic analysis consisted of measuring the values of F1 and F2 of the nuclei of fully stressed vowels in four speech styles represented in the recordings:

1. Spontaneous speech (the bulk of the interview)
2. Semantic differentials
3. Word list
4. Minimal pairs

One of the main goals of this project was to study the precise place of articulation of vowels in phonological space. A second goal was to determine the presence or absence of phonemic distinctions between vowels in the dialect. This was done through impressionistic and acoustic analysis. The latter is based on the well-known (Peterson and Barney 1952) correlation between the position of the tongue and the values of the so-called first (F1) and second (F2) formants of a vowel, that is, the values of the main resonant frequencies of the vocal tract in a particular configuration, seen as the black bands in a spectrogram, as in figure 2.7.[1] That configuration depends largely on the position of the tongue, as the shape of the tongue is otherwise fixed; lip rounding is another gesture used to change the configuration. Particular values of F1 and F2 correspond to particular positions of the tongue. Vowel height is inversely correlated with the value of F1—the higher the value of F1, the lower the vowel—the range being between approximately 250 Hz and 900 Hz. For F2, a higher value corresponds to a more front vowel, the range being between approximately 800 Hz and 2900 Hz.

The acoustic analysis method used in this study, following Labov, Yaeger, and Steiner (1972) and *The Atlas of North American English* (*ANAE* 2006), consists in selecting a single point in time within the vowel nucleus and obtaining the F1 and F2 values at that point as the best indication of the central tendency of the nucleus of the vowel, that is, its most important perceptual cue. In other words, each vowel token produced by a speaker and analyzed in this study is described by a set of two numbers, the value of F1 and the value of F2 in Hertz, corresponding to the degree of height and frontness of the nucleus of the vowel. In addition, measurements of the F1 and F2 of glides were obtained for the long mid vowels /ow/, as in *go* and *goat*, and /ey/, as in *pay* and *gate*.

The selection of the point of measurement for vowel nuclei follows the principles laid out in *ANAE* (2006, chap. 5.5). The single point of measurement within a vowel nucleus should coincide with the point of inflection, that is, the point where the tongue reverses in its movement away from its initial position. This point best represents the overall quality of the vowel in terms of its perception. For short vowels and for long upgliding vowels, the point of inflection in the nucleus is usually the lowest position the tongue reaches before moving up again for the production of the glide or a consonantal transition. This is indicated by the highest value of F1, which is where the measurement is taken, together with the F2 at the same point. For vowels whose central tendency is a movement toward and then away from the front or back periphery of the system, the point of inflection corresponds to the maximum F2 value for vowels whose nuclei move toward the front or the minimum F2 value for vowels moving toward the back periphery, which is where the measurement is taken, together with the corresponding F1 at that point. Short-*a* before nasals, as in *ban* and *Dan*, or the short front vowels /i/ and /e/, as in *sit* and *set*, respectively, when they are tensed as a result of the operation of the Southern Shift, are examples of vowels with such points of inflection.

The F1/F2 measurements are the results of the Linear Predictive Coding (LPC) analysis implemented in Praat, checked against FFT spectra. The "maximum formant" value was set to a default value of 5500 Hz for women's voices and 5000 Hz for men's voices. The default number of poles used was 10, but in cases where the number of formant tracks produced by the LPC analysis appeared to be either too small or too large, the number of poles was varied between 6 and 10 for women and between 10 and 14 for men. There are a total of 15,253 vowel tokens measured, with an average of 355 tokens per speaker.

In order to adjust for the differences between the sizes of the vocal tracts of different speakers, especially between men, women, and children, the F1/F2 values obtained for each speaker were normalized using the log mean normalization method proposed by Nearey (1977) and used by the *ANAE* (2006, 39–40). As children, women, and men have different sizes of vocal tracts, their F1 and F2 values for the same vowels are normally different: highest for children, lower for women, and lowest for men. The Nearey normalization algorithm has been found to eliminate those F1/F2 differences due to the different length of vocal tracts of different groups of speakers and yet to preserve differences having social bases, such as gender, age, or social class (Labov 2001, chap. 5.2). By normalizing the vowel systems of people with different lengths of vocal tracts, we are able to compare them directly and thus to trace the course of sound change more accurately.

Unnormalized vowel systems of women are larger and more spread out than those of men. A normalization procedure using the Nearey algorithm places the center of the vowel system of each speaker in the same position, while expanding men's systems and contracting women's systems by increasing or decreasing the mean F1 and F2 values of each speaker. This is done by using the uniform scaling factor *F*, which is greater than 1 for men and less than 1 for women:

$$F = \exp(G - S)$$

F is the antilog of the difference between the geometric mean of all formants for all speakers (*G*) and the individual log mean for a particular speaker (*S*). The geometric mean of all speakers is derived by the following formula:

$$G = \frac{\sum_{k=1}^{p}\left(\sum_{j=1}^{m}\left(\sum_{i=1}^{n}\ln(F_{i,j,k})\right)\right)}{m \times \sum_{i=1}^{p} n_i}$$

where *p* is the number of speakers measured, *m* is the number of formants, which is 2 (F1 and F2), and *n* is the number of vowel tokens measured for a given speaker. This study uses the same value of the G parameter as is used in the *ANAE*, based on 345 Telsur speakers, where $G = 6.896874$. The individual long mean S for an individual speaker is derived by the following formula:

$$S = \frac{\sum_{j=1}^{m}\left(\sum_{i=1}^{n}\ln(F_{i,j})\right)}{m \times n}$$

These calculations were done automatically for each speaker using the Plotnik program created by Labov (2006) at the Linguistics Laboratory at the University of Pennsylvania. The input to the procedure is a text file with the F1 and F2 values in Hertz for all the vowel tokens measured for a given speaker, and the output is a text file with new, normalized F1 and F2 values in Hertz for that speaker. The procedure is initiated by going to "Data," then "Normalization," then "Norm one" in the Plotnik program.

The F1/F2 values obtained for individual vowel tokens were then averaged for each phoneme and allophone for each speaker. There were a number of tokens (words) measured for each allophone for each speaker. Some allophones and phonemes of particular interest, such as /owF/ in free position, as in *go*, and /owC/ in checked position, as in *goat*, were represented by more tokens than the required minimum. The values for those tokens were averaged, and for each speaker there is a set of mean F1 and F2 values for each vocalic phoneme and allophone, such as /ow/ in checked and free position; /uw/ after coronals, as in *do*, and after noncoronals, as in *food*; short-*a* before nasals, as in *ban*; and before nonnasals, as in *bad*, and so on. The vowel plots presented in the chapters to follow include both individual vowel tokens and the means of phonemes and allophones. The means and the vowel plots of the 43 Charlestonians analyzed acoustically were created with Labov's (2006) Plotnik program.

The levels of *r*-lessness and of /ay/-monophthongization were measured impressionistically. The rates of constricted /r/ observed in the speech of the 100 informants were calculated as the percentage of constricted postvocalic /r/ in the first 15 tokens beginning at the 10-minute point in the interview. Tokens of /əhr/, as in *heard* or *work*, are excluded, as /r/ in this environment behaves differently from /r/ following other vowels: /r/ in words such as *heard* and *work* is realized with constriction consistently in all speakers. Also excluded were words with two /r/s, such as *corner* or *grammar*, due to a well-known dissimilating effect of another /r/ in the same word. Finally, the name of the city, *Charleston*, was excluded, as its /r/ is often vocalized, even in speakers who are otherwise largely *r*-ful, most likely due to the presence of the following liquid.

An index of *ay*-monophthongization has been calculated for each of the 100 speakers in the sample. It is the proportion of tokens with monophthongal realizations to all tokens of /ay/ before voiced obstruents and in word-final position. The personal pronoun *I* is excluded unless it is fully stressed.

In addition, two rapid and anonymous surveys were conducted in downtown Charleston, one for *r*-lessness and the other for /ay/-monophthongization. Postvocalic /r/ was elicited by asking about the time of day around 4 o'clock and by asking for directions to George Avenue and to Wentworth Avenue. These roads are actually named George Street and Wentworth Streets; the modified names were used to increase the likelihood that the full names would be pronounced by the informants giving directions. A total of 49 tokens of postvocalic /r/ were elicited by this means, 33 by women and 16 by men. Tokens of /ay/ were elicited by asking the time of day from between 4:45 and 5:25 in the afternoon. As expected, the word *five* was often produced in response. A total of 52 tokens of /ay/ were elicited, 30 from women and 22 from men.

The data in this project were analyzed statistically in Data Desk 6.1 and in Microsoft Excel. The regression analyses whose results are presented below included a single linguistic factor and three social factors: age, gender, and social class. Age was entered as either a single continuous variable or in decades, in which case each decade had its own regression coefficient, except for the lowest decade, which served as the residual category. Similarly, social class was entered as either one variable or as five separate variables, whereby each social class received its own coefficient in relation to the residual category. In a number of the analyses, some of the five social classes were combined with each other: working with lower-middle class and upper-middle with the upper class, resulting in three social classes in the regression analysis.

Multiple regression analysis is a particularly useful analytical tool for data in which the dependent variable is continuous, as, for example, F1 and F2 values, corresponding to the position of the tongue in the production of a vowel or an index representing the level of a linguistic feature, such as a real number between 0 and 1 or an integer between 1 and 100. The dependent variable in the analyses to follow is a linguistic factor (e.g., the F1 or F2 of a particular vowel), and the independent variables are three social factors (age, social class, and gender). Age is entered as either a single continuous variable or in decades, representing speakers' age in ranges (0–9). Social class is entered as a single variable (with values from 1 to 5) or as five separate variables (or as three variables with some social classes combined together), with the working class as the residual category. Analyzing the data in ranges, such as decades, can be more enlightening than using a single category, such as years, when the relationship between age and the level of a linguistic feature is not linear. The progression of a linguistic change in apparent time can then be described more accurately, which is reflected in the higher value of r^2, which indicates the amount of variation explained given the variables entered into the analysis. Finally, as is common in sociolinguistic studies, gender is represented as 1 or 0, with 1 standing for "female." In consequence, the regression analysis calculates the size of the effect of the speaker being a female.

The results of a multiple regression analysis are the regression coefficients, which represent the size of the effect of a given variable and their significance level, that is, the probability that the calculated association is due to chance. A coefficient is not considered significant unless the probability is less than .05, so such coefficients are not reported. If the value of the coefficient for a given independent variable is positive, then the effect of that variable is also positive, that is, the greater the value of the independent variable (such as age), the greater the expected value of the linguistic factor. If the coefficient is negative, then decreasing age, for example, will produce a higher value of the dependent (linguistic) variable. In other words, a younger speaker would have a higher expected value of F2, that is, a more front vowel. The values of the age coefficients reported below have been multiplied by 25, in order that differences between generations (25 years per generation) may be more readily observed.

When one independent variable, such as social class, is entered as a number of variables with one being the residual category, the regression coefficients for the individual categories represent the difference between a given class and the residual category. For example, if the residual category is working class, then the coefficients for the other social classes represent the difference between the respective social classes and the working class, all other things being equal. Similarly, the gender (female) coefficient represents the size of the difference in the independent variable between females and males. For example, if the value of the female coefficient is 30 and the dependent variable is the F2 of a particular vowel, then, all other things being equal, women can be expected to be more front than men by 30 Hz.

Multiple regression analysis allows us to obtain the expected value of the dependent (linguistic) variable, for example, the F2 of a vowel, for a given set of social characteristics, that is, given particular values of the independent variables. This is particularly useful for comparing different social groups with each other, for example, different age groups or social classes. The expected value of the dependent variable is derived from adding the regression constant to the sum of the products of the regression coefficients and the specified values of the independent variables, or, for a given category, such as age group or social class, it is the sum of the regression constant and the regression coefficient for that category.

4. RETREAT OF THE
TRADITIONAL FEATURES

4.1. RETREAT OF THE TRADITIONAL FEATURES

THE MOST DISTINCTIVE FEATURE of the traditional dialect was the quality of the long mid vowels /ey/ and /ow/, as in *gate* and *goat*, respectively, as described in chapter 3. As opposed to the vast majority of American English dialects, where the vowels are upgliding, the long mid vowels in Charleston are traditionally usually monophthongal in free position, as in *day* and *go*, or ingliding in checked position, as in *gate* and *goat*. In addition, their nuclei are tense, fairly high, and peripheral.

The speech of the informants in the sample shows that this distinctive feature of the traditional dialect has now largely disappeared and occurs only in the speech of some speakers around the age of 60 and older. For the vast majority of the speakers (85 out of 100), the long mid vowels, both front and back, are upgliding and considerably less peripheral than those of the oldest generation, with the nucleus of /ow/ being in central position for the majority of the speakers.[1] Figure 4.1 includes a graph showing the distribution of the traditional realization of the long mid vowels by age in decades. The vowels were judged impressionistically for all the speakers in the sample, with those having the traditional monophthongal or ingliding pronunciation receiving a score of 1, and those with upgliding realizations receiving a score of 0. The graph shows averaged results for 100 speakers, for both /ey/ and /ow/, as the two vowels behave alike: if a speaker has ingliding /ey/, he or she also has ingliding or monophthongal /ow/. A regression analysis of the rate of ingliding which included age, social class, and gender reveals that age is the only significant factor in the realization of the long mid vowels in the sample—gender and social class do not play a role.

An inspection of figure 4.1 suggests that the distribution of the rate of ingliding follows an S-shaped curve. It has been suggested

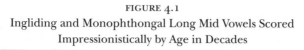

FIGURE 4.1

Ingliding and Monophthongal Long Mid Vowels Scored
Impressionistically by Age in Decades

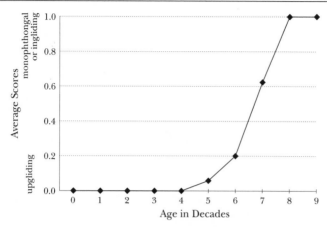

that linguistic changes follow an S-shaped curve, that is, that new forms replace established ones slowly in the beginning, then they accelerate the replacement in the middle stages of the change, and finally slow down (e.g., Weinreich, Labov, and Herzog 1968; Bailey 1973; Labov 1994, 2001). Figure 4.2 presents a logistic transform (Kroch 1989) of the data points for decades 3–9 with a trendline. The fit is quite close, with an r^2 of .96, indicating that 96% of the variance is explained by the logistic function, with only 4% noise. A trendline representing a linear relationship for the corresponding period in figure 4.1 has an r^2 of .89, indicating that we obtain a better fit to a logistic than to a linear relationship. This provides support for the hypothesis that linguistic changes follow an S-shaped curve.

As mentioned above, for the relatively few speakers who have the traditional realization of the long mid vowels, the nuclei are high and peripheral: front for /ey/, as in *take*, and high and back for /ow/, as in *goat*. Figures 4.3–4.6 present the long mid vowels of 4 such speakers, aged 77 to 90.

Figures 4.7–4.18 present spectrograms of the two vowels for four of the speakers with the traditional realization: monophthongal or ingliding, rather than upgliding. The trajectories of F1 and

FIGURE 4.2

Logistic Transform of Ingliding and Monophthongal Long Mid Vowels Scored Impressionistically by Age for Decades 3–9

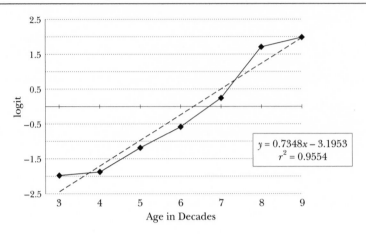

$$y = 0.7348x - 3.1953$$
$$r^2 = 0.9554$$

FIGURE 4.3

Victoria G., 90, Charleston, S.C., Upper-Middle Class: Long Mid Vowels

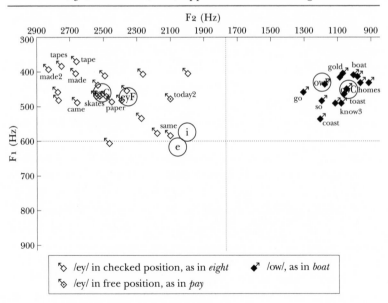

FIGURE 4.4

John E., 80, Charleston, S.C., Middle Class: Long Mid Vowels

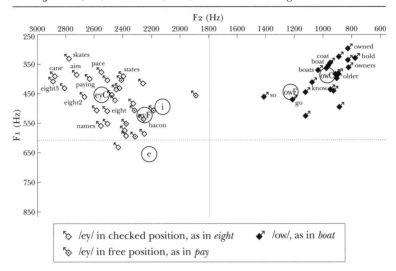

FIGURE 4.5

Elizabeth O., 82, Charleston, S.C., Upper Class: Long Mid Vowels

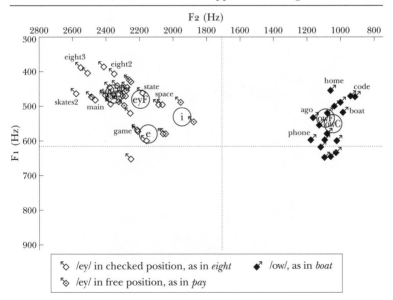

FIGURE 4.6
FIGURE 4.6
Richard A., 77, Charleston, S.C., Upper Class: Long Mid Vowels

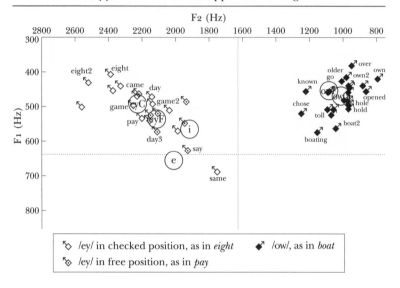

FIGURE 4.7
Victoria G., 90, Charleston, S.C., Upper-Middle Class: *tape*

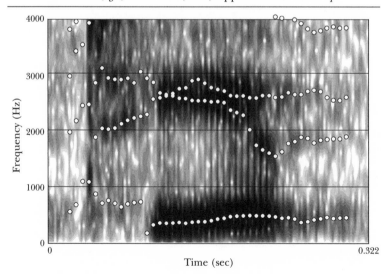

FIGURE 4.8

Victoria G., 90, Charleston, S.C., Upper-Middle Class: *skates*

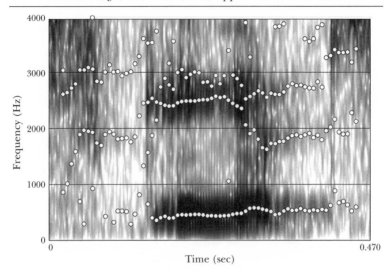

FIGURE 4.9

Victoria G., 90, Charleston, S.C., Upper-Middle Class: *go*

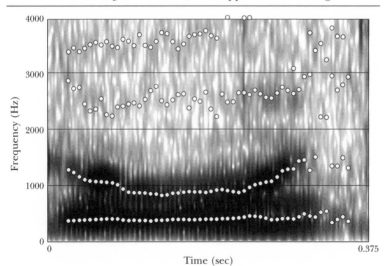

FIGURE 4.10
Victoria G., 90, Charleston, S.C., Upper-Middle Class: *know*

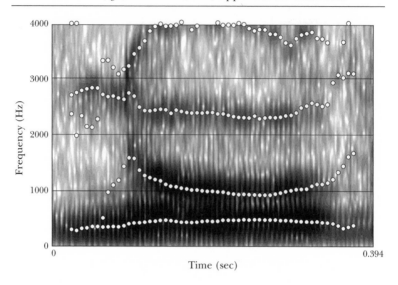

FIGURE 4.11
John E., 80, Charleston, S.C., Middle Class: *boat*

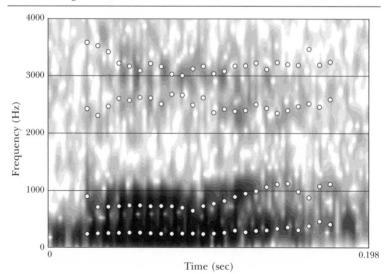

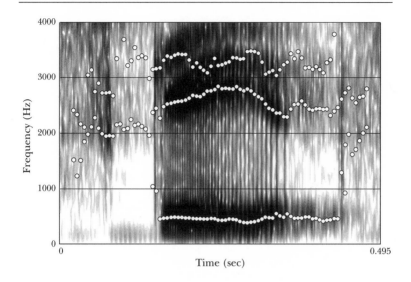

FIGURE 4.12

Elizabeth O., 82, Charleston, S.C., Upper Class: *skates*

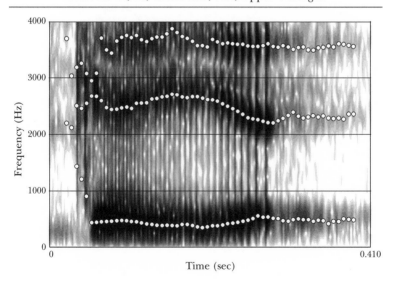

FIGURE 4.13

Elizabeth O., 82, Charleston, S.C., Upper Class: *gate*

FIGURE 4.14

Elizabeth O., 82, Charleston, S.C., Upper Class: *code*

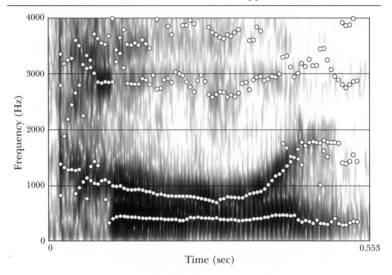

FIGURE 4.15

David W., 77, Charleston, S.C., Lower-Middle Class: *eight*

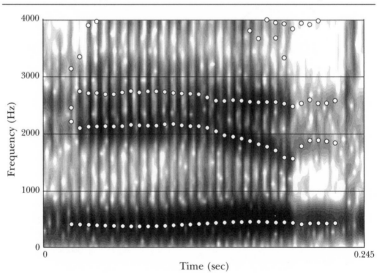

FIGURE 4.16
David W., 77, Charleston, S.C., Lower-Middle Class: *games*

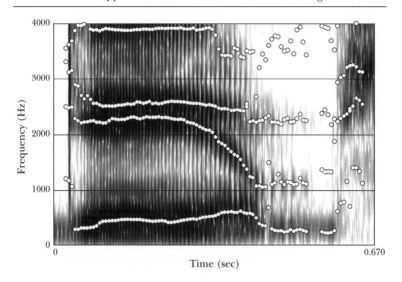

FIGURE 4.17
David W., 77, Charleston, S.C., Lower-Middle Class: *boats*

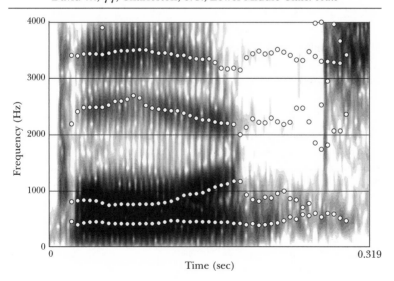

FIGURE 4.18
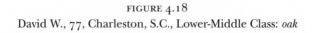
David W., 77, Charleston, S.C., Lower-Middle Class: *oak*

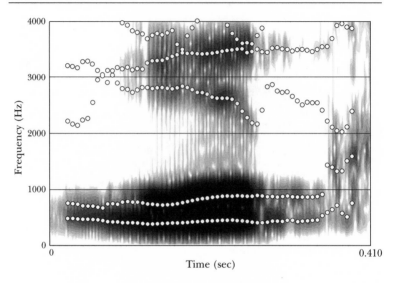

F2 indicate the direction of the glides toward the center of the vowel space, just as they did in the speech of William McTeer discussed in chapter 2.

For the vast majority of speakers, that is, those younger than 60 and some over 60, the long mid vowels are similar to those in other dialects of American English in that they are upgliding rather than monophthongal or ingliding—front upgliding in the case of /ey/, as in *take*, and back upgliding in the case of /ow/, as in *goat*—and the nuclei are lower and less peripheral. Furthermore, the nucleus of /ow/ has now moved toward the center of the vowel space, except before a lateral (see chapter 9), as shown in the vowel charts in figures 4.19–4.22. Diane O., 53, in figure 4.19 is the daughter of Elizabeth O. above (figure 4.5), and Peter O., 15, in figure 4.20 is her grandson. Judy A., 23, in figure 4.21 is a granddaughter of Richard A. above (figure 4.6). Figures 4.23–4.26 present the spectrograms of words with /ey/ and /ow/ produced by Diane O., 53, showing the upgliding character of the two vowels, as they are realized in the dialect today.

FIGURE 4.19

Diane O., 53, Charleston, S.C., Upper Class: Long Mid Vowels

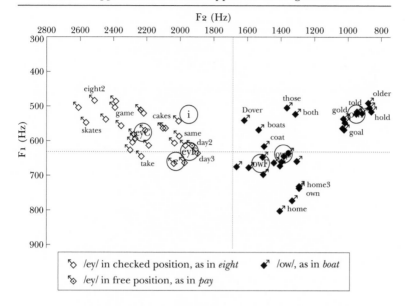

FIGURE 4.20

Peter O., 15, Charleston, S.C., Upper Class: Long Mid Vowels

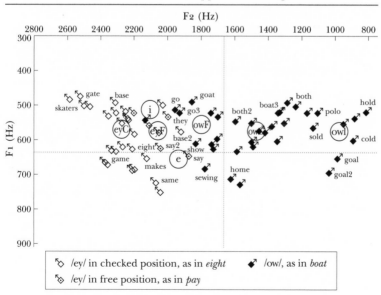

FIGURE 4.21

Judy A., 23, Charleston, S.C., Upper-Middle Class: Long Mid Vowels

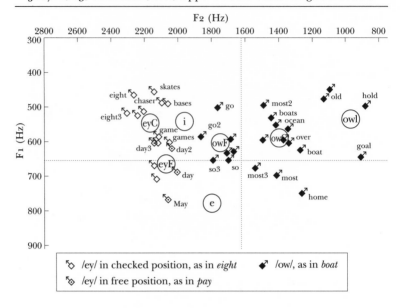

FIGURE 4.22

Margaret C., 46, Charleston, S.C., Middle Class: Long Mid Vowels

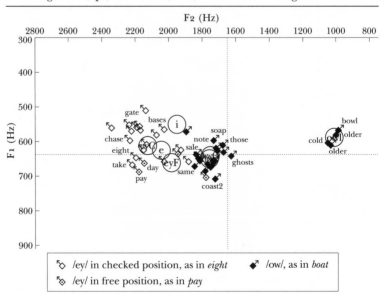

FIGURE 4.23
Diane O., 53, Charleston, S.C., Upper Class: *eight*

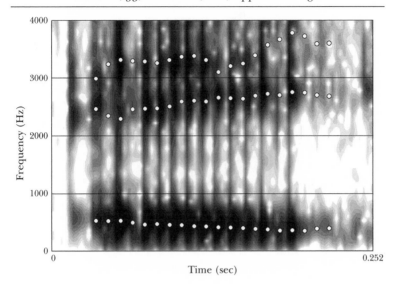

FIGURE 4.24
Diane O., 53, Charleston, S.C., Upper Class: *skates*

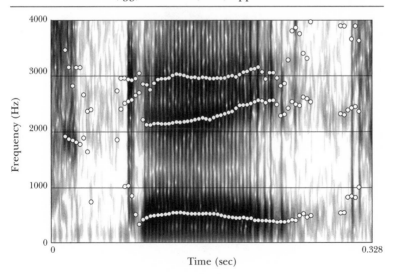

FIGURE 4.25
Diane O., 53, Charleston, S.C., Upper Class: *coat*

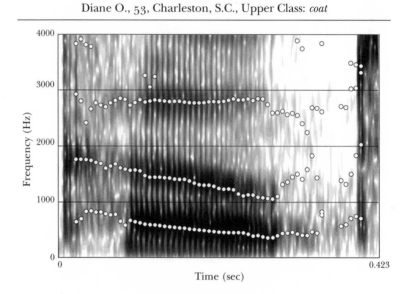

FIGURE 4.26
Diane O., 53, Charleston, S.C., Upper Class: *so*

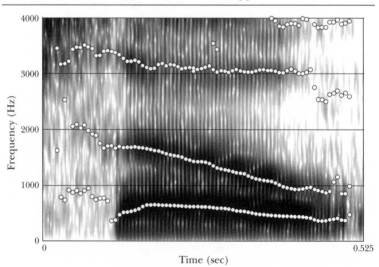

Another distinctive feature of the sound system of the traditional Charleston dialect is Canadian Raising, that is, the raising of the nuclei of /ay/ and /aw/ before voiceless consonants, as in *fight* and *house*, respectively (see chapter 2). The speech of the Charlestonians in the sample shows that this feature has now largely disappeared from the dialect in that it is generally absent in speakers below the age of 40 and is rare for speakers below 70.[2] The retreat of Canadian Raising parallels the disappearance of inglides on long mid vowels discussed above, as the chronology of the two changes in apparent time is very similar. The progress of the retreat of Canadian Raising in apparent time can be seen in figure 4.27, showing averaged rates by age in decades, measured impressionistically—a speaker received a score of 1 if any tokens of either vowel sounded raised. An inspection of figure 4.27 suggests that the distribution of the retreat of Canadian Raising follows an S-shaped curve. Indeed, the best fit is obtained through the logistic function (figure 4.28), indicating that the relationship is logistic rather than linear.

The graphs for /ay/ and /aw/ are very similar, but there is a slightly higher level of /aw/ raising overall: there are four speakers who show the raising of /aw/ but not the raising of /ay/, suggesting that either Canadian Raising for /ay/ had started disappearing earli-

FIGURE 4.27
Canadian Raising Scored Impressionistically by Age in Decades

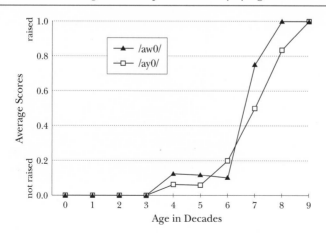

FIGURE 4.28

Logistic Transform of Canadian Raising Scored Impressionistically
by Age for Decades 3–9

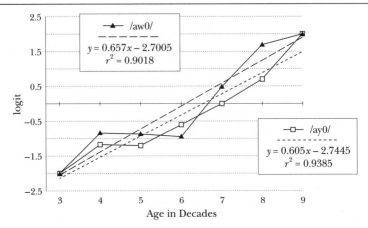

er or that the level of /aw/ raising was higher than that of /ay/ raising
in the traditional dialect, which is not implausible, as this feature
may have appeared in Charleston due to extensive contacts with
Virginia (see chapter 11). In any case, judged impressionistically,
there is no raising of either vowel for speakers younger than 40.

A regression analysis of the impressionistic results reveals that
the raising of /aw/ and /ay/ measured impressionistically on a scale
between 0 and 1 is affected by age and social class (tables 4.1 and
4.2), with the upper class lagging behind in the retreat of this feature for middle-aged speakers, as shown in figures 4.29 and 4.30.

TABLE 4.1

Regression Analysis of /ay/ Raising before Voiceless Consonants
Scored Impressionistically

r^2 (adjusted) = 37.0%		
Variable	*Coefficient*	*Prob*
Constant	−0.400	≤ 0.0001
Social class	0.072	0.0004
Age (in 25-year generations)	0.191	≤ 0.0001

TABLE 4.2

Regression Analysis of /aw/ Raising before Voiceless Consonants,
Scored Impressionistically

	r^2 (adjusted) = 42.3%	
Variable	*Coefficient*	*Prob*
Constant	−0.429	≤ 0.0001
Social class	0.062	0.004
Age (in 25-year generations)	0.232	≤ 0.0001

FIGURE 4.29

/aw/ Raising before Voiceless Consonants Scored Impressionistically
by Age and Social Class

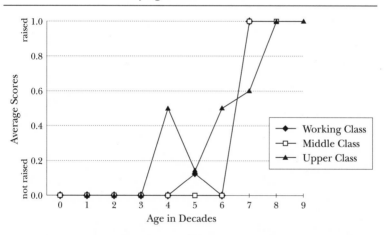

The retreat of Canadian Raising as expressed by the raising of
the vowel nucleus in phonetic space is confirmed by acoustic analysis. A regression analysis of the F1 value of /aw/ before voiceless consonants reveals that the nucleus can be expected to lower (with F1
rising) by 29 Hz for each successive generation of 25 years (table
4.3)—as figure 4.31 shows, the F1 of /aw0/ is below 750 Hz for the
majority of speakers over 70 years for age, whereas for the youngest
generation, it is above 825 Hz. Although age does not prove to be a
significant factor in the raising of /ay/ before voiceless consonants,
figure 4.32 shows three speakers at the age of 70 and older whose
vowel is much higher in acoustic space, at around 700 Hz, than the

FIGURE 4.30

/ay/ Raising before Voiceless Consonants Scored Impressionistically
by Age and Social Class

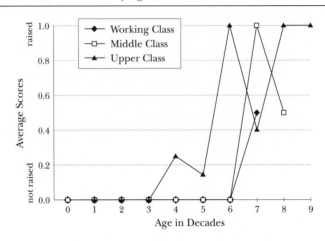

TABLE 4.3

Regression Analysis of F1 of /aw/ Raising before Voiceless Consonants

r^2 (adjusted) = 27.3%		
Variable	*Coefficient*	*Prob*
Constant	845	≤ 0.0001
Age (in 25-year generations)	−29	0.003
Sex	47	0.01

TABLE 4.4

Regression Analysis of F1 of /ay/ Raising before Voiceless Consonants

r^2 (adjusted) = 20.5%		
Variable	*Coefficient*	*Prob*
Constant	768	≤ 0.0001
Sex	47	0.001

rest of the sample. As already indicated by the impressionistic measurements above, the raising of /ay/ before voiceless consonants
seems to have retreated earlier from the dialect than the raising
of /aw/ in the same environment. Figures 4.33–4.37 include vowel
charts of three speakers representing the traditional system, with

FIGURE 4.31

F1 of /aw/ before Voiceless Consonants by Age and Gender

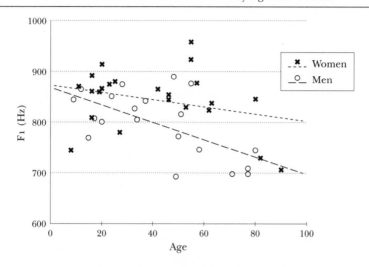

FIGURE 4.32

F1 of /ay/ before Voiceless Consonants by Age and Gender

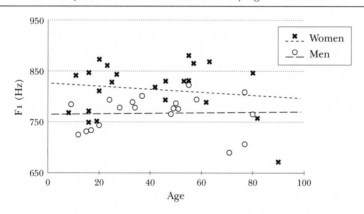

Canadian Raising, whereas figures 4.38–4.41 show two examples of speakers representing the dialect in its present form, without marked raising of /ay/ and /aw/ before voiceless consonants.

Another social factor which has proved significant in the raising of /ay/ and /aw/ before voiceless consonants is the gender of the

FIGURE 4.33
Victoria G., 90, Charleston, S.C., Upper-Middle Class: /ay/

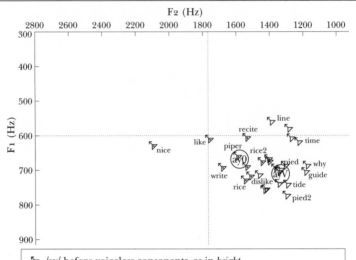

/ay/ before voiceless consonants, as in *height*

/ay/ before voiced consonants and word finally, as in *hide* and *high*

FIGURE 4.34
Victoria G., 90, Charleston, S.C., Upper-Middle Class: /aw/

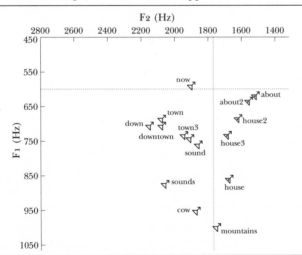

/aw/ before voiceless consonants, as in *south*

/aw/ before voiced consonants and word finally, as in *town* and *how*

FIGURE 4.35
Richard A., 77, Charleston, S.C., Upper Class: /aw/

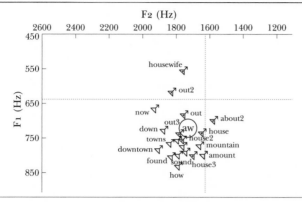

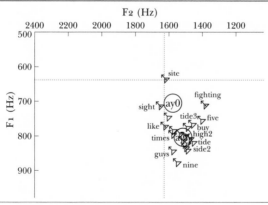

FIGURE 4.36
Richard A., 77, Charleston, S.C., Upper Class: /ay/

FIGURE 4.37

David W., 77, Charleston, S.C., Lower-Middle Class: /aw/

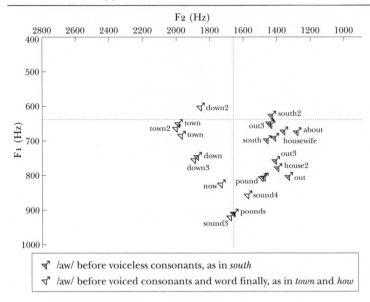

FIGURE 4.38

Debbie D., 27, Charleston, S.C., Lower-Middle Class: /aw/

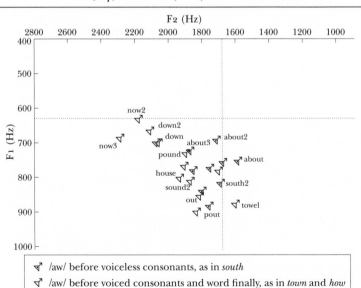

FIGURE 4.39

Debbie D., 27, Charleston, S.C., Lower-Middle Class: /ay/

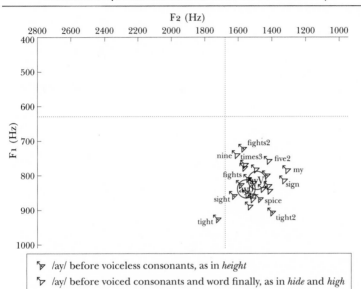

/ay/ before voiceless consonants, as in height

/ay/ before voiced consonants and word finally, as in hide and high

FIGURE 4.40

Judy A., 23, Charleston, S.C., Upper-Middle Class: /aw/

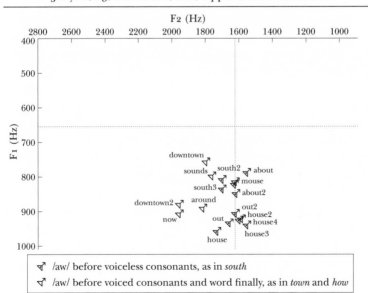

/aw/ before voiceless consonants, as in south

/aw/ before voiced consonants and word finally, as in town and how

FIGURE 4.41

Judy A., 23, Charleston, S.C., Upper-Middle Class: /ay/

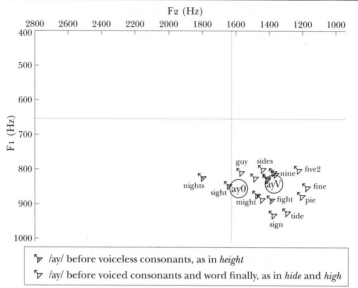

> ⯈ /ay/ before voiceless consonants, as in *height*
> ⯈ /ay/ before voiced consonants and word finally, as in *hide* and *high*

speaker. Regression analyses reveal that women can be expected to have higher normalized F1 values for both /ay0/ and /aw0/ by 47 Hz (tables 4.3 and 4.4, figures 4.31 and 4.32). In other words, the nuclei of the two vowels are less raised in women's speech in comparison with those of men. There are a few, especially older, women with clearly raised nuclei of /aw0/ and /ay0/, such as Victoria G., 90, in figures 4.33 and 4.34 above, which confirms Kurath and McDavid's finding that in the traditional dialect Canadian Raising was present in the speech of both genders (*PEAS* 1961, maps 27 and 29). Although Canadian Raising, as defined by pronounced raising of the nuclei of /ay0/ and /aw0/, has now retreated from the dialect for both genders, there is a fairly clear acoustic difference in the height of the nuclei of the two vowels between men and women, as shown in the different regression lines in figures 4.31 and 4.32. As mentioned above, men can be expected to have the nuclei of the two vowels raised by 47 Hz in comparison with women. This difference, not unlike the one found in Philadelphia (Labov 2001; Conn

FIGURE 4.42

Emily C., 20, Charleston, S.C., Middle Class: /ay/

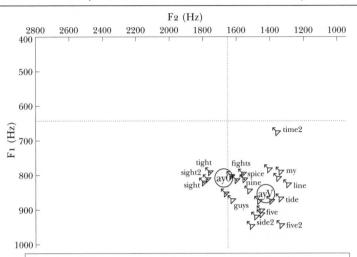

FIGURE 4.43

Peter O., 15, Charleston, S.C., Upper Class: /ay/

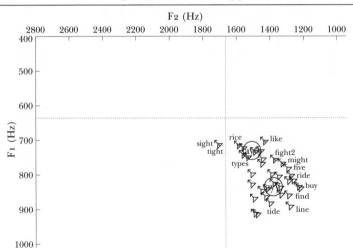

2005), is illustrated by the positions of the nuclei of /ay/ in the speech of Emily C., 20, and Peter O., 15, in figures 4.42 and 4.43.

This leads us to the question of why the gender difference did not prove significant in the results for Canadian Raising measured impressionistically, and at the same time, why social class did not prove to be a significant factor in the regression analysis of the value of F_1. First, acoustic analysis is capable of distinguishing much subtler differences between vowels than can be ascertained through impressionistic analysis—differences around 47 Hz in the F_1 dimension are indeed just below the level of perception. More important, the measurement strategies in the two analyses were different: in the impressionistic analysis, a speaker received a score of 1 in either /ay/ or /aw/ raising if there was at least one token which sounded markedly raised. In other words, outliers played an important part in categorizing a speaker as having Canadian Raising or not. In the acoustic analysis, on the other hand, the mean values of all the tokens of either allophone for each speaker were used—consequently, the role of outliers was diminished, as they were averaged in with the other tokens.[3] Although it remains to be seen which of the two, means or outliers, plays a more important role in the perception and spread of linguistic change (see Labov, Baranowski, and Dinkin 2006), using both methods of analysis results in a more accurate picture of the variation and change of a linguistic variable, in this case, the raising of /ay/ and /aw/ before voiceless consonants. In summary, Canadian Raising as defined by the marked raising of /ay0/ and /aw0/, to a position as high as the middle of the vowel system, has now retreated from the dialect, with the upper class lagging somewhat behind, though there is a gender difference in that men's nuclei of /ay0/ and /aw0/ can be expected to be higher than women's by 47 Hz.

Finally, another feature of the traditional Charleston dialect which has now largely disappeared is a lack of distinction between /ihr/ and /ehr/, as in *fear* and *fair*, respectively. The two classes were merged in the traditional system but are now distinct for the vast majority of Charlestonians. The unmerging of the two phonemes is discussed in chapter 5.

4.2. THE TRADITIONAL DIALECT AND GULLAH

The retreat of the traditional features is closely related to the question of the origins of the dialect and the uniqueness of its phonological system. It is not entirely clear what those origins are, but it seems that at least some of the distinctiveness may stem from the influence of Gullah, a creole spoken by the African slaves and their descendants on the coast and Sea Islands of South Carolina and Georgia. While the presence of Canadian Raising may be attributed to the extensive contacts with Virginia during the formation of the traditional dialect, there is no clear source in the adjacent dialects of English of arguably the most distinctive characteristic of the dialect, the monophthongal and ingliding long mid vowels, which are present in Gullah (Turner 1945; Weldon 2004).

The important role of the Gullah culture in the history of the region is widely acknowledged in Charleston, though Gullah as such has now largely disappeared from the city—the one area pointed out by Charlestonians as a place where the language can still be heard is the Market area, known for its Gullah-speaking sweetgrass-basket makers. Otherwise, Gullah is said to be spoken by the oldest inhabitants on some of the islands, such as Wadmalaw Island and Johns Island.

The linguistic influence of Gullah on the dialect of white Charlestonians is reflected in the use of the term *Geechee* or *Gullah-Geechee* by a number of informants during the interviews to refer to the language of some Charlestonians, not necessarily those of African American descent. Indeed, the term *Geechee*, as it is used in Charleston, seems to refer to the language of white Charlestonians with elements of Gullah in their speech, while the term *Gullah* itself seems to be used to refer to the creole spoken by the descendants of American slaves, though it is not clear how common this distinction is.[4] In the excerpt below, Kathy A., 42, a lower-middle-class Charlestonian, talks about the connection between the speech of her and her friends and the speech of African American inhabitants of the area:

For instance, if you're from Charleston, you still have that accent.... It's very unique to the city. And even more so, the islands, which you're on

James Island now, and Johns Island. They even have what we call Geechee talk.... Now, some people might think it sounds like a racist talk. And it is from– There is Gullah. And it's obviously from African women. And then Geechee is more of a– what we– If I'm sitting with my best friend Jenny and we start talking really fast and we get going, and it is– You can't understand it if you're not from here. [laughter] But when I'm on the job, and, you know, I try to sound more professional, though. I don't always do it because they laugh at me on this radio all the time. You know, they call me a redneck. [laughter] They're all rednecks if we're all from here. [laughter] ... It's a very strange talk. It's just like a street– It almost sounds like you're imitating black people but you're not. You see, we grew up here on the islands, and we grew up with black people, so that's how we all talk to one another.

When asked whether the way Charlestonians talk is changing, she points out that many outsiders have moved into the city recently, which has contributed to the disappearance of the local accent:

Definitely, it's going away. Well, when you walked in here, did you notice that the man that was leaving said, "Oh, you're still from Charleston, that's very rare." It's rare to find people here that are from here. It's very rare, and so people from Ohio and New York love to move here, so there's a lot of people from up North, so we're losing the accent, we're losing all of it.

Margaret C., 46, a middle-class Charlestonian, is also aware of the linguistic influence of Gullah on Charleston, though she suggests that it played an active role in her mother's generation rather than her own:

I remember as a kid, well, Anna, when she'd come to our house, my mother and she could communicate very clearly, and I didn't talk too much to her 'cause I was playing and stuff, but every now and then I'd become like not sure of what she was saying, but, the market, the city market used to sell vegetable, VEGEtables, as my mother calls them and what the black people call them, and uh, and if wanted fresh tomatoes or squash or anything, we would go into the city, because we were all living on James Island and we'd go to the market and get the vegetables. There were no tourist shops in the market. I think there was probably fish and other stuff too, but anyway– I remember as a kid, there would be all black vendors; I mean there were no white people selling in the market. And I couldn't understand a word of what they were saying, but my mother was able to communicate fluently with them. And she was speaking her same language, and they were speaking their same language, but they understood each other. A lot of what my mother's dialect is comes from the Gullah.

The acknowledgment of the role of Gullah on the language of white Charlestonians is not limited to the middle or working classes. It seems to be just as strong among members of the highest-status social group. It may seem paradoxical that an upper-class dialect like that of Charleston could be linked to the stigmatized speech patterns of ex-slaves in the plantations of the Sea Islands, but the latter were often employed in the households of Charleston's upper class, and the white children would pick up elements of Gullah from the speech of their maids and nannies.[5] This is exactly what is reported by a number of upper-class Charlestonians during their interviews, for example, by Charles C., 71, in the excerpt below:

It's a language that came with living in close proximity to our black citizens, and picking up on the way they pronounced things. They spoke Gullah– language, which was simple language, but uh, and very musical, really– but, it's hard to catch on to it, but you pick up inflections from their speech, and I was fortunate enough to have a nurse, a black nurse, who became a member of our family, and uh– She was from the islands and so I picked up on it, and when I went off to Boy Scout camp, people started teasing me about the way I talked, because it was so different from the rest of the state. It didn't have a real Southern infl–

He further reports having to modify his speech later on in life when he had developed business contacts with people outside of Charleston, which led to his losing his Charleston accent:

[When you travel outside of the area, do people identify you as a Charlestonian?] They used to, but I had gotten involved in the business world, and so I had to learn to speak English. Otherwise you would definitely know I was from Charleston. I would call a house a hoose, a car a cjar, a boat a bought–

Another upper-class Charlestonian, Robert B., 49, who was interviewed with his father, Christopher B., 79, acknowledges Gullah as in important influence on Charleston. He also confirms other informants' reports on the virtual disappearance of Gullah from the city:

You've really got two very very distinct influences, which cross on some, in some areas, which of course is the Gullah, which is not at all the Charleston accent, but it becomes a heavy component of what we all, you know, speak and are exposed to, meaning the Charleston accent, which is, I think, a somewhat unique accent in that it does not have the traditional Southern, "Ah! He's from Alabama. Ah, he's from Georgia," the Southern drawl. It's a little bit peculiar, I'm not quite sure what it is.... My experience growing up is that as children we really learned almost to speak two completely different dialects—you learned, you know, the Charleston brogue, or whatever, but then you also learned really to be comfortable speaking in a Gullah dialect, and as children we could sort of switch back and forth. I can't do that now, because ... you have to be around people to sort of practice your tongue, and you lose it after some years. And the ability to speak the Gullah dialect, really, there's very little Gullah left now, and I can remember as a child, I think we, and [to father] you I'm sure the same thing, you could switch into it quite comfortably and talk with people in Gullah and then switch out of it, but it's probably been thirty years since I've had people with whom I could do that, so I've lost that.... [Gullah] was something we were all around, something we were all used to, yet we had very distinct influences at home as to the pronunciation of words and things like that. It was clear that we were taught, you know, not to speak the Gullah, yet we also learned it with our interactions, and it wasn't just the black maids but, you know, people that you would encounter all over. And of course the Gullah influences in the city of Charleston really started disappearing in the 1950s and 1960s. By the early 70s there was almost no Gullah found in the city; you could still find it on the islands but–

This confirms Rogers's (1969, 79) suggestion about the connection between Gullah and the language of Charleston's upper class:

What happened in the nineteenth century was that the aristocrats, by the time of the nullification, had cut themselves off from the rest of the world and associated more and more closely with their native slave population; a bit of Gullah, therefore, found its way into the eighteenth century English speech of the aristocrats, leaving a residue which is peculiarly Charlestonian—high Gullah, one might call it. It still persists in a few old families.

According to Steve M., 24,[6] an upper-middle-class speaker, upper-class Charlestonians not only acknowledge the linguistic influence of Gullah on the dialect of the city but are in fact quite proud to incorporate elements of Gullah into their speech. He suggests that now that Gullah can no longer be found in the city, some upper-class Charlestonians may actually seek out Gullah-speaking maids on the nearby islands, where the language can still be found:

For some folks, there were a number of families at the time whom, I think a lot of people would refer to as sort of your old Charleston families, who were, even though we lived amongst them, my parents were what I would call sort of transplants to the area, who would own properties aside from the peninsula and other places, say around the Edisto, and their maids a lot of time tended, or Johns Island for instance, when they owned property there, tended to have been selected from groups of African Americans that spoke a language that's generally referred to as Gullah. And the interesting thing about it is that you find some individuals, young ones, but mostly men and women between the ages of 35 and say 60, I would say, that picked up on the uniqueness of that language that was spoken by their maids, and especially, I think, a lot of times when the maids would get together with other maids, when say, get together with their friends and various maids would show up, and they would use that language between one another ... and I think that a lot of people really picked up on it, and it was a lot more of a prized subject then than it is now.... As far as those language go, on the peninsula of Charleston you had a little bit of influence from Gullah traditions in language, but it wasn't as prevalent with people whom [*sic*] simply just lived on the peninsula and found maids, who also lived on the peninsula as it was with people that sourced their housekeepers, maids, whatever you want to refer to them as, from the Johns Island and the Edisto areas.... There are some people whom [*sic*] were very influenced by it–

In conclusion, it is plausible that some of the distinctiveness of Charleston's traditional phonological system may stem from the extensive contact between the two ethnic groups, which constituted two different speech communities: Charleston's English-speaking whites and its Gullah-speaking African Americans. Consequently, the disappearance of Gullah from the city may have contributed to the retreat of the most distinctive feature of the traditional dialect, the monophthongal and ingliding long mid vowels.

Another contributing factor may have been the opening of Charleston to the outside world that occurred in the first few decades of the twentieth century, as reported by Robert and Christopher B. in chapter 11, followed by the opening of the naval base (see chapter 1), resulting in an increase in business and educational contacts between Charlestonians and speakers of other Southern dialects. Furthermore, the economic revival of Charleston in the last few decades and its rediscovery as a major tourist destination has led to an influx of new inhabitants from outside the South—Ohio and New York being two of the regions often mentioned by the informants as the sources of the migrants. As a result, a large proportion of the current inhabitants of the city are people who were not born in South Carolina, as shown by the map based on the 2000 U.S. Census data in figure 4.44. It is likely that such large-scale migrations into the dialect area of Charleston have had an effect on its phonological system and contributed to the disappearance of the traditional features, facilitating the process of regionalization. However, further research, supported by accurate demographic data, is needed to substantiate this hypothesis.

FIGURE 4.44
Percentage of Residents Born in South Carolina

☐ 3.1–17.1%   ☑ 31.7–48.4%   ☐ 50.1–60.1%   ▨ 61.9–75.3%   ■ 77.4–94.2%

5: POSTVOCALIC /r/ IN CHARLESTON

Charleston, just like the rest of the Low Country of South Carolina, was until the mid-twentieth century an *r*-less dialect. This was first noted by Primer (1888) and confirmed by McDavid (1955) and Kurath and McDavid (*PEAS* 1961). Postvocalic /r/ was vocalized and realized as schwa, so that words such as *door* and *more* were pronounced as [doə] and [moə], respectively (*PEAS* 1961, 117). The South has seen a rapid change toward rhoticity in the last few decades (Feagin 1990), and as shown by the *Atlas of North American English*, it is now a largely *r*-ful dialect (*ANAE* 2006, map 7.1). The change has affected the coastal areas, such as South Carolina's Low Country, including the city of Charleston.

The change from *r*-less to *r*-ful in Charleston was already reported in O'Cain (1972). Table 5.1 presents the average incidence of the constriction of /r/ per informant in each class and age group in O'Cain's study (1972, 93) and reveals a rise in the rate of consonantal /r/ in apparent time, the highest being 23.1% for the 20-year-olds. It also indicates that the change toward constricted /r/ was being led by the lower class.

The rates of constricted /r/ observed in the speech of the informants in the present study were calculated as the percentage of constricted postvocalic /r/ in the first 15 tokens beginning at the 10-minute point in the interview—it is assumed that at this point the informants were likely to be more relaxed than at the begin-

TABLE 5.1

Incidence of Constricted /r/ by Age and Social Class in O'Cain (1972, 93)

	Age						
	70	60	50	40	30	20	10
Percentage of Constricted /r/	1.0	3.0	4.0	13.8	10.2	23.1	19.6
				Class			
	Upper		Middle		Lower		
Percentage of Constricted /r/	0.7		9.7		14.2		

ning of the interview and thus likely to produce more informal and less self-conscious speech. The interviewer speaks an *r*-less variety of English. The count includes tokens of both word-final and preconsonantal /r/. Tokens of /əhr/, as in *heard* or *work*, that is, stressed syllabic /r/ in closed syllables, are excluded, as /r/ in this environment behaves differently from /r/ following other vowels: /r/ is constricted in words such as *heard* and *work* consistently in all speakers, in all ages, though admittedly the constriction is stronger in younger speakers. Also excluded were words with two /r/s, such as *corner* or *grammar*, due to a well-documented dissimilating effect of another /r/ in the same word (Kenyon 1994). Finally, the name of the city, *Charleston*, was excluded, as its /r/ is often vocalized, even in speakers who are otherwise largely *r*-ful.

Figure 5.1 presents a scatterplot of the rates of /r/ for all 100 speakers in the sample, and figure 5.2 presents averaged rates for 10-year age groups, showing the progress of the change in apparent time. It suggests that the change follows an S-shaped curve, and indeed the best fit is obtained through the logistic function, as indicated by the r^2 value (figure 5.3).

FIGURE 5.1
Rates of Constricted /r/ by Age

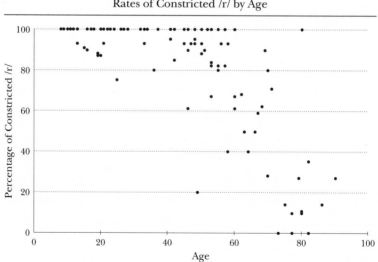

FIGURE 5.2

Mean Rate of Constricted /r/ by Age in Decades

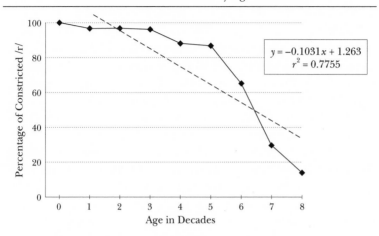

$$y = -0.1031x + 1.263$$
$$r^2 = 0.7755$$

FIGURE 5.3

Logistic Transform of Constricted /r/ by Age in Decades

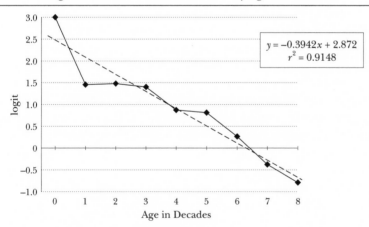

$$y = -0.3942x + 2.872$$
$$r^2 = 0.9148$$

These results show that the change is now nearly completed, with the majority of speakers below 60 being largely *r*-ful. This suggests that the change in Charleston originated in the generation growing up before World War II, which agrees with O'Cain's conclusion (1972, 94).

A regression analysis of the rate of constricted /r/ was conducted, which took into consideration the effect of age, gender, and
social class on the constriction of /r/. Age turns out to be the only
significant factor (table 5.2). The age coefficient indicates that the
rate of /r/ in Charleston can be expected to decrease by 25% with
each generation of 25 years, which is a strong effect in apparent
time. In fact, it is stronger than the effect of age for the adoption
of constricted /r/ in the South in general, as reported by the *ANAE*
(2006, table 7.1), which is −14% for each 25 years. *ANAE* also reports a weak effect for level of education (6% increase of /r/ for
every 4 years of school), but in Charleston age emerges as the only
significant factor. Neither the highest nor the lowest social classes
are leading in the adoption of constricted /r/ in Charleston. Even
though O'Cain (1972) reports that the change may have originated in the lower class or, as *ANAE* suggests, it may have been a
change from above in the South in general, at this late stage in the
development of the change, nearing completion, the vast majority
of Charlestonians can be expected to be fully *r*-ful and social class
differences can no longer be discerned.

The completion of the change toward *r*-fulness is borne out
by the results of the rapid and anonymous survey conducted in
downtown Charleston. Postvocalic /r/ was elicited by asking about
the time of day around 4 o'clock and by asking for directions to
George Avenue and to Wentworth Avenue (which are in fact called
George and Wentworth Streets; the modified names were used in
order to increase the likelihood that the names would actually be
pronounced by the informants giving directions). A total of 49 tokens of postvocalic /r/ were elicited: 33 were produced by women,
and 16 by men. Except for one vocalized /r/ produced by a man in
his 50s, all tokens were realized with a constricted /r/.

TABLE 5.2
Regression Analysis of the Rate of Constricted /r/

r^2 (adjusted) = 55.2%		
Variable	*Coefficient*	*Prob*
Constant	1.2238	< 0.0001
Age (in 25-year generations)	−0.25	< 0.0001

Finally, there is the question of /əhr/, as in *work* or *hurt*, which seems to follow a different pattern from other vowels followed by /r/. In the traditional dialect, as reported by Kurath and McDavid (*PEAS* 1961), Charleston and most of South Carolina had an unconstricted /r/ in words such as *work* and *thirty*, and the vowel usually had a front upglide and was transcribed as [ɜɪ] (*PEAS* 1961, map 25), not unlike the sound in *thirty* in New York City (Labov 1966). However, this variant has now entirely disappeared—it is not found in the speech of any of the informants in the sample. Instead, all the speakers in the sample have a constricted /r/ in words such as *heard* and *work*, though, as mentioned above, the constriction is generally stronger in the younger generations. The fact that constricted /r/ in /əhr/ seems to be categorical in Charleston—it is constricted even for those speakers who are otherwise *r*-less—suggests that its phonemic representation has changed as well: it may be interpreted as a syllabic /r/, rather than a sequence of a vowel followed by /r/, just as it seems to be represented in most dialects of American English.

The reversal of the pattern of /r/ constriction in Charleston is part of the general retreat of /r/ vocalization in the Low Country, noted by McDavid (1948), and throughout the South (Feagin 1990). *R*-lessness has traditionally been the prestige pronunciation in the South, associated with the plantation caste of the Low Country, the highest-status social group. At the same time, /r/-constriction was a feature of the Upcountry, settled largely from the Midland and likely influenced by the speech of the strongly rhotic Scotch-Irish. White speakers in that area tended to be poor, and their speech patterns carried low social prestige.

As the South, including the Upcountry of South Carolina, became more affluent, the social perception of rhoticity, formerly associated with poor whites, changed as well. As Feagin (1990, 141) puts it, "The parents might resent the presence of a rich plumber's daughter in the classroom, but the children were more impressed with her affluence than her parents' origin." Other factors contributing to the retreat of *r*-lessness have been increased migration of Northerners to the South—in the case of Charleston this included a large influx of military personnel (McDavid 1948; see chapter

1)—and the growing separation of *r*-less African Americans, many migrating to the North, and Southern whites, who have increasingly adopted the national rhotic pattern of white speakers outside of the South (Feagin 1990).

6. NEARLY COMPLETED MERGERS

6.1. MERGER OF /ohr/ AND /ɔhr/

Charleston's traditional dialect maintained a distinction between the vowel classes of /ohr/, as in *mourning* and *hoarse*, and of /ɔhr/, as in *morning* and *horse*. As shown in map 44 of *PEAS*, a distinction between the two vowels was found in most of the country as recently as the first half of the twentieth century: the two vowels were different from each other in the North and the South, with only the north Midland showing a merger.

The vowel class of /ohr/ was originally long open *o* before /r/ in Middle English; as a result of the Great Vowel Shift, the vowel was raised to [o]. The vowel class of /ɔhr/, on the other hand, is a reflex of short open *o* before /r/ and in a dialect maintaining a distinction, it is pronounced lower than /ohr/. A number of words beginning with labials moved to the long *o* class, such as *fort* and *porch*; consequently, spelling ceased to be a reliable predictor of which words belong to which of the two vowel classes. Table 6.1 includes

TABLE 6.1
/ohr/ and /ɔhr/ Words
(based on Kenyon and Knott 1953, from *ANAE*)

/ohr/	/ɔhr/
hoarse	horse
four	for
fort	sort
mourning	morning
ore	or
lore	lord
port	storm
porch	fork
sport	corn

examples of words with the two vowels according to the classification in Kenyon and Knott (1953).

An acoustic analysis of the speech of William McTeer shows a clear separation between the two vowels (figure 2.15) and corroborates the report by Kurath and McDavid (*PEAS* 1961), whereby Charleston, just like the rest of the South and the North, had a distinction between words such as *morning-mourning* and *horse-hoarse*. Figure 6.1 shows that for the vast majority of the country, the two vowels are now merged, with the pairs in table 6.1 being identical in perception and production.

Charleston has also undergone this merger, which is now almost complete in the dialect; only the oldest speakers in the sample report a distinction and even fewer pronounce the two vowels differently. Figure 6.2 summarizes the results of the minimal-pair tests for the pair *horse-hoarse*. Each informant was asked to read a minimal pair, such as *horse-hoarse*, and asked whether the two words

FIGURE 6.1

Merger of /ɔhr/, as in *horse*, and /ohr/, as in *hoarse*
(Telsur Project, Univ. of Pennsylvania)

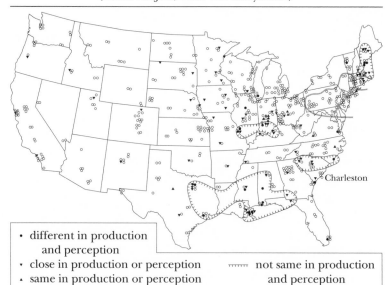

- · different in production
  and perception
- · close in production or perception   ˌˌˌˌˌˌ not same in production
- ▴ same in production or perception   and perception
- ○ same in production and perception   ˍˍˍˍ same in *PEAS*, map 44

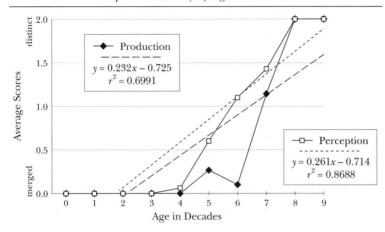

FIGURE 6.2

Merger of *horse* and *hoarse* in Minimal-Pair Tests Scored
Impressionistically by Age in Decades

sounded different (2 points), close (1 point), or the same (0 points)
to him or her. The graphs present the averaged scores for 97 informants. An inspection of figure 6.2 suggests that the change follows
an S-shaped curve—indeed, the best fit is obtained through the
logistic function (figure 6.3).

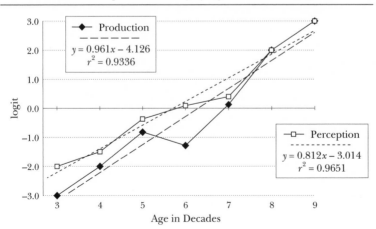

FIGURE 6.3

Logistic Transform of the *horse-hoarse* Merger in Minimal-Pair Tests
Scored Impressionistically by Age for Decades 3–9

In production most speakers in their 70s or older show a distinction between /ɔhr/ and /ohr/, common in most of North America up to the mid-twentieth century, whereas for the vast majority of speakers younger than 60, the two vowels are completely merged, which mirrors the phonemic status of the two vowels in the vast majority of American English dialects today. The line in figure 6.2 is essentially flat at 0 (the index value for merged) for speakers younger than 70, which means that the change from a distinction to a merger is almost complete in the dialect.

Acoustic analysis shows that for speakers who make a distinction between the two vowels, they are often clearly separated in phonetic space, with /ohr/ being higher and slightly backer than /ɔhr/, as in the speech of Victoria G., 90, figure 6.4, or Richard A., 77, figure 6.5. It is worth noting that the two speakers are largely *r*-less—the connection of the merger with increasing rhoticity is discussed in chapter 12.

For most other speakers below the age of 70, who report the words *morning-mourning* and *horse-hoarse* to sound identical and whose pronunciations are judged to sound identical, the vowels

FIGURE 6.4

Victoria G., 90, Charleston, S.C., Upper-Middle Class: /ɔhr/ and /ohr/

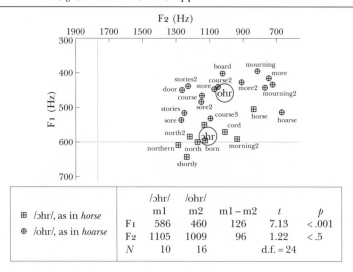

		/ɔhr/	/ohr/			
		m1	m2	m1 − m2	*t*	*p*
⊞ /ɔhr/, as in *horse*	F1	586	460	126	7.13	< .001
⊕ /ohr/, as in *hoarse*	F2	1105	1009	96	1.22	< .5
	N	10	16		d.f. = 24	

FIGURE 6.5

Richard A., 77, Charleston, S.C., Upper Class: /ɔhr/ and /ohr/

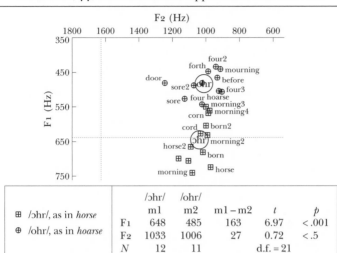

		/ɔhr/	/ohr/			
⊞ /ɔhr/, as in *horse*		m1	m2	m1 – m2	*t*	*p*
	F1	648	485	163	6.97	< .001
⊕ /ohr/, as in *hoarse*	F2	1033	1006	27	0.72	< .5
	N	12	11		d.f. = 21	

overlap in phonetic space and their means are very close to each other. The merged vowel is usually in high back position, as in the speech of Fred W., 50, figure 6.6, and Catherine A., 25, figure 6.7.

A regression analysis of the results of the minimal-pair tests for the pair *horse-hoarse* in production reveals that in addition to an age effect, which is expected, there is also a social class effect, whereby the difference between the lowest-status group and the highest-status group amounts to .55 on a 2-point scale (table 6.2). The effect is then much smaller than the one found for the PIN-PEN merger (table 7.4 below).

Figure 6.8 presents the progress of the merger in apparent time separately for three social classes. The upper-class numbers have been pooled together with those of the upper-middle class, and the middle class has been combined with the lower-middle class. This graph reveals that all three social groups behave in exactly the same way for speakers younger than 50—they are all merged—but the rate of distinction rises slightly for upper-class speakers in their 50s,[1] though the difference from the other classes in this age range is not statistically significant.

FIGURE 6.6

Fred W., 50, Charleston, S.C., Working Class: /ɔhr/ and /ohr/

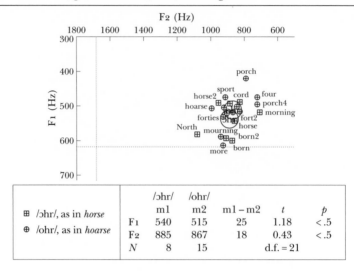

		/ɔhr/	/ohr/			
		m1	m2	m1 – m2	t	p
⊞ /ɔhr/, as in *horse*	F1	540	515	25	1.18	< .5
⊕ /ohr/, as in *hoarse*	F2	885	867	18	0.43	< .5
	N	8	15		d.f. = 21	

FIGURE 6.7

Catherine A., 25, Charleston, S.C., Working Class: /ɔhr/ and /ohr/

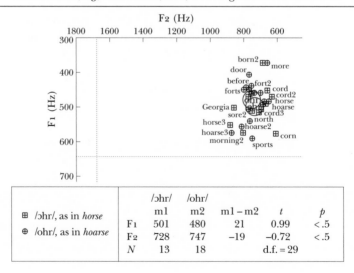

		/ɔhr/	/ohr/			
		m1	m2	m1 – m2	t	p
⊞ /ɔhr/, as in *horse*	F1	501	480	21	0.99	< .5
⊕ /ohr/, as in *hoarse*	F2	728	747	–19	–0.72	< .5
	N	13	18		d.f. = 29	

TABLE 6.2

Regression Analysis of the *horse-hoarse* Merger in Minimal-Pair Tests
for Production Scored Impressionistically

r^2 (adjusted) = 41.8%		
Variable	*Coefficient*	*Prob*
Constant	–0.7923	< 0.0001
Social class	0.106	0.007
Age (in 25-year generations)	0.017	< 0.0001

FIGURE 6.8

Merger of *horse* and *hoarse* in Minimal-Pair Tests for Production
Scored Impressionistically by Age in Decades and Social Class

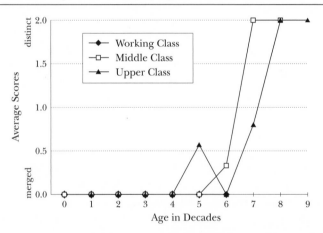

To conclude, Charleston has merged /ɔhr/ and /ohr/, with resulting homonymy of pairs such as *morning-mourning, horse-hoarse,*
and *for-four.* The merger is almost complete, and Charleston shares
this merger with the vast majority of American English dialects today.

6.2. MERGER OF /iw/ AND /uw/

Another almost completed merger found in Charleston is the
merger of /iw/, as in *dew, tune,* and *new,* and /uw/, as in *do, goose,* and
moose. The vowel in words such as *dew* and *new* has its origins in

Middle English /iu/, which was derived from a number of different sounds, such as French /iw/, /iu/, /u/, and /ui/, as well as Old English /iw/, as in *Tiwesdøg* 'Tuesday' (Jespersen 1949, 3.8). According to Jespersen, the sound was a rising diphthong with an initial glide [ju], which was later variably lost. In North America it was retained after labials and dorsals but usually lost after apicals, as in *tune* and *new*, except for the South, where Kurath and McDavid report [ju] to be the predominant form (*PEAS* 1961, map 164). The glide has now largely disappeared after apicals even there, as suggested by Phillips (1981, 1994) and Pitts (1986). The Telsur project detected no glides in either the North or the South (*ANAE* 2006, 58), and the resulting vowel, for which the symbol /iw/ is used, has been undergoing a merger with the class of /uw/ as in *do, boot*, and *goose*. The vowels are now almost completely merged in American English, with only two regions in the South still maintaining the distinction—central North Carolina and the Gulf States: southern Georgia, Alabama, and Mississippi (*ANAE* 2006, 59). Charleston has also been undergoing a merger of /iw/ and /uw/, which is now almost complete—the two vowels are distinct only for some speakers over the age of 60. The minimal-pair test used the words *dew-do* to test the contrast between the two vowels in perception and production for the 100 speakers in the sample. The progress of the merger in apparent time can be seen in figure 6.9, which summarizes the results of the minimal-pair test for *dew-do*. An inspection of figure 6.9 suggests that the relationship is exponential, rather than logistic or linear (figure 6.10).

Table 6.3 presents the results of a regression analysis of the results, which reveals that age is the only significant factor; the merger has been adopted by both genders and all social groups in Charleston.

Acoustic analysis confirms the results of the minimal-pair tests: the nuclei of /iw/ and /uw/ are very close in phonetic space for most speakers; only for some of the oldest speakers in the sample are they clearly separated, as in the speech of Victoria G., 90, and John E., 80—for both of them *dew* and *do* are distinct in perception and production (figures 6.11 and 6.12).

FIGURE 6.9

Merger of *dew* and *do* in Minimal-Pair Tests for Production
Scored Impressionistically by Age in Decades

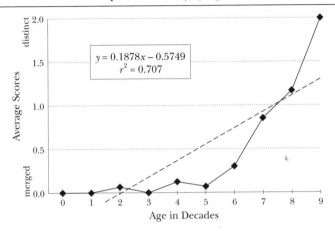

$$y = 0.1878x - 0.5749$$
$$r^2 = 0.707$$

FIGURE 6.10

Exponential Fit of the *dew-do* Merger in Minimal-Pair Tests for Production
Scored Impressionistically by Age in Decades

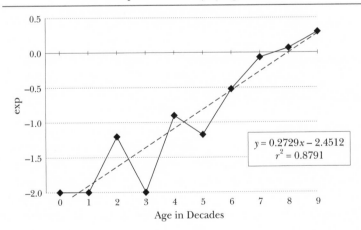

$$y = 0.2729x - 2.4512$$
$$r^2 = 0.8791$$

TABLE 6.3

Regression Analysis of the *dew-do* Merger in Minimal-Pair Tests
for Production Scored Impressionistically

r^2 (adjusted) = 23.4%		
Variable	*Coefficient*	*Prob*
Constant	−0.346	0.0046
Age (in 25-year generations)	0.013	< 0.0001

FIGURE 6.11

Victoria G., 90, Charleston, S.C., Upper-Middle Class: /iw/ and /uw/

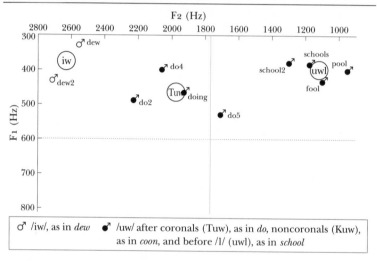

For the majority of speakers under 60, the two vowels are very close to each other acoustically, and they often overlap entirely. For some of the speakers who did not distinguish between *do* and *dew* in a minimal-pair test, the nucleus of /iw/, as in *dew*, is nevertheless somewhat fronter than the nucleus of /uw/, as in *do*. The distance between the means of the two vowels is usually fairly small, but it can be statistically significant in the F2 dimension, as in the speech of Catherine A., 25, in figure 6.13. Her mean /iw/ is 200 Hz in front of her mean /uw/. However, for most speakers the two vowels overlap completely, as in the speech of Kathy A., 42, and Kevin P., 20 (figures 6.14 and 6.15). It is worth noting that in the speech

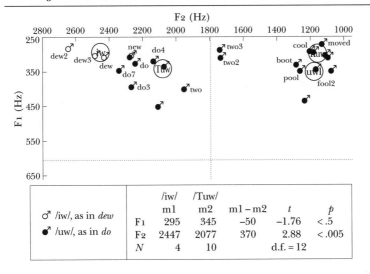

FIGURE 6.12

John E., 80, Charleston, S.C., Middle Class: /iw/ and /uw/

		/iw/	/Tuw/			
		m1	m2	m1 − m2	*t*	*p*
♂ /iw/, as in *dew*	F_1	295	345	−50	−1.76	< .5
⬧ /uw/, as in *do*	F_2	2447	2077	370	2.88	< .005
	N	4	10		d.f. = 12	

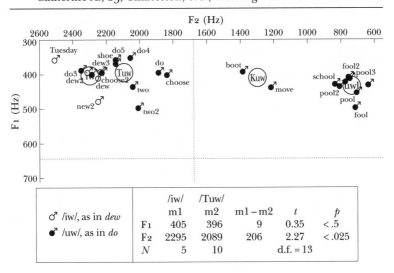

FIGURE 6.13

Catherine A., 25, Charleston, S.C., Working Class: /iw/ and /uw/

		/iw/	/Tuw/			
		m1	m2	m1 − m2	*t*	*p*
♂ /iw/, as in *dew*	F_1	405	396	9	0.35	< .5
⬧ /uw/, as in *do*	F_2	2295	2089	206	2.27	< .025
	N	5	10		d.f. = 13	

FIGURE 6.14

Kathy A., 42, Charleston, S.C., Lower-Middle Class: /iw/ and /uw/

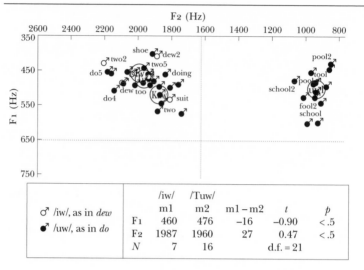

		/iw/	/Tuw/			
♂ /iw/, as in *dew*		m1	m2	m1 – m2	*t*	*p*
♂ /uw/, as in *do*	F1	460	476	–16	–0.90	< .5
	F2	1987	1960	27	0.47	< .5
	N	7	16		d.f. = 21	

FIGURE 6.15

Kevin P., 20, Charleston, S.C., Working Class: /iw/ and /uw/

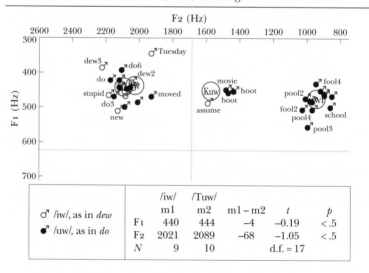

		/iw/	/Tuw/			
♂ /iw/, as in *dew*		m1	m2	m1 – m2	*t*	*p*
♂ /uw/, as in *do*	F1	440	444	–4	–0.19	< .5
	F2	2021	2089	–68	–1.05	< .5
	N	9	10		d.f. = 17	

of Kathy A., 42, the vowel class of /uw/ after noncoronals (labeled /Kuw/), as in *move* and *boot*, is in front of the center of her vowel system and is only slightly behind the allophone after coronals (/Tuw/). This marks a very advanced stage in the fronting of /uw/ and is an important feature of Charleston's phonological system today, to be discussed below.

One interesting outlier in the merger of /iw/ and /uw/ in Charleston is Robert B, 49, an upper-class speaker, who distinguishes between *do* and *dew* in a minimal-pair test, both in perception and in production, and for whom the two vowels are clearly separated in acoustic space (figure 6.16). His phonological system is conservative in a few other respects, such as the raising and tensing of short-*a* before nasals and the presence of Canadian Raising in /aw/. However, just like most other Charlestonians in the sample, he shows advanced fronting of /uw/ before coronals, as in *do* and *two*, and his /uw/ before noncoronals is at the center of his vowel space, rather than at the back. As figure 6.9 shows, however, Robert B. is an outlier in the merger of /iw/ and /uw/, which is an almost completed change in the phonological system of Charleston.

FIGURE 6.16
Robert B., 49, Charleston, S.C., Upper Class: /iw/ and /uw/

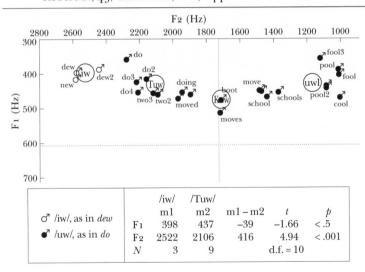

		/iw/	/Tuw/			
		m1	m2	m1 − m2	*t*	*p*
♂ /iw/, as in *dew*	F1	398	437	−39	−1.66	< .5
🌑 /uw/, as in *do*	F2	2522	2106	416	4.94	< .001
	N	3	9		d.f. = 10	

6.3. MERGER OF *MERRY* AND *MARY*

The traditional dialect of Charleston, just like most of the eastern United States up to the mid-twentieth century (*PEAS* 1961, maps 49–51), maintained a difference between the non-high front vowels before /r/ represented by the words *merry*, *Mary*, and *marry*. Synopses 135 and 136 in *PEAS* describe the vowels in the three words in Charleston as /ɛ/, /e/, and /ə/, respectively. The different positions of the three vowels can be seen only in the speech of some of the speakers over the age of 50, such as John E., 80, and Richard A., 77 (figures 6.17 and 6.18, resp.). In the second half of the twentieth century, most of the East Coast, with the exception of southeastern New England and the mid-Atlantic region of New York and Philadelphia, joined the rest of North America in merging either two of the vowels, *merry* and *Mary*, or even all three in some regions. The South is one of the areas where a two-way merger of *merry* and *Mary* is common, while *marry* often remains distinct (*ANAE* 2006, map 8.4).

FIGURE 6.17
John E., 80, Charleston, S.C., Middle Class: *Merry-Mary-marry*

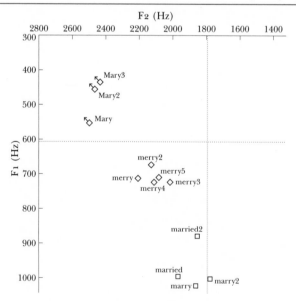

FIGURE 6.18

Richard A., 77, Charleston, S.C., Upper Class: *Merry-Mary-marry*

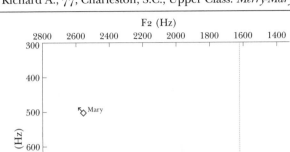

The results of the minimal-pair test for the pair *merry-Mary* show that for the vast majority of speakers under the age of 70 the two vowels are merged in perception and production (figure 6.19). An inspection of figure 6.19 suggests that the merger follows a logistic progression. Indeed, the best fit is obtained through the logistic function (figure 6.20).

A regression analysis of the results of the minimal-pair test for production reveals that in addition to an age effect, there is also a weak social class effect (table 6.4).

Figure 6.21 presents the progress of the merger in apparent time separately for three social groups: the upper class (combined with the upper-middle class), the middle class (combined with the lower-middle class), and the working class. There is a slight bump for upper-class speakers in their 50s toward a distinction, similar to the one observed in the merger of /ɔhr/ and /ohr/, as in *horse* and *hoarse*. For seven upper-class speakers in this age range, three distinguish between *merry* and *Mary* and one is close. This suggests that middle-age speakers in the upper class in Charleston may be more conservative in the adoption of this merger, though the num-

FIGURE 6.19

Merger of *merry* and *Mary* in Minimal-Pair Tests Scored
Impressionistically by Age in Decades

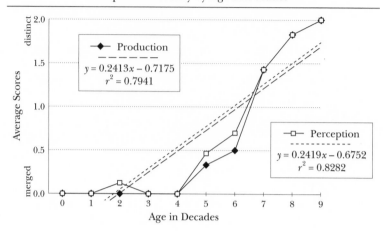

FIGURE 6.20

Logistic Transform of the *merry-Mary* Merger in Minimal-Pair Tests
Scored Impressionistically by Age in Decades

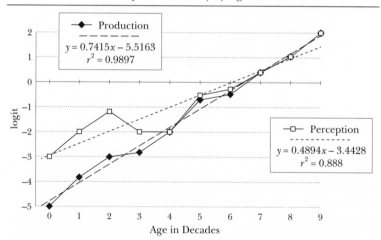

bers are too small to be definitive. In any case, it is clear that for all
social classes below the age of 50 the vowels of *merry* and *Mary* are
now completely merged, as they are for the vast majority of speakers of North American English.

TABLE 6.4

Regression Analysis of the *merry-Mary* Merger in Minimal-Pair Tests
for Production Scored Impressionistically

r^2 (adjusted) = 44.8%

Variable	Coefficient	Prob
Constant	−0.781	< 0.0001
Age (in 25-year generations)	0.498	< 0.0001
Social class	0.0944	0.024

FIGURE 6.21

Merger of *merry* and *Mary* in Minimal-Pair Tests Scored
Impressionistically by Age in Decades and Social Class

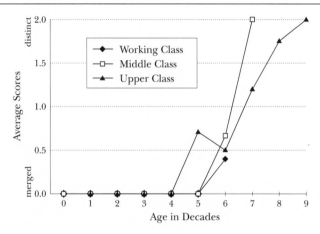

The merger is confirmed by acoustic analysis. For the speakers
for whom *merry* and *Mary* are identical in perception and production in the minimal-pair test, the two vowels are very close or overlap completely in phonetic space, as in the speech of Emily C., 20,
and Kathy A., 42 (figures 6.22 and 6.23). Figure 6.24 shows the two
vowels in the speech of Diane O., 53, an upper-class speaker for
whom *merry* and *Mary* were close in a minimal-pair test—the vowels
do not overlap, but they are fairly close acoustically.

FIGURE 6.22

Emily C., 20, Charleston, S.C., Middle Class: *Merry-Mary*

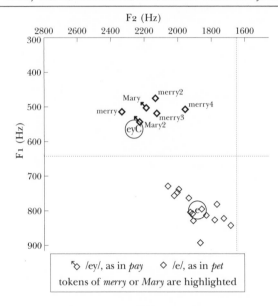

FIGURE 6.23

Kathy A., 42, Charleston, S.C., Lower-Middle Class: *Merry-Mary*

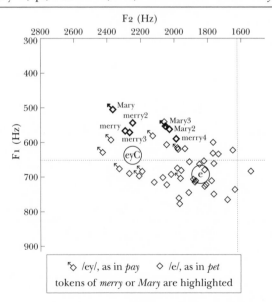

FIGURE 6.24

Diane O., 53, Charleston, S.C., Upper Class: *Merry-Mary*

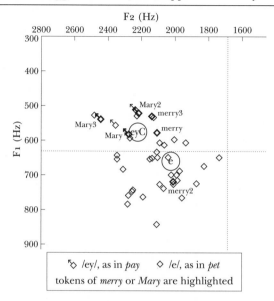

tokens of *merry* or *Mary* are highlighted

6.4. MERGER OF /ihr/ AND /ehr/

The merger of high front vowels before tautosyllabic /r/ was a prominent feature of Charleston's phonological system in its traditional form; it was first listed by Primer (1888). The lack of contrast between /ihr/, as in *dear*, and /ehr/, as in *hair*, resulted in homophony of pairs such as *fear-fair*, *beer-bear*, *hear-hair*, *dear-dare*, and so on. It appears that it must have started giving way to a distinction between the two vowels fairly early on, as McDavid (1955) describes the lack of contrast as belonging to a relic area, and Kurath and McDavid describe the two vowels as distinct in the two synopses for Charleston that they include in *PEAS*: the vowel of *ear* (/ihr/) is realized as [iə], whereas the vowel of *stairs* (/ehr/) is realized as [eə] and [ɛə]. However, in describing the vowels in *ear*, *here*, *beard*, and *queer*, they say that "in the tidewater area of South Carolina ... *care* /keə/ sometimes rimes with *ear* /eə/" (*PEAS* 1961, 117). Similarly, in commenting on the synopses of the Lower South they add that "[i]n *care*, *stairs*, etc. the Low Country has /e/, articulated as [e~ɛ^].... Since *ear, beard* often have /e/ in this subarea, *ear* sometimes rimes with *care*; but most speakers who have /e/ in ear have /æ/ in care" (*PEAS* 1961, 22). In maps 34 to 40 of *PEAS*, Charleston shows some over- lap between the vowels of *care, stairs,* and *chair,* on the one hand, and *ear, here, beard,* and *queer,* on the other—both word classes are sometimes realized as [e].

The speech of William McTeer, described in chapter 2, shows a lack of distinction between /ihr/ and /ehr/: in a minimal-pair test, *beer* and *bear* sound identical to him, and he produces them as the same. In addition, words such as *hear, care,* and *deer* produced in spontaneous speech overlap with each other and with *beer* and *bear* in the F_1/F_2 dimension. This confirms the early descriptions of the dialect in that a merger of /ihr/ and /ehr/ could be found in the Charleston area in the first half of the twentieth century. The merged vowel of the traditional dialect is in lower position, that is, it is close to the vowel of *fair, bear,* and *hair* in dialects of English which do not have the merger. This is similar to West Indian English but different from New Zealand English (Holmes and Bell 1992; Maclagan and Gordon 1996; Gordon and Maclagan 2001) and the English of Tristan da Cunha and of St. Helena, three other dialects known for a merger of /ihr/ and /ehr/, where the two phonemes are merged in high position, that is, the merged vowel sounds close to *fear, bear,* and *here* in other dialects of English (Trudgill 2004, 146).

The vast majority of the speakers in O'Cain's (1972) study had a distinction between /ihr/ and /ehr/, which confirmed McDavid's (1955) and Kurath and McDavid's (*PEAS* 1961) conclusions that a distinction between the two vowels was now the predominant form and that the merger was a relic feature in Charleston. O'Cain's sample was stratified into three social classes: upper, middle, and lower. He concludes that "the implementation of the *fear:fair* con- trast (Table 3) is quite strong in MW, LW.... It is distinctly less well established among other classes, especially among younger speak- ers of the UW[hite]" (1972, 78). He goes on to suggest that the motivation for the lower rate of contrast in the latter group was "differential regard for the old ways of the community" (78). However, the results presented in his table 3 (O'Cain 1972, 136–37) do not provide strong support for his conclusion. His lower-class sample had 24 white speakers, his middle-class sample had 29 speakers, and his upper-class sample had 8 speakers. In the upper class, two speakers had a lack of contrast for some of the words in the two vowel classes: a 70-year-old speaker had [e] in *fear, fair,* and *hair* (though he had /ɪ/ in *ear*), and a 20-year-old upper-class speaker had [e] in *ear, beard,* and *hair.* The other two classes show a merger for some (but not all) of the words for some (but not all) of the speakers between 30 and 60, though one 20-year-old lower-class speaker shows the same vowel in *ear* and *hair,* namely [ɚ]. While O'Cain's results show clearly that a contrast between /ihr/ and /ehr/ was already the predominant form at the time of his study, there seems to be little support for the claim that the contrast was less established in the upper class.

The speech of the informants in this study shows that a distinction between /ihr/ and /ehr/ is indeed by far the most common form used in Charleston today and that a merger of the two vowels generally occurs only in the speech of some of the oldest members of the community. A regression analysis of the results of the minimal-pair test reveals (tables 6.5 and 6.6) that there is no social class

TABLE 6.5

Regression Analysis of the *beer-bear* Merger in Minimal-Pair Tests
for Production Scored Impressionistically

r^2 (adjusted) = 41.7%		
Variable	*Coefficient*	*Prob*
Constant	2.555	< 0.0001
Age (in 25-year generations)	−0.023	< 0.0001

TABLE 6.6

Regression Analysis of the *fear-fair* Merger in Minimal-Pair Tests
for Production Scored Impressionistically

r^2 (adjusted) = 38.4%		
Variable	*Coefficient*	*Prob*
Constant	2.551	< 0.0001
Age (in 25-year generations)	−0.023	< 0.0001

effect, and for two of the three pairs used in the minimal-pair tests, there is no gender effect either. As with the other mergers, each informant's replies were scored on a two-point scale, ranging from 0 for merged to 2 for completely distinct.

In other words, a contrast between the two vowels or lack thereof cannot be expected to occur more in one social group in comparison with the others. The progress of the distinction between /ihr/ and /ehr/ in apparent time based on two minimal-pair tests is shown in figure 6.25. A lack of distinction between the two vowels is especially clear for speakers over 70—there is a steep rise in the rate of the distinction for 60- and 50-year-olds, with a clear contrast for the vast majority of speakers below the age of 50. An inspection of figure 6.25 suggests that the retreat of the merger follows an S-shaped curve, with the best fit obtained through the logistic function (figures 6.26 and 6.27).

The change from a merger to a distinction is also shown acoustically as an increase in the Cartesian distance in Hertz between the two vowels in apparent time (figure 6.28).[2] Table 6.7 presents the results of a regression analysis of the distance between the /ihr/ and /ehr/ classes, which included age, gender, and social class. Age turns out to be the only significant factor: the Cartesian distance between

FIGURE 6.25

Merger of /ihr/ and /ehr/ in Minimal-Pair Tests Scored Impressionistically by Age in Decades

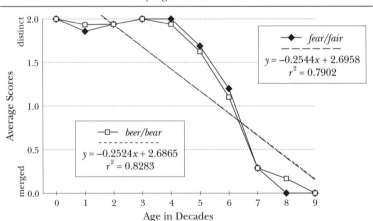

FIGURE 6.26

Logistic Transform of the *beer-bear* Merger in Minimal-Pair Tests
for Production Scored Impressionistically by Age for Decades 3–9

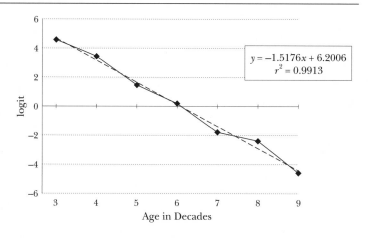

$$y = -1.5176x + 6.2006$$
$$r^2 = 0.9913$$

FIGURE 6.27

Logistic Transform of the *fear-fair* Merger in Minimal-Pair Tests
for Production Scored Impressionistically by Age for Decades 3–9

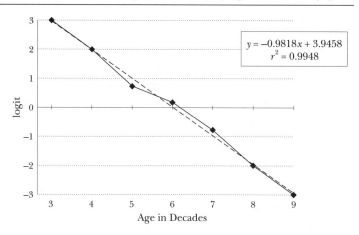

$$y = -0.9818x + 3.9458$$
$$r^2 = 0.9948$$

the two vowels can be expected to increase by 109 Hz with each
successive generation of 25 years.

Interestingly, the two vowels may be the same for some pairs
of words, such as *beer* and *bear* or *fear* and *fair*, but they will sometimes be different for other words, for example, *here* and *hair*, for

FIGURE 6.28

Cartesian Distance between the Means of /ihr/ and /ehr/ by Age

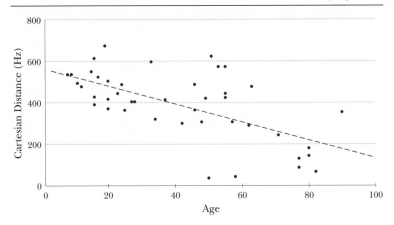

TABLE 6.7

Regression Analysis of Cartesian Distance between /ihr/ and /ehr/
for 43 Speakers

r^2 (adjusted) = 37.8%		
Variable	*Coefficient*	*Prob*
Constant	571	≤ 0.0001
Age (in 25-year generations)	–109	≤ 0.0001

the same speaker.[3] Figure 6.29 presents the two vowels before /r/ in the speech of Victoria G., 90, who is largely *r*-less. She does not distinguish between *beer* and *bear* or *fear* and *fair* in a minimal-pair test—the vowel in both words in each pair sounds closer to the canonically lower one, that is, closer to /e/. Her *dear* is also rather low and sounds like *dare*. However, her *here* is higher and fronter than her *hair* and the other words mentioned above. She distinguishes between *here* and *hair* in a minimal-pair test in perception and production, although there is some noticeable F1/F2 overlap between the nuclei of the vowels in the two words, and *hair* is more fronted than other /ehr/ words.

Another example of a partial merger is John E., 80. For him *beer* and *bear*, and *fear* and *fair* are identical in both perception and

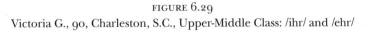

FIGURE 6.29

Victoria G., 90, Charleston, S.C., Upper-Middle Class: /ihr/ and /ehr/

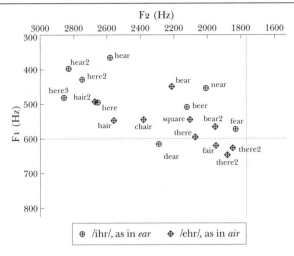

production, but *here* and *hair* are distinct—the vowel in *here* sounds fronter and higher than the vowel in *hair,* which can be seen in an acoustic vowel display, although *hair* is also fronter than other /ehr/ words (figure 6.30).

For a number of speakers, on the other hand, the merger is complete; they do not distinguish between members of the three pairs: *fear-fair, beer-bear, here-hair* in perception and in production, and the tokens of the two vowels overlap completely in the F1/F2 dimension, as in the speech of Fred W., 50 (figure 6.31). However, for the vast majority of the speakers in the sample the two vowels before /r/ are clearly distinct: they distinguish between them in both perception and production in a minimal-pair test, which is confirmed by acoustic analysis, showing clear separation of the nuclei of /ihr/, which is higher and fronter, and /ehr/, as in the speech of Margaret C., 46, and Vincent J., 33 (figures 6.32 and 6.33).

There seems to be some social awareness of the merger in the community, and possibly some social evaluation, which suggests that the /ihr/-/ehr/ merger in Charleston may be a counterexample to the idea that mergers are not subject to overt social observation

FIGURE 6.30

John E., 80, Charleston, S.C., Middle Class: /ihr/ and /ehr/

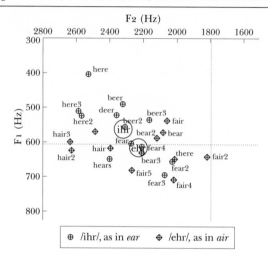

FIGURE 6.31

Fred W., 50, Charleston, S.C., Working Class: /ihr/ and /ehr/

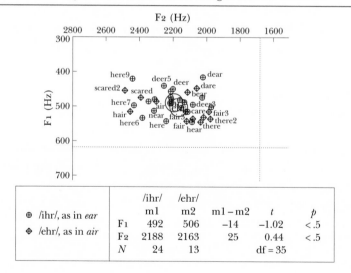

		/ihr/	/ehr/			
⊕ /ihr/, as in *ear*		m1	m2	m1 − m2	*t*	*p*
	F1	492	506	−14	−1.02	< .5
⊕ /ehr/, as in *air*	F2	2188	2163	25	0.44	< .5
	N	24	13		df = 35	

FIGURE 6.32

Margaret C., 46, Charleston, S.C., Middle Class: /ihr/ and /ehr/

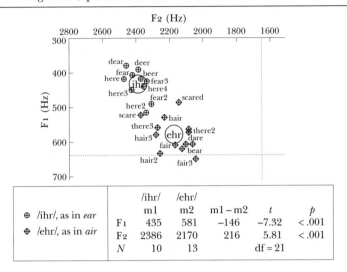

	/ihr/	/ehr/			
	m1	m2	m1 – m2	*t*	*p*
⊕ /ihr/, as in *ear*					
⊕ /ehr/, as in *air*	F1	435	581	–146	–7.32	<.001
	F2	2386	2170	216	5.81	<.001
	N	10	13		df = 21	

FIGURE 6.33

Vincent J., 33, Charleston, S.C., Lower-Middle Class: /ihr/ and /ehr/

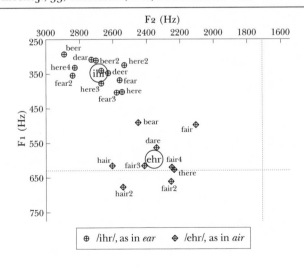

⊕ /ihr/, as in *ear*   ⊕ /ehr/, as in *air*

and comment. Those speakers over 60 who have the merger in their spontaneous speech or in the reading of a word list also show it in a minimal-pair test: they admit that *beer* sounds identical with *bear, fear* sounds identical to *fair*, and *here* sounds identical to *hair*. Most of them are aware of the fact that this is the traditional way of speaking in Charleston, and they show no self-correction toward a distinction. John M., 73, an upper-class Charlestonian with a complete merger in perception and production, comments: "*beer*, as much as *pen*, I was teased about, still am but not as much. When I was in the Navy, I would say I want a brew, in order to avoid the usual laughter and good-natured teasing I got about the way that I pronounced the word, and I tried to learn to say BEER [high vowel]."

Some speakers below the age of 60 who have a distinction are also aware of the merger as the traditional form in the dialect. For example, Jonathan C., 28, an upper-class speaker, commented that his mother and his grandfather had pronounced *beer* and *bear* and *here* and *hair* in the same way; he has a clear distinction between the two vowels. Margaret C., 46, a middle-class Charlestonian, also commented that those pairs of words sounded the same in her mother's speech; she has a clear distinction (figure 6.32). Another middle-class speaker, Martin P., 50, commented that *beer* and *bear* were the same for his grandmother—again, his speech shows a clear distinction between the two vowels. Edward H., 56, an upper-class Charlestonian with a clear distinction, said, "Those sound different to me but for some Charleston people they would be pronounced very similarly."

Figures 6.34 and 6.35 present vowel plots for two upper-class speakers: Richard A., 77, and his daughter Sally A., 55. A minimal-pair test reveals that he has a complete merger in perception and production, which is confirmed by acoustic analysis, whereas she shows a clear distinction in a minimal-pair test and the two vowels are separated in phonetic space. Similarly, figures 6.36 and 6.37 include vowel charts for two generations of another upper-class family: Elizabeth O., 82, and her daughter, Diane O., 53. The mother does not distinguish between /ihr/ and /ehr/ in a minimal-pair test and the vowels overlap in the F_1/F_2 dimension, whereas the vowels are completely distinct for her daughter, in both perception and

FIGURE 6.34

Richard A., 77, Charleston, S.C., Upper Class: /ihr/ and /ehr/

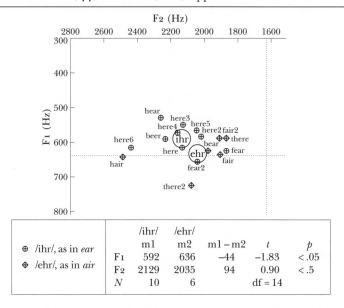

		/ihr/	/ehr/			
		m1	m2	m1 – m2	*t*	*p*
⊕	/ihr/, as in *ear*					
		F1	592	636	–44	–1.83	< .05
⊕	/ehr/, as in *air*	F2	2129	2035	94	0.90	< .5
		N	10	6		df = 14	

FIGURE 6.35

Sally A., 55, Charleston, S.C., Upper Class: /ihr/ and /ehr/

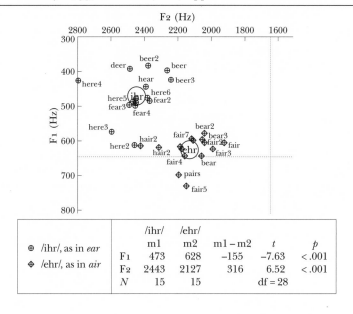

		/ihr/	/ehr/			
		m1	m2	m1 – m2	*t*	*p*
⊕	/ihr/, as in *ear*					
		F1	473	628	–155	–7.63	< .001
⊕	/ehr/, as in *air*	F2	2443	2127	316	6.52	< .001
		N	15	15		df = 28	

FIGURE 6.36

Elizabeth O., 82, Charleston, S.C., Upper Class: /ihr/ and /ehr/

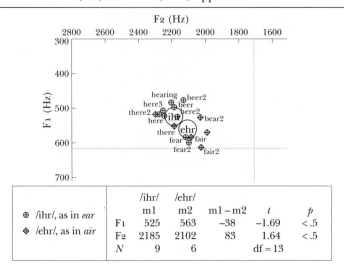

		/ihr/	/ehr/			
⊕ /ihr/, as in *ear*		m1	m2	m1 – m2	*t*	*p*
	F1	525	563	–38	–1.69	< .5
◈ /ehr/, as in *air*	F2	2185	2102	83	1.64	< .5
	N	9	6		df = 13	

FIGURE 6.37

Diane O., 53, Charleston, S.C., Upper Class: /ihr/ and /ehr/

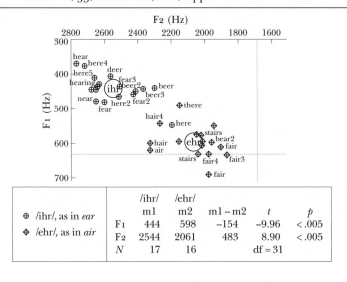

		/ihr/	/ehr/			
⊕ /ihr/, as in *ear*		m1	m2	m1 – m2	*t*	*p*
	F1	444	598	–154	–9.96	< .005
◈ /ehr/, as in *air*	F2	2544	2061	483	8.90	< .005
	N	17	16		df = 31	

production, the vowels being separated from each other acoustically. The change from a lack of contrast to a clear distinction between /ihr/ and /ehr/ was then very abrupt and was complete within one generation.

A few of the speakers commented during the minimal-pair test that they vary between a distinction and a merger of the two vowels, that is, sometimes they pronounce words such as *beer* and *bear* the same and other times they may sound different from each other. For example, Mark N., 45, a middle-class speaker, commented during the minimal-pair test that the words in the pairs might sound the same when he spoke with his brother; he distinguishes between all three pairs of words in a minimal-pair test, though his *here* sounded close to his *hair*. For Simon J., 58, an upper-middle-class speaker, the two vowels before /r/ are close in production, but he claims they sound different to him. He also commented that he used to say *beer* and *bear* in the same way but that now he is more conscious of the difference.

Neil S., 58, a working-class Charlestonian, shows a complete merger in a minimal-pair test, and the two vowels can be seen to overlap completely in the F1/F2 dimension (figure 6.38). He comments that he sometimes pronounces *here* as "here7" in figure 6.38, that is, with a high front vowel, one normal for most other dialects of English. This particular token is fronter and higher than his other tokens of /ihr/, including his other tokens of *here* produced in the minimal-pair test. He adds that he does not do it very often. Similarly, Matthew R., 60, an upper-middle-class Charlestonian, has a distinction for *fear-fair* but a merger for *beer-bear* and *here-hair*. He comments that when he is speaking carefully he probably distinguishes between the words in all of the pairs. When asked about his most natural way of speaking, he produces *beer-bear* and *here-hair* as the same.

Some of the younger Charlestonians, on the other hand, that is, those who have a clear distinction between /ihr/ and /ehr/, are unaware of the traditional lack of distinction between the two vowels in Charleston. Catherine A., 25, for example, has never heard words such as *beer* and *bear* to be pronounced in the same way in Charleston—her /ihr/ and /ehr/ are presented in figure 6.39. Nei-

FIGURE 6.38

Neil S., 58, Charleston, S.C., Working Class: /ihr/ and /ehr/

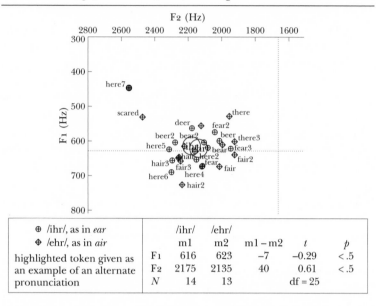

	/ihr/	/ehr/			
⊕ /ihr/, as in *ear*	m1	m2	m1 – m2	*t*	*p*
⊕ /ehr/, as in *air*					
highlighted token given as	F1	616	623	–7	–0.29	< .5
an example of an alternate	F2	2175	2135	40	0.61	< .5
pronunciation	N	14	13		df = 25	

FIGURE 6.39

Catherine A., 25, Charleston, S.C., Working Class: /ihr/ and /ehr/

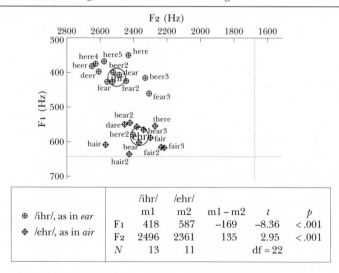

		/ihr/	/ehr/			
		m1	m2	m1 – m2	*t*	*p*
⊕ /ihr/, as in *ear*	F1	418	587	–169	–8.36	< .001
⊕ /ehr/, as in *air*	F2	2496	2361	135	2.95	< .001
	N	13	11		df = 22	

ther has William V., 37, a middle-class speaker, who commented that *beer* and *bear* might sound the same for "real country folks" and that it might be a country way of talking. Like the vast majority of Charlestonians today, he has a clear distinction in perception and production (figure 6.40).

Kathy A., 42, a lower-middle-class Charlestonian showing a distinction in perception and production in a minimal-pair test, notes that in her speech the two sounds are not always identified correctly (the numbers next to the words refer to the tokens in figure 6.41):

beer[2] and *bear*[2] [pauses, smiles] sound different to me, though some people think– OK *beer*[3] is something you drink and *bear*[4] is an animal, [but] some people if they hear me say *bear*[3] they think I'm saying *beer*[4]. That happens all the time. [If you say what?] If I'm saying *beer*[5], they think I'm saying or if I say *bear*[5], they think I'm saying *beer*[6], like the drink.... For some reason I know when I say *bear*[6], they go b– they think I'm talking about *beer*[7] and I'm not talking about *beer*[8].

FIGURE 6.40
William V., 37, Charleston, S.C., Middle Class: /ihr/ and /ehr/

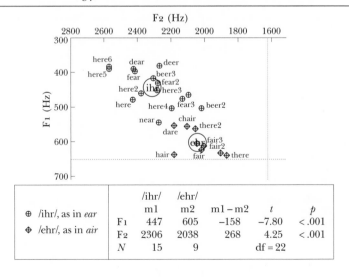

		/ihr/	/ehr/			
		m1	m2	m1 – m2	*t*	*p*
⊕ /ihr/, as in *ear*	F1	447	605	−158	−7.80	< .001
⊕ /ehr/, as in *air*	F2	2306	2038	268	4.25	< .001
	N	15	9		df = 22	

FIGURE 6.41

Kathy A., 42, Charleston, S.C., Lower-Middle Class: /ihr/ and /ehr/

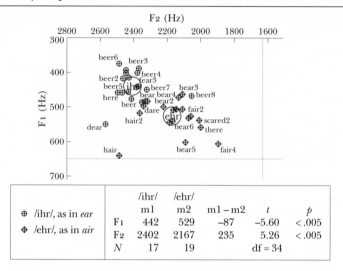

		/ihr/	/ehr/			
⊕ /ihr/, as in *ear*		m1	m2	m1 – m2	t	p
	F1	442	529	−87	−5.60	< .005
✦ /ehr/, as in *air*	F2	2402	2167	235	5.26	< .005
	N	17	19		df = 34	

FIGURE 6.42

Jane Y., 16, Charleston, S.C., Middle Class: /ihr/ and /ehr/

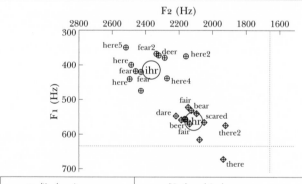

		/ihr/	/ehr/			
⊕ /ihr/, as in *ear*		m1	m2	m1 – m2	t	p
✦ /ehr/, as in *air*						
highlighted token given as	F1	417	565	−148	−6.45	< .001
an example of an alternate	F2	2361	2105	256	4.94	< .001
pronunciation	N	12	11		df = 21	

Finally, Jane Y., 16, a middle-class Charlestonian, shows a clear distinction between /ihr/ and /ehr/ in both a minimal-pair test and the reading of a word list. However, she pronounced the pair *beer-bear* with the same vowel, the same one she had used in other /ehr/ words up to that point (figure 6.42). When asked about it, she corrected herself and pronounced *beer* with a higher vowel. When asked which version was more natural to her, she replied "probably the first version, the dumb version [laughter]." At another point she had said that her geometry teacher pronounced *fear* and *fair* in the same way and sometimes her mother did too.

To sum up, people over 70 are likely to have no contrast between the two vowels, at least for some lexical items. People younger than 70 are likely to have a clear distinction, and there does not seem to be any correlation between the presence of a distinction and the social class of a speaker. The overt comments about the merger indicate that there is some awareness of it in the community, usually as a feature of the traditional dialect, which goes against the idea that mergers are below the level of public consciousness, and as such do not elicit overt comments. While some speakers are aware of the merger as a traditional way of speaking in Charleston, others do not make the connection and may associate a lack of contrast between the two vowels with speech characteristic of rural areas. This is not entirely surprising, because, as Kurath and McDavid (*PEAS* 1961) note, a lack of contrast between the two vowels before /r/ could be found in the tidewater area of South Carolina, and for many decades there was a strong connection between Charleston and the plantations located in the Low Country of South Carolina.

As has been mentioned above, there is no social class effect—the few people below 70 who have no contrast between the two vowels belong to different social classes—and there is no difference between the two genders for the pair *fear-fair* and *beer-bear*. However, regression analysis for the pair *here-hair* reveals a weak gender effect: the level of distinction between /ihr/ and /ehr/ in the two words can be expected to be slightly higher for women than for men (table 6.8).

TABLE 6.8

Regression Analysis of the *here-hair* Merger in Minimal-Pair Tests
for Production Scored Impressionistically

r^2 (adjusted) = 41.8%		
Variable	*Coefficient*	*Prob*
Constant	2.292	< 0.0001
Women	0.292	< 0.017
Age (in 25-year generations)	−0.021	< 0.0001

FIGURE 6.43

Merger of *here* and *hair* in Minimal-Pair Tests for Production
Scored Impressionistically by Age in Decades and Gender

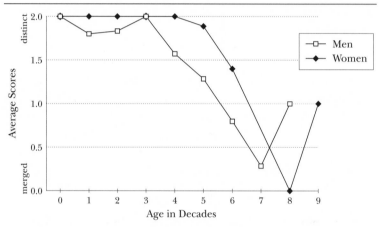

Figure 6.43 presents the progress of the change from a lack of contrast toward a distinction between /ihr/ and /ehr/ in apparent time separately for the two genders. The line for men is slightly lower, indicating that men can be expected to have a slightly higher level of the merger of the two vowels than women for this particular pair of words.

The slight dip away from a complete distinction for the 10–19 age group is due to Tim P., a 12-year-old middle-class boy, who claimed in a minimal-pair test that *here* and *hair* (and the words in the other two pairs used in the test) sounded the same to him and he pronounced them identically, with a vowel close to [e]. However, in his spontaneous speech, there is a clear contrast between

/ihr/ and /ehr/, and the contrast is maintained in the reading of a wordlist. He was interviewed together with his two sisters, and he had heard his parents conduct the test a few days earlier—both parents have a clear distinction between /ihr/ and /ehr/, as do his sisters. When reading the minimal pairs, he insisted that the words sounded identical to him, and he in fact produced them as the same, to which his older sister said, "Right, they do. You talk funny." Tim's vowels are presented in figure 6.44, with the minimal-pair tokens highlighted.

One wonders whether a lack of distinction between the two vowels found in the traditional Charleston dialect has perhaps acquired a new sort of prestige, not as a conservative way of speaking, connected with the upper strata of society, but rather as covert prestige, possibly associated with masculinity, at least for some Charlestonians, such as Tim P. However, there is not enough data at this point to firmly support this hypothesis.

It should be stressed that this small gender difference has been observed for only one pair of words used in the test, *here-hair*, and the difference itself is rather small. In general, a lack of distinction between /ihr/ and /ehr/ is no longer a robust feature of the dialect.

FIGURE 6.44
Tim P., 12, Charleston, S.C., Middle Class: /ihr/ and /ehr/

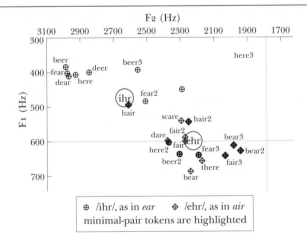

While it has not disappeared entirely, it is evident that for the vast majority of Charlestonians, there is a clear contrast between the two vowels, both in perception and in production.

The introduction of a distinction between /ihr/ and /ehr/ in Charleston appears to be a counterexample to the generalization about mergers known as Garde's Principle (Garde 1961; Labov 1994), whereby mergers are irreversible by linguistic means—in other words, once a merger, always a merger. It is not entirely clear how complete this merger was in the traditional dialect, that is, whether there were no speakers with a distinction and whether those with no distinction always merged the two vowels in production. In other words, there is not enough evidence to exclude the possibility of a near-merger in the traditional dialect, which has now unmerged (Labov, Karen, and Miller 1991; Labov 1994).

While some of the speakers in the sample show a merger for some pairs of words but a distinction for others, there are speakers for whom the merger is complete in perception and production in all contexts, and acoustic analysis reveals a complete overlap in acoustic space.

If it is not a case of a near merger, another explanation of this apparent counterexample to Garde's Principle may be that the reversal of the merger has been due to EXTRALINGUISTIC means. There is some evidence of migrations into Charleston of speakers from other parts of the South, beginning with the opening of the Navy Yard in 1901, intensifying during the time of World War I, and then in the late 1930s and during World War II, continuing after the war as a result of the buildup of military installations in the area, such as the naval base (see chapter 1). In addition, there has been a more recent wave of migrations from outside of the South, following the rediscovery of Charleston as a popular tourist destination within the last few decades. As a result, over half of the inhabitants of the Historic District on the southern tip of the peninsula were born outside of South Carolina (figure 3.10). While the unmerging of two phonemes is virtually impossible for adults, Chambers's (1992) study suggests that children below the age of 7 may acquire a distinction even if such a contrast was not present in their dialect when they were acquiring it. In other words, if there were enough speakers with the distinction from outside of the Charleston area providing input for children growing up in Charleston, the children might have been able to acquire the distinction. On the other hand, as the merger seems to have started unmerging in the 1930s or even slightly earlier—people born around the time of World War II already show a distinction—it is unlikely that the initial wave of migrants during World War I would have been massive enough to provide a trigger for the change.

However, Feagin (1997, 138) suggests that peer pressure had a strong linguistic effect upon upper-class children in Charleston and gives the example of palatalized velar stops, as in [kʲar] and [gʲardn], which, while considered prestigious in South Carolina in the 1940s, were ridiculed by lower-class white children. Feagin notes that "upper class children attending the public schools in Charleston acquired the unpalatalized forms, providing another example of how non-prestigious forms can wipe out prestigious forms" (138). As indicated by the accounts of the Charlestonians cited above, there was similar peer pressure in the case of the /ihr/-/ehr/ merger: those pronouncing *beer* in the same way as *bear*, for instance, would be teased, sometimes leading them to choose another word entirely, such as *brew*. This suggests that in rare circumstances, given enough social pressure, mergers may become unmerged and that the loss of the /ihr/-/ehr/ merger in Charleston may indeed be a counterexample to Garde's Principle.

7. MERGERS IN PROGRESS

7.1. THE LOW-BACK MERGER

CHARLESTON IS UNDERGOING the low-back merger: a merger of the short-*o* class (/o/), as in *cot* and *Don*, and the long open *o* class (/oh/), as in *caught* and *dawn*, resulting in homophony of words such as *cot-caught*, *Don-dawn*, and *hock-hawk*. This is a merger covering vast territories of North America and is consistent in Canada, the West, western Pennsylvania, and eastern New England. In the South the nuclei of the two vowels usually overlap in the F1-F2 dimension, but the vowels remain distinct, as the /oh/ class (*caught*) has developed a back upglide and the nucleus is often unrounded. As such the vowel is best represented as /aw/; there is no overlap with the vowel of *house* and *mouth*, as its nucleus is now strongly fronted to /æw/ (*ANAE* 2006, chap. 18.4). The Telsur project reports a number of scattered points in the South with the low-back merger, but only before nasals, as in *Don-dawn* (figure 7.1).

Charleston has traditionally had two distinct phonemes, with no reports of a back upglide for /oh/, as in *caught* (*PEAS* 1961, maps 22–24). This is confirmed by the speech of William McTeer presented in chapter 2, representing the dialect at the beginning of the twentieth century, where the nuclei of the two vowels are clearly separated in phonetic space and the long open *o* has no back upglide. There is no evidence of a back upglide in the speech of the speakers in this project. The results of the minimal-pair tests conducted for 97 informants in the sample show that Charlestonians vary in the extent to which they merge the two vowels, and regression analysis shows that the only significant factor is age (tables 7.1 and 7.2)

In other words, the older the speaker, the more likely he or she is to maintain a distinction. Speakers over 50 almost uniformly distinguish between *cot* and *caught*, whereas for speakers below that age, the merger progresses at a fast rate. For children and teenag-

FIGURE 7.1

The Low-Back Merger

(Telsur Project, Univ. of Pennsylvania)

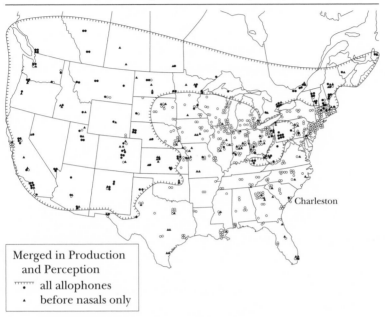

Merged in Production
and Perception

⊓⊓⊓⊓⊓ all allophones

▴　before nasals only

TABLE 7.1

Regression Analysis of the *Don-dawn* Merger in Minimal-Pair Tests
Scored Impressionistically

r^2 (adjusted) = 24.0%		
Variable	*Coefficient*	*Prob*
Constant	−0.098	0.563
Age (in 25-year generations)	0.488	< 0.0001

TABLE 7.2

Regression Analysis of the *cot-caught* Merger in Minimal-Pair Tests
Scored Impressionistically

r^2 (adjusted) = 42.7%		
Variable	*Coefficient*	*Prob*
Constant	−0.034	0.831
Age (in 25-year generations)	0.702	< 0.0001

ers, then, the two phonemes are almost completely merged (figures 7.2 and 7.3).

The age coefficient for *cot-caught* is 0.7 for each 25 years of age, indicating that the merger can be expected to advance 0.7 units on the two-point scale for each successive generation of 25 years. The age coefficient for the merger before nasals is lower, at .49, which is due to the fact that /o/ and /oh/ before nasals tend to merge earlier than before oral consonants. This is seen in the difference between the two graphs in figures 7.2 and 7.3: for many people over the age of 50, the two vowels are either merged or close before nasals, as opposed to allophones preceding an oral consonant, hence the difference in the steepness of the slopes in the two graphs. The finding that the most advanced allophone is before nasals conforms to what we find in other areas where the low-back merger is in progress (*ANAE* 2006).

It is worth noting that no clear gender or social class differences emerge. All social groups and both genders are undergoing the change at an equal rate. In addition, the speakers' reports in the minimal-pair test and their pronunciations of the minimal pairs are almost identical, that is, their perception is matched by

FIGURE 7.2

Merger of *cot* and *caught* in Minimal-Pair Tests Scored
Impressionistically by Age in Decades

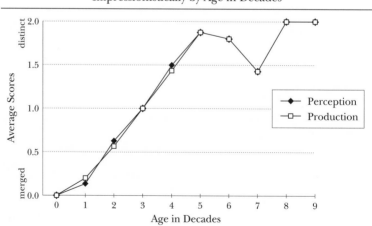

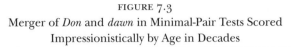

FIGURE 7.3
Merger of *Don* and *dawn* in Minimal-Pair Tests Scored
Impressionistically by Age in Decades

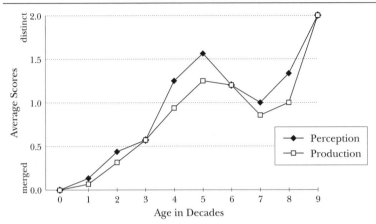

their production, at least in these elicitation tasks. This means that the speakers' judgments are not likely to have been influenced by either stigmatization or prestige connected to the variable in question, which suggests that the low-back merger in Charleston, just like many other mergers in general, is taking place below the level of social awareness.

The progress of the low-back merger in apparent time is shown in figures 7.4–7.8, which present acoustic measurements of the two vowels across a few generations. The captions include the results on the perception of the two vowels for the particular speaker, based on the minimal-pair tests. For the oldest speakers, the two nuclei are clearly separated in acoustic space with little or no overlap between individual tokens. Middle-aged speakers, such as Frank T. (figure 7.7), are transitional speakers, for whom the two vowels are merged for one allophone, usually before nasals, but distinct for others. There is some overlap between individual tokens, though the means remain separate. For speakers around 20 or younger, the means are very close, with a high degree of overlap between the tokens.

It is worth noting that even for speakers who have a complete merger in perception, such as Pam K., 16, in figure 7.9, the means

FIGURE 7.4

Victoria G., 90, Charleston, S.C., Upper-Middle Class: /o/ and /oh/

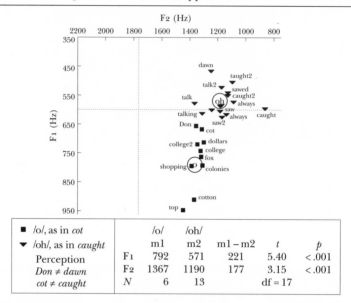

		/o/	/oh/			
■ /o/, as in *cot*		m1	m2	m1 – m2	*t*	*p*
▼ /oh/, as in *caught*						
Perception	F1	792	571	221	5.40	< .001
Don ≠ dawn	F2	1367	1190	177	3.15	< .001
cot ≠ caught	*N*	6	13		df = 17	

FIGURE 7.5

Valerie R., 62, Charleston, S.C., Working Class: /o/ and /oh/

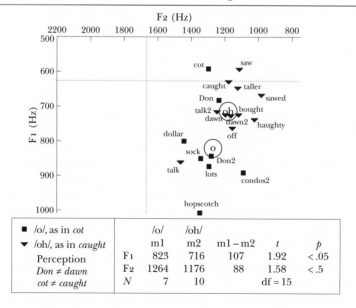

		/o/	/oh/			
■ /o/, as in *cot*		m1	m2	m1 – m2	*t*	*p*
▼ /oh/, as in *caught*						
Perception	F1	823	716	107	1.92	< .05
Don ≠ dawn	F2	1264	1176	88	1.58	< .5
cot ≠ caught	*N*	7	10		df = 15	

FIGURE 7.6

Judy O., 55, Charleston, S.C., Lower-Middle Class: /o/ and /oh/

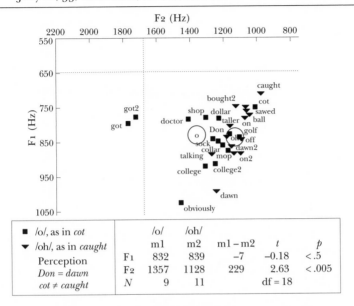

		/o/	/oh/			
■ /o/, as in *cot*		m1	m2	m1 − m2	*t*	*p*
▼ /oh/, as in *caught*	F1	832	839	−7	−0.18	< .5
Perception	F2	1357	1128	229	2.63	< .005
Don = dawn	*N*	9	11		df = 18	
cot ≠ caught						

FIGURE 7.7

Frank T., 48, Charleston, S.C., Working Class: /o/ and /oh/

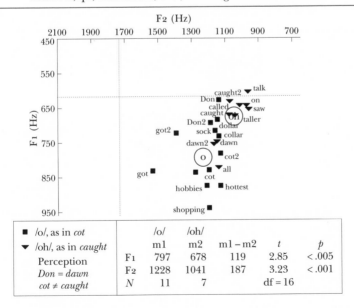

		/o/	/oh/			
■ /o/, as in *cot*		m1	m2	m1 − m2	*t*	*p*
▼ /oh/, as in *caught*	F1	797	678	119	2.85	< .005
Perception	F2	1228	1041	187	3.23	< .001
Don = dawn	*N*	11	7		df = 16	
cot ≠ caught						

FIGURE 7.8

Heather G., 19, Charleston, S.C., Working Class: /o/ and /oh/

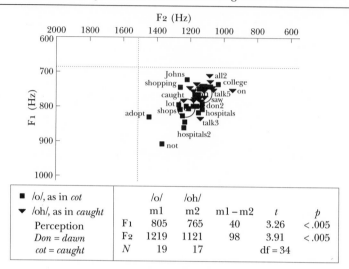

		/o/	/oh/			
■ /o/, as in *cot*		m1	m2	m1 – m2	*t*	*p*
▼ /oh/, as in *caught*						
Perception	F1	805	765	40	3.26	< .005
Don = dawn	F2	1219	1121	98	3.91	< .005
cot = caught	N	19	17		df = 34	

FIGURE 7.9

Pam K., 16, Charleston, S.C., Upper Class: /o/ and /oh/

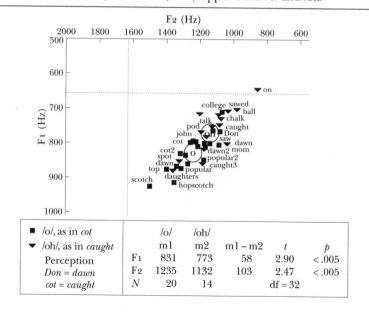

		/o/	/oh/			
■ /o/, as in *cot*		m1	m2	m1 – m2	*t*	*p*
▼ /oh/, as in *caught*						
Perception	F1	831	773	58	2.90	< .005
Don = dawn	F2	1235	1132	103	2.47	< .005
cot = caught	N	20	14		df = 32	

do not overlap entirely, though there is substantial overlap between individual tokens of the two phonemes. The results of the minimal-pair tests for perception and production are almost identical: if the two vowels are merged, they are merged equally in perception and production. However, acoustic measurements that include many more tokens than just the ones elicited in the minimal-pair test show a difference between the two means even for speakers who report a merger in perception (though it is not statistically significant for some of them). This difference indicates that the merger is occurring earlier in perception than in production. Asymmetry in this direction is not unexpected; in fact, in the majority of cases of merger that have been described, perception precedes production (Di Paolo and Faber 1990; Herold 1990).

Table 7.3 includes the results of a regression analysis for the Cartesian distance in Hertz between the two means in the speech of 43 speakers analyzed acoustically. The distance ranges from 456 for Charles C., 77, to 44 for Peter O., 15. As in the case of the minimal-pair test, age emerges as a highly significant factor. Figure 7.10 includes a scatterplot of the Cartesian distance between the two vowels against the age of the speaker.

For every 25 years of age, the distance between the means of /o/ and /oh/ can be expected to decrease by 86 Hz. This, along with the results of the minimal-pair tests, indicates that the low-back merger is a fairly vigorous change in the dialect, as it displays a strong expansion in apparent time. As such, it is likely to expand across the whole population in the future. One structural consequence of the merger is that once the two vowel classes have been merged completely, long open *o* is unlikely to develop a back upglide common

TABLE 7.3

Regression Analysis of Cartesian Distance between /o/ and /oh/
for 43 Speakers

r^2 (adjusted) = 43.1%		
Variable	*Coefficient*	*Prob*
Constant	153	< 0.0001
Age (in 25-year generations)	86	< 0.0001
Gender	−62	0.0449

FIGURE 7.10

Cartesian Distance between the Means of /o/ and /oh/ by Age and Gender

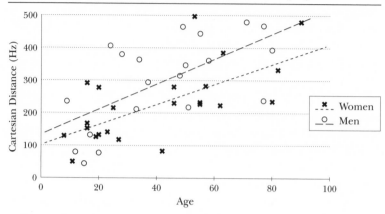

in the Inland South and to be affected by the parallel shifting of the back upgliding vowels.

Regression analysis of the acoustic measurements reveals that gender is another significant factor in the low back merger in Charleston. The distance between the means of /o/ and /oh/ can be expected to be smaller by 62 Hz for women in comparison with men (table 7.3, figure 7.10).[1] In other words, women lead in the adoption of this merger in the dialect, expressed as the decreasing distance between the acoustic means of the two phonemes. This result adds to the evidence from other studies (Herold 1990; *ANAE* 2006) indicating that women lead in the acquisition of the low back merger, and in this way confirms women's position as the leaders of linguistic change.

7.2. THE PIN-PEN MERGER

The merger of /i/ and /e/ before /n/ and /m/, as in *pin-pen* and *him-hem*, is a well-known feature of Southern phonology (Brown 1991; Montgomery and Eble 2004). It is now expanding beyond the South as defined by the operation of the Southern Shift and is present in Oklahoma, Kansas, Missouri, and southern Indiana. It is also found in scattered points across the United States, for example, in a number of cities in California, such as Bakersfield and Fresno (*ANAE* 2006).[2] It is, however, most consistent in the South and, as such, partly defines Southern phonology. The extent of the merger across North America is shown in figure 7.11.

The origin of the PIN-PEN merger is believed to go back to at least the mid-nineteenth century, though it appears to have expanded particularly rapidly in the first half of the twentieth century (Brown 1991; Bailey 2004). Charleston's traditional dialect, as described by McDavid (1955) and Kurath and McDavid (*PEAS* 1961), had a distinction between /i/ and /e/ before nasals. The speech of William McTeer, described in chapter 2, confirms those reports: the two submeans before nasals are clearly separated, and he distinguishes between the two vowels in a minimal-pair test. O'Cain (1972) reports on the beginning of the PIN-PEN merger

FIGURE 7.11
Merger of /i/ and /e/ before Nasals, as in *pin/pen*
(Telsur Project; Univ. of Pennsylvania)

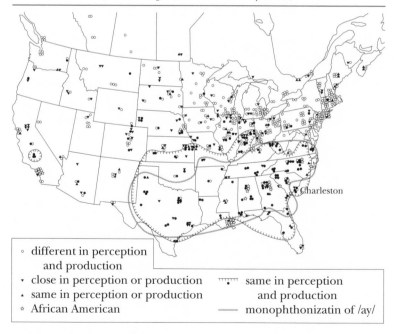

° different in perception
  and production
• close in perception or production   ⊤⊤⊤⊤ same in perception
▲ same in perception or production   and production
✩ African American   —— monophthonizatin of /ay/

in Charleston: his upper-class informants had a distinction, whereas middle-class speakers below 20, as well as working-class speakers below age 30, exhibited the merger (O'Cain 1972, 138–39). O'Cain concludes that "the new lack of contrast in *pin:pen*, then, is not only characterized by its geographical origin, the interior of the state, but by its social origin as well, outside the speech of the cultivated."

Charleston is indeed undergoing the merger of /i/ and /e/ before nasal consonants. For many speakers age 60 and older, there is a distinction in both production and perception. There is some overlap in phonetic space, and the two nasal submeans are clearly separated, as in the speech of John E., 80, in figure 7.12 and David W., 77 in figure 7.13. For speakers under age 60, however, the two allophones are often identical in perception and, especially, in production. For those, there is considerable overlap of phonetic space, and the two nasal submeans are close together, as in the speech of Margaret C., 46, in figure 7.14, and Jane Y., 16, in figure 7.15 (vowels before nasals are highlighted).

FIGURE 7.12

John E., 80, Charleston, S.C., Middle Class: /i/ and /e/ before Nasals

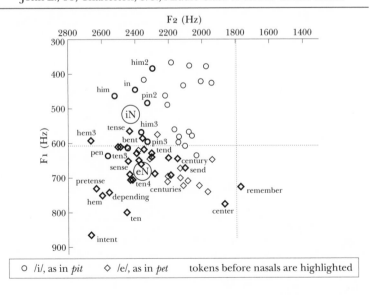

○ /i/, as in *pit*   ◇ /e/, as in *pet*   tokens before nasals are highlighted

FIGURE 7.13

David W., 77, Charleston, S.C., Lower-Middle Class: /i/ and /e/ before Nasals

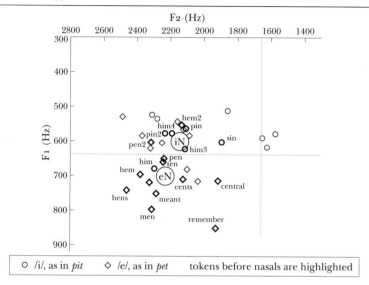

FIGURE 7.14

Margaret C., 46, Charleston, S.C., Middle Class: /i/ and /e/ before Nasals

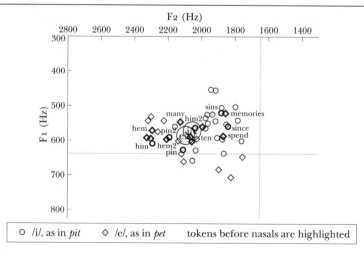

FIGURE 7.15

Jane Y., 16, Charleston, S.C., Middle Class: /i/ and /e/ before Nasals

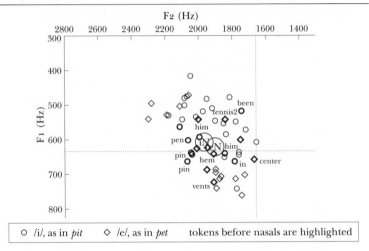

The minimal-pair test elicited the pronunciation of and judgment on two pairs of words: *pin-pen* and *him-hem*. The scores were constructed on a 2-point scale in the same way as for the other mergers described above. Regression analysis of the results of the minimal-pair tests reveals that age and social class are significant factors (table 7.4).

The age coefficient of .016 means that with every 25 years of age, the merger can be expected to progress .4 units on a 2-point scale, which makes it a fairly vigorous change. However, the social class effect is sizable and indicates that different social classes are responding differently to the merger. Graphing the progress of the

TABLE 7.4

Regression Analysis of the *pin-pen* Merger in Minimal-Pair Tests
Scored Impressionistically

r^2 (adjusted) = 44.8%		
Variable	*Coefficient*	*Prob*
Constant	−0.699	0.0004
Social class	0.2523	< 0.0001
Age (in 25-year generations)	0.408	< 0.0001

merger in apparent time separately for three social groups reveals that the upper class is lagging behind in this change (figures 7.16–7.19). The numbers are too small to analyze each of the five social

FIGURE 7.16

Merger of *him* and *hem* in Minimal-Pair Tests for Perception Scored Impressionistically by Age in Decades and Social Class

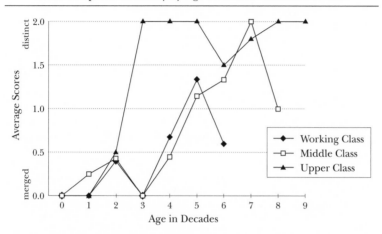

FIGURE 7.17

Merger of *him* and *hem* in Minimal-Pair Tests for Production Scored Impressionistically by Age in Decades and Social Class

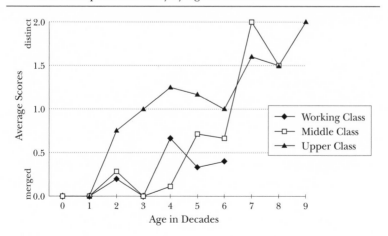

FIGURE 7.18

Merger of *pin* and *pen* in Minimal-Pair Tests for Perception
Scored Impressionistically by Age in Decades and Social Class

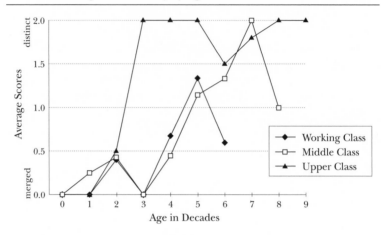

FIGURE 7.19

Merger of *pin* and *pen* in Minimal-Pair Tests for Production
Scored Impressionistically by Age in Decades and Social Class

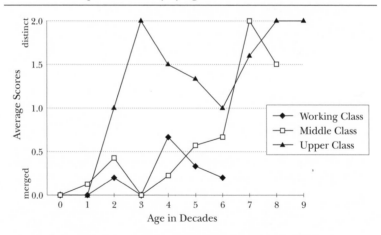

classes separately across nine decades. Therefore the numbers for
the upper and the upper-middle class are pooled together, as are
the numbers for the lower-middle and the middle classes.

As figures 7.16–7.19 show, for middle- and working-class speakers age 60 and under, the two allophones are usually either completely merged or close in production, for both pairs elicited in the test, *pin-pen* and *him-hem*. Middle-aged speakers belonging to the highest-status group, on the other hand, maintain a distinction at a higher rate than the other social groups, especially for *pin-pen*. This social class difference becomes even more pronounced in perception, where 30- to 50-year-old members of the upper class judge the two allophones to be completely distinct in their pronunciation. At the same time, it should be noted that for speakers aged 20 or younger of any social class, the two vowels before nasals are completely merged. The conservative behavior of the highest-status social group is confirmed acoustically in figure 7.20.

These results suggest that if Charleston is becoming part of the South phonologically, by adopting one of its characteristics, the PIN-PEN merger, then it is happening through the lower classes; in other words, the highest-status social group is resisting the direction of the change. This confirms O'Cain's conclusion about the

FIGURE 7.20

Cartesian Distance between Means of /iN/ and /eN/ by Age and Social Class for Speakers up to Age 65

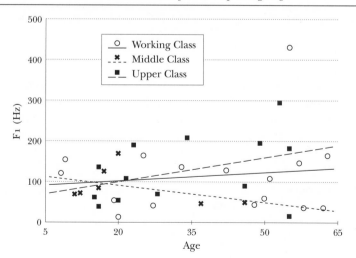

origin of the change as being located "outside of the speech of the cultivated" (O'Cain 1972, 139). This result also corresponds to Labov, Ash, and Boberg's findings (*ANAE* 2006, 68) about the PIN-PEN merger in the South in general, whereby education is correlated inversely with the merger: the higher the education, the higher the level of distinction between the two allophones.

Two upper-class speakers made overt comments about the merger, suggesting that there may be some awareness of it in the community. One is John M., 78, who says the following when doing the minimal-pair test for *pin* and *pen*:

Now here are the two that I've had so much trouble with. And when I say I'm teased about it, believe me that.... When I was a young boy, I guess I resented it and was embarrassed by it but after that it's been a source of amusement. *Pin* and *pen*, I hear the difference and other people tell me there's no difference the way I pronounce them.

The other overt comment comes from Elizabeth O., 82, who distinguishes between *pin* and *pen* in production and perception:

pin and *pen* [pronounced differently]; I think they sound differently and that's one of the first words that I can remember hearing in college that I didn't know what somebody from Greenville was asking for. They came in and said, "You got a pen?" and I said, "A what?!" and they said, "a pin" and "Do you want a pin or a pen?!" So, that I think I definitely pronounce differently and people in Greenville don't [laughter].

These overt comments, combined with the social class effect discussed above, together with the difference between the judgments about the pronunciation of the two vowels by the upper class and their actual productions, suggest that, at least for some people, the merger is above the level of social awareness and may be subject to sociolinguistic evaluation. This goes against the observation that mergers are generally below the level of social awareness and as such are devoid of social affect (Labov 1994). While this generalization has been found to be true of the most thoroughly studied merger currently in progress in American English, the low-back merger, and may be true of most mergers, it may not be accurate in the case of the merger of /i/ and /e/ before nasals. As this merger is found primarily in the South and partly defines the region phonologically, it may be that, at least for some people in Charleston, possibly members of the upper class, it is associated with the speech patterns of the South, or more specifically the Upcountry, as opposed to Charleston and the tidewater areas of South Carolina. Consequently, although the PIN-PEN merger itself does not draw any negative comments and thus has not reached the level of stigmatization or even stereotyping, it may be on its way to becoming a sociolinguistic marker rather than just an indicator.

It is worth adding that the social class effect observed in Charleston and the difference between production and perception is unlikely to be caused by the fact that upper-class people, being usually more educated, may tend to pay more attention to phonological distinctions which are reflected in the spelling. Crucially, the low-back merger does not display a similar social class effect: the upper class is undergoing the change at the same rate as the rest of the population.[3] The low-back merger is not limited to one dialect region and thus is not associated with any particular social or geographical group. It is the connection with the South as a dialect region that makes the sociolinguistic status of the PIN-PEN merger distinct from other mergers described to date.

7.3. MERGER OF *MERRY* AND *MARRY*

As maps 49–51 in *PEAS* show, most of the eastern United States distinguished between the vowel in *merry*, *Mary*, and *marry* in the first half of the twentieth century. Most of the region has joined the rest of the United States in merging the three vowels into one over the last few decades.[4] As the *ANAE* shows, New England and the South are two regions where *merry* and *Mary* have merged, but *marry* tends to remain distinct (map 8.4).

The traditional dialect of Charleston distinguished between the three vowels, as did the rest of the South and the eastern United States in general. As chapter 5 shows, the dialect has undergone a merger of the vowels in *merry* and *Mary*, which is now almost complete, as it is for most of the South today. The data in this project show that Charleston is currently undergoing a merger of the vowels in *merry* and *marry*, and that this change is more recent than the

FIGURE 7.21

Christine D., 57, Charleston, S.C., Working Class: *Merry-Mary-marry*

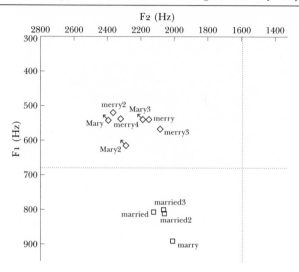

FIGURE 7.22

Brian R., 55, Charleston, S.C., Upper-Middle Class: *Merry-Mary-marry*

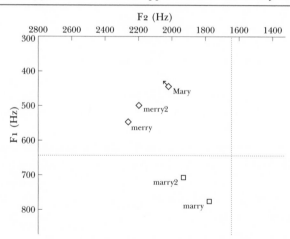

merry-Mary merger. This is to be expected, as in other areas which have undergone the two mergers, *merry* and *Mary* have been found to merge first. Figures 7.21 and 7.22 show the position of the three vowels in the speech of Christine D. and Brian R., in which *marry* is in low position, clearly separated from *merry* and *Mary*.

As the minimal-pair test reveals, *merry* and *marry* are distinct in perception and production for the vast majority of speakers over age 40, and they are completely distinct for Charlestonians over 70. Figure 7.23 presents the progress of the merger in apparent time. The graph suggests that the merger follows an S-shaped curve in apparent time—the best fit is obtained through the logistic function (figure 7.24).

What is particularly striking is the abrupt change between 40- and 30-year-olds: for the vast majority of speakers younger than 40, the vowels of *merry* and *marry* are identical in perception and production. The line representing a change from a distinction toward a merger of *merry* and *marry* is much steeper than the line showing the progress of the merger of *merry* and *Mary* in figure 6.19 in chapter 6. A comparison of the two graphs shows that the *merry-marry* merger is a more recent and more vigorous change, which is

FIGURE 7.23

Merger of *merry* and *marry* in Minimal-Pair Tests Scored
Impressionistically by Age in Decades

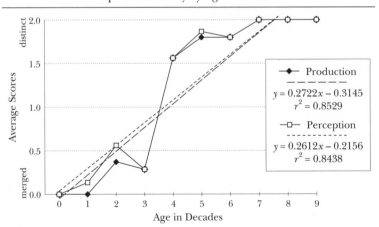

Production

$y = 0.2722x - 0.3145$
$r^2 = 0.8529$

Perception

$y = 0.2612x - 0.2156$
$r^2 = 0.8438$

FIGURE 7.24

Logistic Transform of the *merry-marry* Merger in Minimal-Pair Tests
Scored Impressionistically by Age in Decades

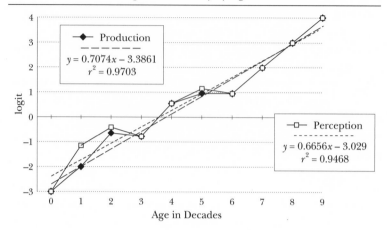

TABLE 7.5

Regression Analysis of the *merry-marry* Merger in Minimal-Pair Tests
for Production Scored Impressionistically

	R squared (adjusted) = 61.1%	
Variable	*Coefficient*	*Prob*
Constant	–0.3567	0.0096
Age (in 25-year generations)	0.8577	< 0.0001

borne out by regression analysis (table 7.5): the age coefficient for the *merry-marry* merger is higher than the age coefficient for the merger of *merry* and *Mary* (0.86 vs. 0.50 for every 25 years on the two-point scale). Age emerges as the only significant factor in the progress of this change.

Acoustic analysis shows that for speakers younger than 40 all three vowels, *merry*, *Mary*, and *marry*, overlap in the F1-F2 dimension, as in the speech of Claire S., 16 (figure 7.25). Figure 7.26 presents the vowels of Rosemary S., 46, Claire S.'s mother, who maintains a distinction between *merry* and *marry*. Another mother-daughter pair is presented in the next two figures: Margaret C., 46,

FIGURE 7.25

Chris S. (daughter of Rosemary S.), 16, Charleston, S.C.,
Upper-Middle Class: *Merry-Mary-marry*

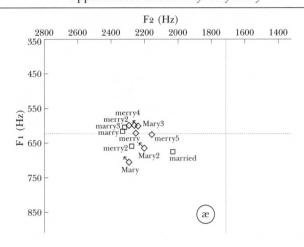

FIGURE 7.26

Rosemary S., 46, Charleston, S.C., Upper-Middle Class: *Merry-Mary-marry*

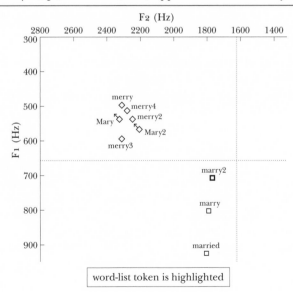

FIGURE 7.27

Margaret C., 46, Charleston, S.C., Middle Class: *Merry-Mary-marry*

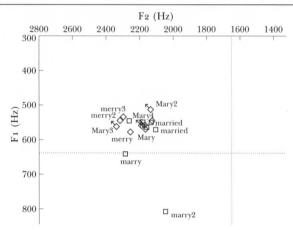

a middle-class Charlestonian (figure 7.27), showing a *merry-marry* distinction in a minimal-pair test (though not in spontaneous speech—note the tokens of *married* in figure 7.27), and Emily C., 20 (figure 7.28), showing a merger of all three vowels.

There is one token of *marry* in figure 7.28 (Emily C.) which is lower than the other ones; it also sounds lower. That is the token produced in a minimal-pair test when the two words are read next to each other for the first time. However, when she defines each of the words after reading the pair, both *merry* and *marry* sound identical and overlap with the merged vowels produced in spontaneous speech and in the reading of a word list. Emily C. is one of only two cases in the whole sample of a discrepancy between a speaker's production in either a minimal-pair test or in spontaneous speech and their judgment about the way *merry* and *marry* sound—the other was 16-year-old Heather M., a middle-class Charlestonian, who also claimed the two words sounded different, even though she pronounced them identically in a minimal-pair test.

Finally, the only overt comment indicating awareness of the merger of *merry* and *marry* was made by Kathy A., 42, a lower-middle class speaker, who pronounced *merry* and *marry* (as well as *Mary*) identically in spontaneous speech and in a word list (figure 7.29), and judged them to sound identical to her. Her first reading of

FIGURE 7.28
Emily C. (daughter of Margaret C. above), 20, Charleston, S.C.,
Middle Class: *Merry-Mary*

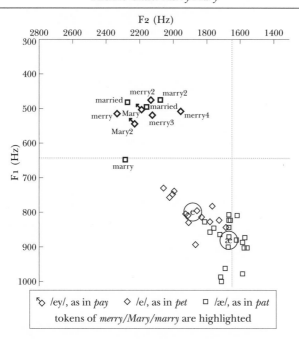

the *merry-marry* pair revealed a contrast between the vowels, *marry* sounding much lower, but she quickly added "I only say *marry* [sounding low; "marry" in figure 7.29] because I know I should, but that's not the way I... I say *marry* [identical to *merry*; "marry2" in figure 7.29]." She then says that for her *merry* and *marry* sound the same and produces them with the vowel identical to that of *merry*. Other than these few cases out of the 97 informants who participated in the minimal-pair tests, there seems to be little awareness or social evaluation of the *merry-marry* merger. The change is not complete yet, as speakers over age 40 can be expected to have a distinction, but it is quite vigorous; for the vast majority of Charlestonians under age 40, all three vowels in words such as *merry, Mary,* and *marry* are likely to sound identical, regardless of social class or gender.

FIGURE 7.29

Kathy A., 42, Charleston, S.C., Lower-Middle Class: *Merry-Mary-marry*

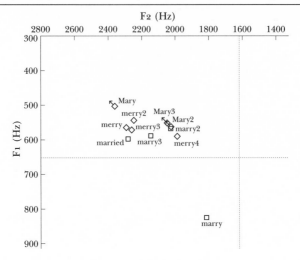

8. CHARLESTON
AND THE SOUTHERN SHIFT

8.1. /ay/-MONOPHTHONGIZATION

T HE DEFINING FEATURE of Southern phonology is the Southern Shift (Labov 1994; *ANAE* 2006), beginning with the monophthongization of /ay/, which leaves the subsystem of upgliding vowels and thus triggers the lowering and laxing of the other front upgliding vowels, /ey/ and /iy/. In the traditional form of the Charleston dialect, the vowel of *guy* and *tide* is a front upgliding vowel, that is, the nucleus is followed by a clear upglide, as opposed to the most common realization found in the South, a monophthong. Map 29 of *PEAS* shows that an upgliding vowel was characteristic of the coastal areas of South Carolina and Georgia, whereas most of the coast of North Carolina, as well as the Upcountry of South Carolina, had a monophthongal or ingliding vowel ([aᵊ~ɑᵊ]), just like most of the South. In synopses 135 and 136 in *PEAS*, showing the sound systems of two cultured speakers in Charleston, the vowel in *five* is transcribed as [ɑɪ], and Kurath and McDavid comment that the Low Country of South Carolina had an upgliding diphthong in free position and before voiced consonants (*PEAS* 1961, 22). These observations about the realization of /ay/ in the traditional dialect are borne out by the speech of William McTeer, described in chapter 2: his /ay/ is an upgliding diphthong, and there are no traces of monophthongization.

Before voiceless consonants, on the other hand, /ay/ was also a front upgliding diphthong, but the nucleus was raised and centralized in Charleston, and beyond it in coastal South Carolina, Virginia, parts of New England, and upstate New York[1] (*PEAS* 1961, map 27), which is a process commonly referred to as Canadian Raising (see chapter 4). This is reflected in one of the *PEAS* synopses for Charleston (136), which shows [ɐɪ] for the vowel in *twice*—the other synopsis (135) reports a vowel identical to the one before voiced consonants, that is, [ɑɪ].

The upgliding realization of /ay/ in free position and before voiced consonants is one of the most important features setting the traditional form of Charleston's dialect apart from the rest of the South—the monophthongization of /ay/ was the triggering event in the Southern Shift, and it is also the most salient phonological feature of the South as a dialect region. The speech of the informants in the present study shows that this has remained unchanged, in that for the most part /ay/ in Charleston is still an upgliding vowel, as opposed to the rest of the South, where it is monophthongal before voiced consonants and word-finally (*ANAE* 2006, chap. 18).

An index of *ay*-monophthongization has been calculated for each of the 100 speakers in the sample. It is the proportion of tokens with monophthongal realizations to all tokens of /ay/ before voiced obstruents and in word-final position. The personal pronoun *I* is excluded, unless it is in stressed position. As mentioned above, it turns out that the level of *ay*-monophthongization for the community as a whole is very low, 6.2%, and for the vast majority of speakers in the sample the rate of /ay/-monophthongization is zero—there are no tokens of completely monophthongal /ay/ before voiced obstruents or in word-final position in their speech—as shown in the histogram in figure 8.1.

The very low level of /ay/-monophthongization observed in the speech of informants in sociolinguistic interviews is mirrored by the results of a rapid and anonymous survey conducted in downtown Charleston. Tokens of /ay/ were elicited by asking the time of day from between 4:45 and 5:25 in the afternoon. As expected, the word *five* was often produced in response. A total of 52 tokens of /ay/ were elicited: 30 from women and 22 from men. Only one of those produced by women was monophthongal (3.33%), and two of the ones produced by men (9%), which results in a rate of 5.8% for the whole sample. Given the complementary sources of error of the two methods of elicitation, the sociolinguistic interview and the rapid and anonymous survey, obtaining very similar results, both showing a very low level of /ay/-monophthongization, gives us added confidence about the accuracy of the findings.

FIGURE 8.1

Histogram of the Rate of /ay/-Monophthongization
before Voiced Obstruents and Word Finally, as in *tide* and *tie*

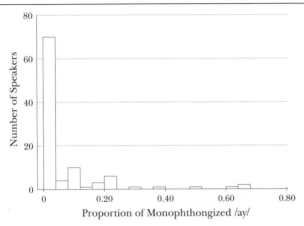

Furthermore, the results of the present study corroborate the findings of the *ANAE* based on the Telsur project, whose four Charleston informants show no *ay*-monophthongization. The lack of /ay/-monophthongization sets Charleston apart from the rest of the South, as shown in figure 8.2.

Regression analysis reveals an effect of two social factors on the level of *ay*-monophthongization in Charleston: age and social class. The age coefficient is positive, indicating that the level of *ay*-monophthongization is decreasing in apparent time: for each successive generation of 25 years the rate of monophthongization can be expected to fall by 4.75% (table 8.1). The effect is then rather weak and the amount of variation explained is only 11.5%. The decrease, seen in figure 8.3, conforms to the *ANAE* finding for the South in general, where the rate of *ay*-monophthongization has also been found to be falling at the rate of 12.7% with each 25 years of age (*ANAE* 2006, table 18.3).

There is also an effect of social class on the level of /ay/-monophthongization in Charleston. The coefficient is negative, indicating that the higher the social class, the lower the level of /ay/-monophthongization expected. The effect is fairly weak, as the expected

FIGURE 8.2

Glide Deletion of /ay/ before Voiced Obstruents and Word Finally
(after *ANAE*)

TABLE 8.1

Regression Analysis of /ay/-Monophthongization
before Voiced Obstruents and Word Finally

r^2 (adjusted) = 11.5%		
Variable	*Coefficient*	*Prob*
Constant	0.098	0.0058
Age (in 25-year generations)	0.048	0.0259
Social class	−0.031	0.0007

difference between the lowest and the highest of the five social classes is 15%. It does, however, reinforce the hypothesis that phonological features characteristic of the South as a dialect region, such as the PIN-PEN merger and /ay/-monophthongization, can be expected to be highest in the lowest-status social group. This can also be seen in the scatterplot in figure 8.3, where the four highest outliers are working-class speakers. At the same time, it needs to be stressed that even in the lowest-status social group the average level of *ay*-monophthongization is fairly low, as indicated by the mean rates by social class in figure 8.4; it is lower than the rate

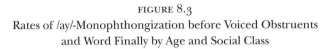

FIGURE 8.3

Rates of /ay/-Monophthongization before Voiced Obstruents
and Word Finally by Age and Social Class

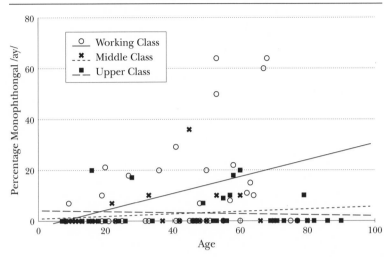

of /ay/-monophthongization in the rest of the South (*ANAE* 2006, chap. 18).

The rates of monophthongization presented above are based on the proportion of tokens which are clearly monophthongal. All the other tokens of /ay/ before voiced obstruents and in word-final position are upgliding, though the glides are usually not as pronounced and not as long as they would be in any Northern dialect. Some of them could be described as shortened glides, but the majority of the tokens of this allophone of /ay/ are characterized by an unusually long nucleus, followed by a short but distinct upglide. This realization of /ay/ is, of course, different from that of any non-Southern dialect, where the nucleus is much shorter and the upglide is very clear, but more importantly, it is also different from the most common realization of this allophone in the rest of the South, as shown by the *ANAE* (2006, chap. 18), which is a monophthong. Figures 8.5–8.7 show a comparison of /ay/ before a voiced obstruent and in word-final position as pronounced by two Charleston speakers and by Steve S., 42, an Inland South speaker from Greenville, S.C., currently living in Charleston.[2] Steve S. shows a complete

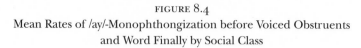

FIGURE 8.4

Mean Rates of /ay/-Monophthongization before Voiced Obstruents
and Word Finally by Social Class

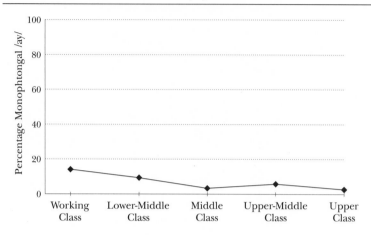

monophthong, whereas the two Charleston speakers show a very long nucleus followed by a front upglide.

There does not seem to be any relation between the occurrence of a long nucleus and social class—it is found in the speech of all social groups. Figure 8.8 shows a spectrogram of the word *side* pronounced by Sally A., 55, an upper-class Charlestonian, in which the nucleus is exceedingly long and is followed by a short but clear upglide. The quality of this allophone of /ay/ in Charleston is very distinctive and as such has not been reported for other dialects of American English, although a similarly prolonged nucleus is found in the Pamlico Sound region of North Carolina (Thomas 2001).

It also contrasts sharply with the allophone of /ay/ before voiceless consonants in Charleston, whereby the nucleus is much shorter and there is always a clear and distinct upglide, as shown in the spectrograms of the word *sight* spoken by two of the Charleston speakers presented above (figures 8.9 and 8.10). In having a sharp distinction between the two allophones of /ay/, Charleston follows the pattern found throughout most of the South, where, except for the region referred to as Inland South (see the map in figure 8.2), /ay/ before voiceless consonants is usually monophthongized only

FIGURE 8.5

Tide: Steve S., 42, Greenville, S.C., Lower-Middle Class (top),
and Kathy A., 42, Charleston, S.C., Lower-Middle Class (bottom)

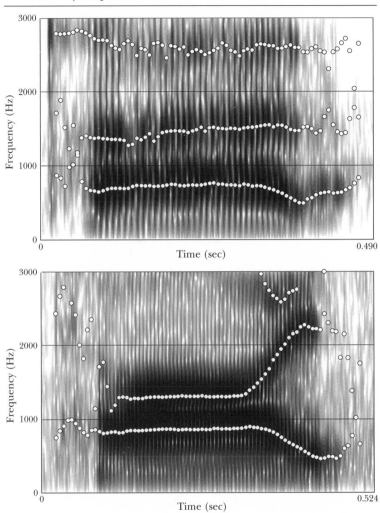

in the speech of the lowest-status social group (Crane 1973; Bernstein, Gregory, and Bailey 1993; Feagin 1994; *ANAE* 2006, chap.
18). In this way, even though Charleston is distinct from the rest of
the South in having little /ay/-monophthongization before voiced

FIGURE 8.6

Side: Steve S., 42, Greenville, S.C., Lower-Middle Class (top),
and William V., 37, Charleston, S.C., Middle Class (bottom)

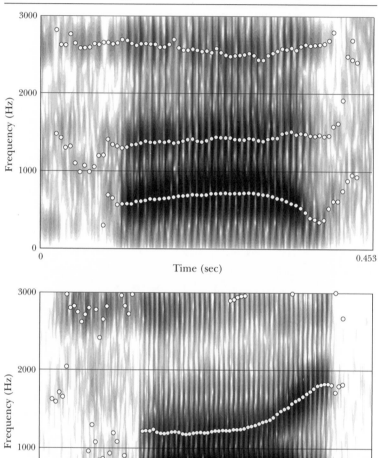

FIGURE 8.7

Tie: Steve S., 42, Greenville, S.C., Lower-Middle Class (top),
and William V., 37, Charleston, S.C., Middle Class (bottom)

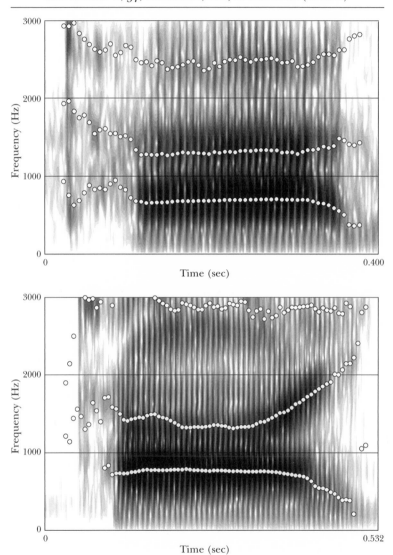

FIGURE 8.8

Sally A., 55, Charleston, S.C., Upper Class: *Side*

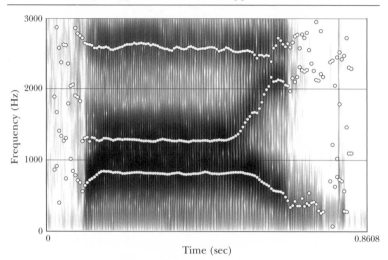

FIGURE 8.9

Sally A., 55, Charleston, S.C., Upper Class: *Sight*

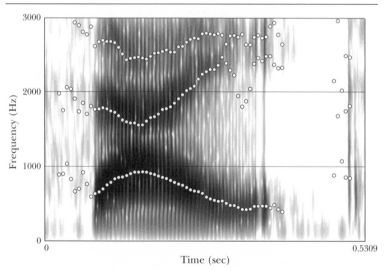

obstruents and in word-final position, it is nevertheless closer to the South than to the North in its realization of /ay/, as it maintains a distinction between the two allophones.

FIGURE 8.10

Kathy A., 42, Charleston, S.C., Lower-Middle Class: *Sight*

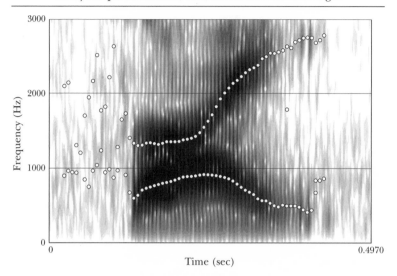

Time (sec)

8.2. THE SOUTHERN SHIFT BEYOND /ay/-MONOPHTHONGIZATION

As the previous section shows, Charleston lacks the triggering factor behind the Southern Shift and its most salient element, /ay/-monophthongization. In the areas of the South where /ay/ has become monophthongal and has thus left the subsystem of front upgliding vowels, the nucleus of the mid front vowel /ey/, as in *pay*, becomes lax and lowers along a nonperipheral track, toward the position vacated by the nucleus of /ay/. This in turn leads to the laxing and lowering of the high front upgliding vowel /iy/, as in *see* and *feet*. At the same time, the front short vowels rise along a peripheral track, becoming tense and ingliding. These vowel movements, developing in accordance with the general principles of vowel shifting proposed by Labov (1994), are schematized in figure 8.11.

As a consequence, the nuclei of the long front vowels and the nuclei of the short front vowels reverse their positions—in what *ANAE* refers to as the second stage of the Southern Shift, the positions of the nuclei of /ey/, as in *pay*, and /e/, as in *pet*, become

FIGURE 8.11

The Southern Shift (from *ANAE*)

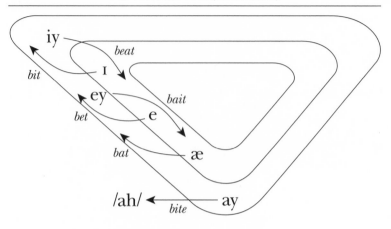

reversed, /e/ now being fronter and higher than /ey/. In the most advanced stage of the Southern Shift (stage 3 in *ANAE* 2006), the nuclei of /iy/, as in *see* and *feet*, and /i/, as in *sit*, become reversed, /i/ being fronter and higher than /iy/. As map 18.6 of *ANAE* shows, the territories in the South engaged in Stage 3 are a subset of the larger region characterized by Stage 2, which in turn is subsumed within Stage 1, /ay/-monophthongization. In other words, those speakers who have reversed the positions of /iy/ and /i/ will have also reversed the positions of /ey/ and /e/, and all of them will show /ay/-monophthongization.

Figure 8.12 presents the Southern Shift in the speech of Steve S., 42, a resident of Charleston who spent the first 18 years of his life in Greenville, South Carolina. His speech is a good example of the vowel shifts discussed above; the bolded tokens of /ay/ are monophthongal.

Stages 1 through 3 of the Southern Shift reflect the chronology of the shift, which in turn is the result of the structural conditioning of the vowel movements. From a structural point of view then, one would not expect to find in Charleston the extreme lowering of /ey/, as in *pay*, found elsewhere in the South without prior /ay/-monophthongization, or a reversal of the positions of /ey/ and /e/.

FIGURE 8.12

Steve S., 42, Greenville, S.C.: The Southern Shift

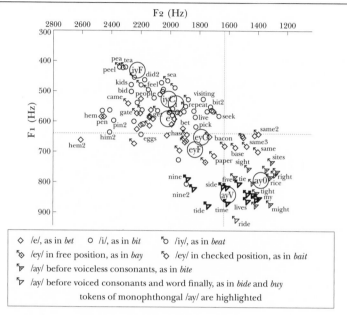

It is possible, however, that through language contact, dialects of neighboring territories affected by the Southern Shift might adopt some elements of the Southern Shift without necessarily following the same chronology. For example, we might not observe the tensing and ingliding of the short front vowels, but it would not be surprising to find some laxing of /ey/, which generally seems to be at a lower level of awareness than some other vowel shifts.

In fact, however, there is little laxing and lowering of /ey/ (*pay*, *gate*, etc.) in Charleston. The nucleus of the vowel is certainly lax, rather than tense, unlike in the traditional form of the dialect, and it is currently lower and less peripheral than it was in the first half of the twentieth century, as observed in the speech of William McTeer (chapter 2) or speakers over 80 in the present sample. Nevertheless, for the majority of speakers interviewed for the present study, the nucleus of /ey/ is not as low as that of most Southern Shift speakers, such as Steve S. presented above, and the nucleus

FIGURE 8.13

Vincent J., 33, Charleston, S.C., Lower-Middle Class: /e/ and /ey/

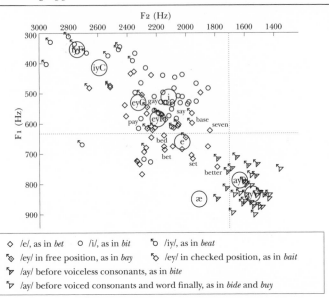

FIGURE 8.14

Jonathan C., 28, Charleston, S.C., Upper Class: /e/ and /ey/

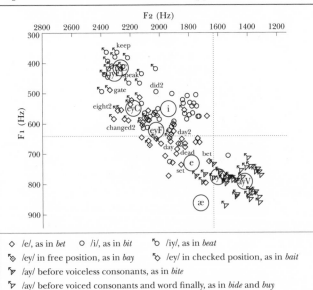

FIGURE 8.15

Mark T., 9, Charleston, S.C., Lower-Middle Class: /e/ and /ey/

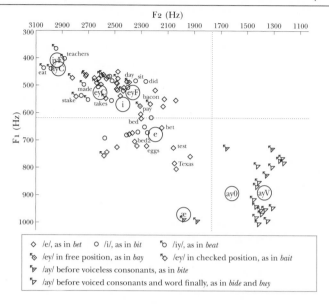

◇ /e/, as in *bet*   ○ /i/, as in *bit*   ⭒ /iy/, as in *beat*
⭒ /ey/ in free position, as in *bay*   ⭒ /ey/ in checked position, as in *bait*
▷ /ay/ before voiceless consonants, as in *bite*
▽ /ay/ before voiced consonants and word finally, as in *bide* and *buy*

FIGURE 8.16

Judy A., 23, Charleston, S.C., Upper-Middle Class: /e/ and /ey/

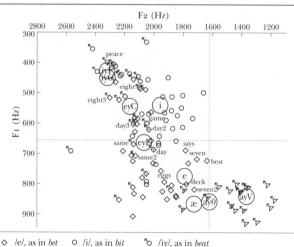

◇ /e/, as in *bet*   ○ /i/, as in *bit*   ⭒ /iy/, as in *beat*
⭒ /ey/ in free position, as in *bay*   ⭒ /ey/ in checked position, as in *bait*
▷ /ay/ before voiceless consonants, as in *bite*
▽ /ay/ before voiced consonants and word finally, as in *bide* and *buy*

of /e/, as in *pet*, is usually, though not always, lower and backer than /ey/, as in *pay*. Figures 8.13–8.16 present the front vowels of four Charleston speakers, showing the canonical relationship between the positions of /e/ and /ey/.

Since Stage 2 of the Southern Shift involves the reversal of the positions of /ey/ and /e/, a measure using the values of $F1$ and $F2$ of the two vowels can be used to show numerically the extent to which a given speaker is participating in Stage 2 of the Southern Shift. The measure, proposed in the *ANAE* and called EEY there, is the sum of two differences: $F2(e) - F2(ey)$ and $F1(ey) - F1(e)$ (*ANAE* 2006, 256). EEY is positive if the canonical positions of /ey/, as in *pay*, and /e/, as in *pet*, have been reversed, indicating a completion of the second stage of the Southern Shift. Figure 18.6 of *ANAE* shows a bimodal distribution of the values of EEY: Southern speakers show a positive mode around 250, whereas speakers from the rest of the country show a negative mode of –450. *ANAE* reports that EEY is positive (Stage 2 completed) for 58% of the speakers in the South, but for only 1.6% of the speakers in the rest of North America (*ANAE* 2006, 251).

In Charleston EEY for /eyF/ (in free position, as in *pay* and *day*) is positive for 19.5% of the speakers whose speech has been analyzed acoustically, and for /eyC/ (in checked position, as in *paid* and *gate*) it is positive for 7% of the speakers. For the majority of speakers in Charleston then, the relative positions of the nuclei of /ey/ and /e/ have not been reversed. The mean values of EEY are negative: –143 for /eyF/ and –344 for /eyC/—they are much closer to the values reported for the non-Southern dialects of North American English than to the positive values observed for the South (*ANAE* 2006, 251) and cited above. Figure 8.17 shows the distribution of the values of EEY for /eyF/ and /eyC/ for Charleston speakers— again, they are much closer to the distribution characteristic of the bulk of the non-Southern dialects than to that of the South: there is a negative mode around –225 for /eyF/ and a lower negative mode of –400.

While the majority of speakers in Charleston have not reversed the relative positions of /ey/ and /e/ and thus cannot be said to have been affected by Stage 2 of the Southern Shift, or even by Stage 1 (/ay/-monophthongization), there are a few speakers for whom /e/,

FIGURE 8.17

Distribution of EEY Measure for 43 Charleston Speakers:
/ey/ in Free Position (left) and Checked Position (right)

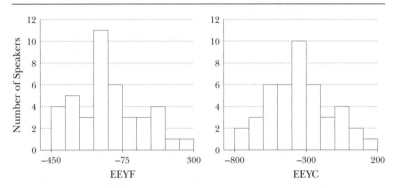

as in *pet*, is actually fronter and higher than the nucleus of /ey/, as in *pay*, shown by the positive value of EEY. Figures 8.18 and 8.19 show the positions of the front vowels of two such speakers.

Regression analysis of the social factors reveals that speakers such as Christine D. and Frank T. are not randomly distributed in the population, as age and social class turn out to play a role in the extent to which Charlestonians are participating in Stage 2 of the Southern Shift. Table 8.2 presents the significant coefficients for /eyF/ and /eyC/.

Although the coefficients are sizable, the amount of data explained, expressed as the value of adjusted r^2, is rather low. Plotting the values of EEY against the age of the speakers reveals an anomaly in an otherwise regular pattern (figures 8.20 and 8.21). There are a number of speakers around age 80 whose EEY values are much lower than what might be expected given the trend line. Those speakers turn out to represent the traditional form of the dialect with high and tense long mid vowels /e:/, as in *day* and *gate*, and /o:/, as in *go* and *boat*, which are monophthongal and often ingliding. As such, those vowels belong to a system which is incompatible with the system of upgliding vowels present in all of American English today, including Charleston. Therefore speakers over age 65 should be excluded from the analysis of the relative positions of short /e/ and upgliding /ey/. Figures 8.22 and 8.23 present scatterplots of the values of EEY against age for speakers up to age 65.

FIGURE 8.18

Christine D., 57, Charleston, S.C., Working Class: /e/ and /ey/

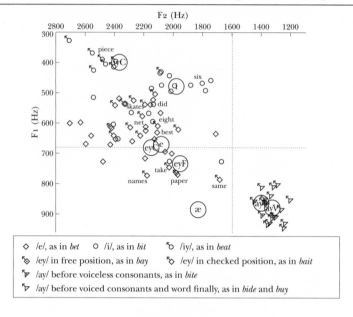

◇ /e/, as in *bet*   ○ /i/, as in *bit*   ❀ /iy/, as in *beat*

❀ /ey/ in free position, as in *bay*   ❀ /ey/ in checked position, as in *bait*

▽ /ay/ before voiceless consonants, as in *bite*

▽ /ay/ before voiced consonants and word finally, as in *bide* and *buy*

FIGURE 8.19

Frank T., 48, Charleston, S.C., Working Class: /e/ and /ey/

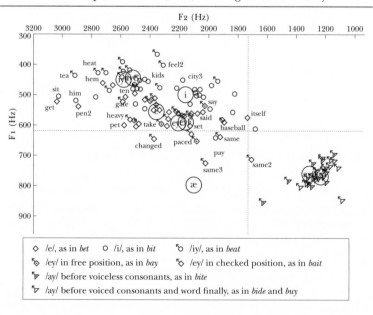

◇ /e/, as in *bet*   ○ /i/, as in *bit*   ❀ /iy/, as in *beat*

❀ /ey/ in free position, as in *bay*   ❀ /ey/ in checked position, as in *bait*

▽ /ay/ before voiceless consonants, as in *bite*

▽ /ay/ before voiced consonants and word finally, as in *bide* and *buy*

TABLE 8.2

Regression Analysis of EEY

EEY for /ey/ in Free Position, as in *pay, day*		
r^2 (adjusted) = 11.3%		
Variable	*Coefficient*	*Prob*
Constant	−251	< 0.0001
Age (in 25-year generations)	67	0.018

EEY for /ey/ in Checked Position, as in *paid, date*		
r^2 (adjusted) = 20.8%		
Variable	*Coefficient*	*Prob*
Constant	−290	0.001
Age (in 25-year generations)	77	0.019
Social Class	−61	0.006

FIGURE 8.20

EEY for /ey/ in Free Position by Age

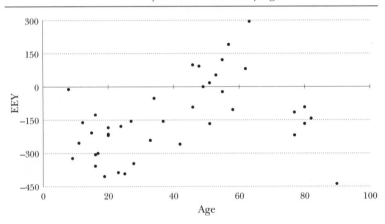

Once speakers over 65 have been removed from the analysis, the age coefficients become twice as large and the amount of variation explained rises to over 50% (table 8.3).

Figures 8.22 and 8.23 above show that the reversal of the relative positions of /e/ and /ey/ is observed only for some speakers over age 45, and the positive age coefficients for the EEY measure indicate that the Southern Shift, however little advanced in Charleston overall, is receding. With each successive generation of 25 years,

FIGURE 8.21

EEY for /ey/ in Checked Position by Age

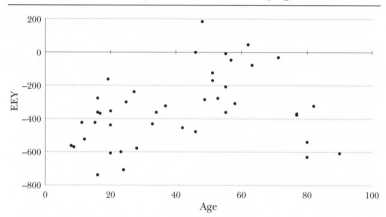

the EEY measure of Stage 2 of the Southern Shift can be expected to fall by around 185 Hz. The same effect has been found for the South as a whole: the *ANAE* (2006, chap. 18) reports a retreat of the Southern Shift in apparent time, expressed in the EEY measure of Stage 2 and in the percentage of /ay/-monophthongization (Stage 1), measured for the whole region; similar findings have been reported by Fridland (1999, 2001) and Thomas (2001).

FIGURE 8.22

EEY for /ey/ in Free Position for Speakers up to Age 65

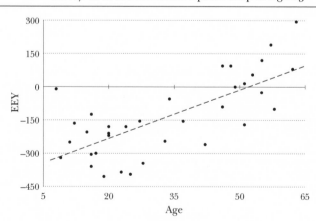

FIGURE 8.23

EEY for /ey/ in Checked Position for Speakers up to Age 65

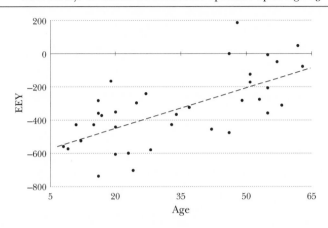

TABLE 8.3

Regression Analysis for EEY for Speakers up to 65

EEY for /ey/ in Free Position, as in *pay, day*
r^2 (adjusted) = 51.8%

Variable	Coefficient	Prob
Constant	−381	< 0.0001
Age (in 25-year generations)	185	< 0.0001

EEY for /ey/ in Checked Position, as in *paid, date*
r^2 (adjusted) = 55.5%

Variable	Coefficient	Prob
Constant	−421	< 0.0001
Age (in 25-year generations)	187	< 0.0001
Social Class	−58	0.002

As shown in table 8.3, social class emerges as another significant factor in the EEY measure for the relative positions of /e/, as
in *pet*, and /eyC/, as in *date*, though not for /eyF/, as in *pay*. The coefficient is negative, which means that the higher the social class, the
lower the expected value of EEY, that is, the higher the social class,
the less affected it is by the Southern Shift. Table 8.4 below shows
the results of the regression analysis of EEY which considered social
class as three separate factors: working class (as the residual; com-

TABLE 8.4
Regression Analysis for EEY for /ey/ in Checked Position, as in *date*,
for Speakers up to Age 65

r^2 (adjusted) = 55.1%		
Variable	Coefficient	Prob
Constant	–543	< 0.0001
Age (in 25-year generations)	200	< 0.0001
Upper class	–165	0.002

bined with the lower-middle class), middle class, and upper class (combining upper-middle and upper class). The negative coefficient of –165.5 Hz means that members of the upper-middle and upper classes can be expected to have the EEY measure lower by 165.5 Hz in comparison with the working class in Charleston— again, showing that the highest-status social groups are least affected by the Southern Shift.

Although overall the Southern Shift is not very advanced in Charleston—there is little /ay/-monophthongization and the reversal of the relative positions of /e/ and /ey/ is observed for only a minority of speakers—both of the measures used to assess the development of the shift indicate that it is most advanced in the lowest-status social group. This coincides with the evidence for the PIN-PEN merger in Charleston discussed above, which pointed to the lowest social class as leading in the adoption of that Southern feature. Taken together, the results for the Southern Shift and the PIN-PEN merger provide support for the hypothesis that if Charleston is acquiring the phonological characteristics of the South, it is happening through the lower social classes, or that it is being resisted by the highest-status social group. At the same time, it should be stressed that, as opposed to the PIN-PEN merger, the Southern Shift, realized through /ay/-monophthongization and the reversal of the relative positions of /e/ and /ey/, has been shown to be receding, rather than advancing, in Charleston, just as it is in the rest of the South.

9. THE FRONTING OF BACK UPGLIDING VOWELS

9.1. THE FRONTING OF /uw/

Aₙₒₜₕₑᵣ ᵢₘₚₒᵣₜₐₙₜ ₛₑₜ of vowel movements found in the South is the parallel fronting of the back upgliding vowels, schematized in figure 9.1. It is not exclusively found in the South—and it is in fact more advanced in the Midland—and thus it is not a defining Southern feature, but it is found there consistently, and it is generally more advanced there than in the rest of North America (*ANAE* 2006, chap.12).

Historically, and in a few conservative dialects of American English at present, the nucleus of /uw/, as in *two* and *boot*, is a high back vowel, but in the majority of American dialects today the vowel has undergone considerable fronting, so that the nucleus is often front of the center of the vowel system as a whole, except before /l/ (see Di Paolo and Faber 1990; Hagiwara 1997; Labov 2001; Thomas 2001; Conn 2002; Feagin 2003; Ward 2003; Hall-Lew 2005; Fridland and Bartlett 2006). As shown by the *ANAE*, there is an impor-

FIGURE 9.1
Parallel Fronting of Back Upgliding Vowels (from *ANAE*)

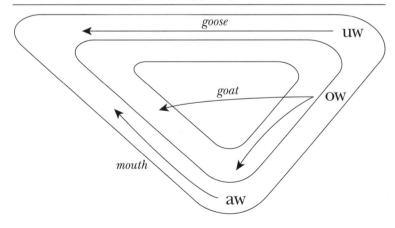

tant allophonic distinction between /uw/ after coronals (/Tuw/), as in *do, soon, noon, shoot,* and *choose,* and /uw/ after noncoronal consonants (/Kuw/), as in *move, boots, food,* and *coop:* tokens of /uw/ with coronal onsets are always fronter than tokens with noncoronal onsets. For the vast majority of *ANAE* informants (389 out of 439), /Tuw/ is front of the normalized center line of 1550 Hz. The mean F2 of /Tuw/ for all of North America is 1811 Hz, whereas the mean F2 of /Kuw/ is 1433 Hz. Finally, another important allophonic distinction is between /uw/ before /l/ and before all other consonants and word-finally: for all dialects of American English except for the South, /uw/ before /l/ does not participate in the fronting and remains firmly at the back of the vowel space (*ANAE* 2006, chap.12; see also Anderson, Milroy, and Nguyen 2002; Fridland and Bartlett 2006).[1]

This common configuration of the three allophones of /uw/ can be seen in the system of Frank T., 48, from Charleston (figure 9.2), where /Tuw/ is front of center, /Kuw/ is further back and behind the center line, and /uw/ before /l/ is at the back of the vowel space.

As map 12.1 of *ANAE* shows, the fronting of /uw/ is generally most advanced in the South, though the Midland is the region with the highest concentration of speakers with the most extreme fronting, that is, with the F2 of /uw/ higher than 2000 Hz. While Charleston does not have the Southern Shift, it does share the fronting of /uw/ with the rest of the South—it is undergoing the fronting of the back upgliding vowels just like the rest of the region, except when followed by /l/. In fact, it is ahead of the South as defined by the Southern Shift—/uw/ in Charleston is as front as in the most advanced Midland cities, such as Kansas City and St. Louis, and is more front than the rest of North America. The mean F2 of /Tuw/ for the 43 speakers analyzed acoustically is 2056 Hz, with a standard deviation of 133 Hz.

A regression analysis of F2 reveals that age and social class play a role in the fronting of /Tuw/ in Charleston (table 9.1). The negative age coefficient indicates that the vowel is fronting in apparent time—younger speakers have higher values of F2, which can be expected to increase by 42 Hz with every successive generation of 25 years.

FIGURE 9.2

Frank T., 48, Charleston, S.C., Working Class: /uw/

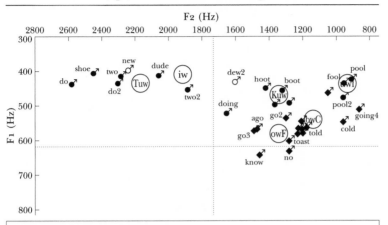

σ̂ /iw/, as in *dew*

🡒 /uw/ after coronals (Tuw), as in *do*, and noncoronals (Kuw), as in *coon*

🡒 /ow/ in free position (owF), as in *go*, and in checked position (owC), as in *coon*

An increase of this size, given the F2 range for high vowels, is not particularly great—the change is nearing completion. While the youngest Charlestonians' /Tuw/ is among the most front in the country, the older generations are not far behind (figure 9.3); their /Tuw/ is already more front than it is in many other dialects of North American English. Another indication that the change is nearing completion is that there is no difference between women and men in the extent of the fronting. Women have been found to lead in changes of this type, that is, in the fronting of back vowels, and are caught up with by men as the change spreads throughout

TABLE 9.1

Regression Analysis of F2 of /uw/ after Coronals but Not before /l/

r^2 (adjusted) = 14.1%		
Variable	*Coefficient*	*Prob*
Constant	2033	< 0.0001
Age (in 25-year generations)	–42	0.043
Social class	30	0.024

FIGURE 9.3
F2 of /uw/ after Coronals by Age

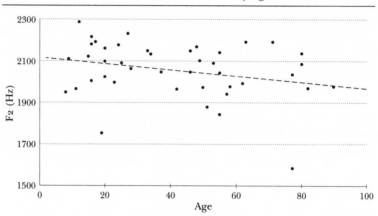

the community (see Luthin 1987; Labov 2001; Ward 2003; Hall-Lew 2004, 2005).

The social class coefficient in table 9.1 is positive, indicating that the higher the social class, the higher the expected F2 of /Tuw/. Figure 9.4 presents the means of F2 of /Tuw/ for the five social classes represented in the sample.

FIGURE 9.4
Mean F2 of /uw/ after Coronals by Social Class

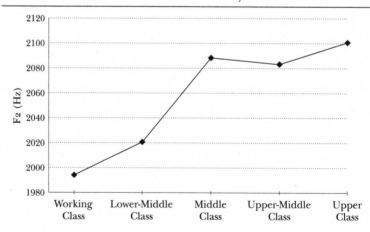

Table 9.2 below presents the regression coefficients for /Tuw/ with social class considered as three separate classes with the working class as the residual. The analysis indicates that the expected difference between the lowest and the highest social classes is 90 Hz, that is, the upper class can be expected to be ahead the working class by 90 Hz in the F2 of /Tuw/.

Figures 9.5–9.7 present the high back upgliding vowels of three Charleston speakers, representing different social classes, showing differential fronting of /Tuw/. Pam K., an upper-class Charlestonian, shows extreme fronting of /Tuw/ at 2179 Hz, except for allophones

TABLE 9.2

Regression Analysis of F2 of /uw/ after Coronals but Not before /l/

r^2 (adjusted) = 10.5%		
Variable	*Coefficient*	*Prob*
Constant	2068	< 0.0001
Age (in 25-year generations)	–38	0.076
Upper class	90	0.044
Middle class	73	0.172
Working class	0	–

FIGURE 9.5

Heather G., 19, Charleston, S.C., Working Class: /uw/

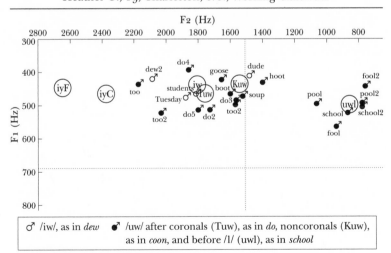

♂ /iw/, as in *dew*   ♂ /uw/ after coronals (Tuw), as in *do*, noncoronals (Kuw), as in *coon*, and before /l/ (uwl), as in *school*

FIGURE 9.6

Emily C., 20, Charleston, S.C., Middle Class: /uw/

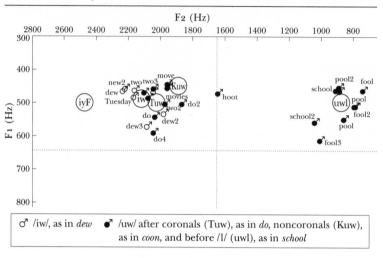

○⃗ /iw/, as in *dew*   ●⃗ /uw/ after coronals (Tuw), as in *do*, noncoronals (Kuw), as in *coon*, and before /l/ (uwl), as in *school*

FIGURE 9.7

Pam K., 16, Charleston, S.C., Upper Class: /uw/

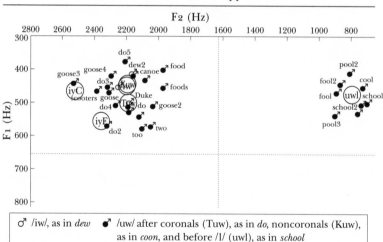

○⃗ /iw/, as in *dew*   ●⃗ /uw/ after coronals (Tuw), as in *do*, noncoronals (Kuw), as in *coon*, and before /l/ (uwl), as in *school*

before /l/, which are firmly at the back of the vowel space. However, what is most striking about her vowel system is the very front position of the noncoronal allophone of /uw/, labeled /Kuw/, as in *move* and *boot*, with a mean F2 of 2186 Hz. As mentioned above, in all dialects of American English, including the South, the allophone with a noncoronal onset is usually less front than the one with a coronal onset, as shown, for example, in the vowel system of Frank T. in figure 9.2, Heather G. in figure 9.5, and Vincent J. and Kevin P. in figures 9.8 and 9.9 below. Map 12.2 of *ANAE* shows the regions with the most advanced fronting of /Kuw/ (not before /l/), defined as having F2 higher than the normalized center line of 1550 Hz for the whole vowel system. The area of /uw/ fronting includes the South, with a mean F2 of 1703 Hz, and parts of the Midland (expected mean F2 = 1713 Hz), with the most advanced fronting reported for some of the large Midland cities, such as Kansas City and St. Louis (*ANAE* 2006, 153); the mean for the whole of North America is 1433 Hz (*ANAE* 2006, chap. 12).

The speech of the informants in this project shows that Charleston is at the forefront of not only /Tuw/ fronting, but also /Kuw/ fronting, with a mean F2 of 1666.5 Hz for /uw/ with noncoronal

FIGURE 9.8
Vincent J., 33, Charleston, S.C., Lower-Middle Class: /uw/

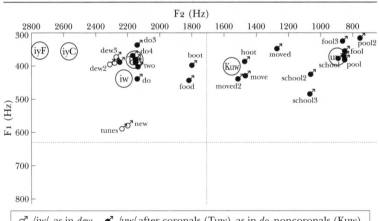

♂ /iw/, as in *dew*   ♂ /uw/ after coronals (Tuw), as in *do*, noncoronals (Kuw), as in *coon*, and before /l/ (uwl), as in *school*

FIGURE 9.9

Kevin P., 20, Charleston, S.C., Working Class: /uw/

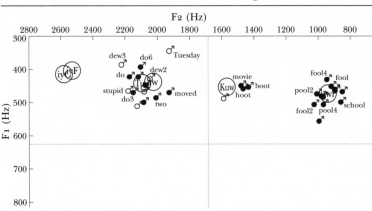

onsets (SD = 295.4 Hz) and not before /l/. Furthermore, for some of the youngest speakers, such as Pam K. in figure 9.7, or the speakers in figures 9.10–9.13, /Kuw/ is as front as the coronal allophone, occupying high front position in the region of 2000 Hz. Such extreme fronting of /uw/ after a noncoronal onset has not been reported for many dialects of North American English. Again, /Kuw/ before the lateral is at the back of the vowel space.

A regression analysis of F2 of /Kuw/ shows that, as in the case of /Tuw/, age and social class play a role in the extent of the fronting (table 9.3).[2] For /Kuw/, however, both coefficients are much larger, indicating that the change is both more vigorous and more socially differentiated; the amount of variation accounted for, as expressed by the value of r^2, is also much greater.

The positive value of the age parameter indicates that the vowel is moving toward the front in apparent time; with each successive generation of 25 years, the F2 of /Kuw/ can be expected to increase by 212 Hz. This is also demonstrated by the slope of the regression line in figure 9.14.

FIGURE 9.10
Geena E., 20, Charleston, S.C., Upper-Middle Class: /uw/

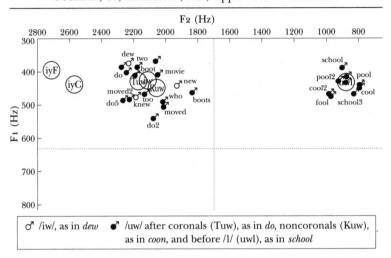

♂ /iw/, as in *dew*   ♂ /uw/ after coronals (Tuw), as in *do*, noncoronals (Kuw), as in *coon*, and before /l/ (uwl), as in *school*

FIGURE 9.11
Margaret C., 46, Charleston, S.C., Middle Class: /uw/

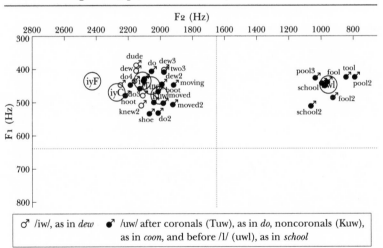

♂ /iw/, as in *dew*   ♂ /uw/ after coronals (Tuw), as in *do*, noncoronals (Kuw), as in *coon*, and before /l/ (uwl), as in *school*

FIGURE 9.12
Jonathan C., 28, Charleston, S.C., Upper Class: /uw/

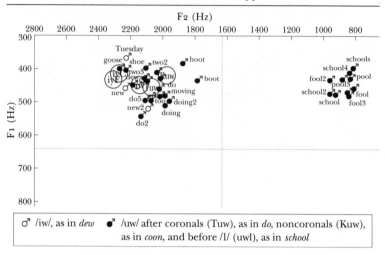

♂ /iw/, as in *dew*   ♂ /uw/ after coronals (Tuw), as in *do*, noncoronals (Kuw), as in *coon*, and before /l/ (uwl), as in *school*

FIGURE 9.13
Jane Y., 16, Charleston, S.C., Middle Class: /uw/

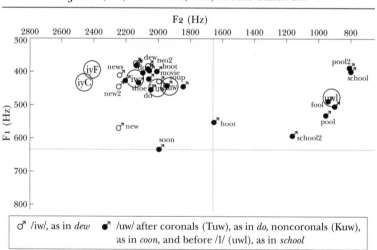

♂ /iw/, as in *dew*   ♂ /uw/ after coronals (Tuw), as in *do*, noncoronals (Kuw), as in *coon*, and before /l/ (uwl), as in *school*

TABLE 9.3
Regression Analysis of F2 of /uw/ after Noncoronals

r^2 (adjusted) = 57.7%

Variable	Coefficient	Prob
Constant	1724	< 0.0001
Age (in 25-year generations)	−212	< 0.0001
Social class	95	< 0.0001

FIGURE 9.14
F2 of /uw/ after Noncoronals by Age

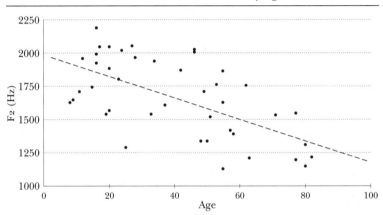

The value of the social class coefficient is positive and three times as large as the coefficient for /Tuw/, indicating greater social differentiation. Table 9.4 presents the influence of social class as three separate factors: working class (the residual), middle class (lower-middle and middle combined), and upper class (upper-middle and upper combined), indicating that the fronting of /uw/ in Charleston is being led by the highest-status groups; the expected difference between the lowest and the highest classes is 316 Hz.

As the social class effect is more robust than in the case of /Tuw/, it is possible to conduct a more detailed regression analysis of the influence of social class on the fronting of /Kuw/. Table 9.5 includes regression coefficients for five social classes and age, whereas figure 9.15 presents the expected values of F2 for the five social classes before the effects of age.

TABLE 9.4

Regression Analysis of F2 of /uw/ after Noncoronals

r^2 (adjusted) = 57.9%		
Variable	*Coefficient*	*Prob*
Constant	1826	< 0.0001
Age (in 25-year generations)	−199	< 0.0001
Upper class	316	< 0.0001
Middle class	188	0.023
Working class	0	–

TABLE 9.5

Regression Analysis of F2 of /uw/ after Noncoronals

r^2 (adjusted) = 57.0%		
Variable	*Coefficient*	*Prob*
Constant	1780	< 0.0001
Age (in 25-year generations)	−198	< 0.0001
Upper class	336	0.001
Upper-middle class	387	0.0004
Middle class	232	0.016
Lower-middle class	92	0.338
Working class	0	–

FIGURE 9.15

Expected Values of F2 for /uw/ after Noncoronals by Social Class
(before the effect of age)

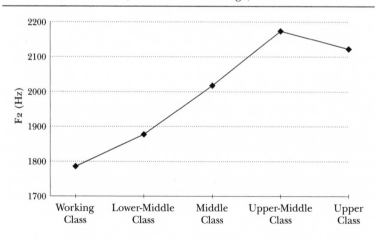

This more fine-grained analysis confirms that the lowest social classes lag behind in the change, but it also reveals a familiar pattern whereby the second-highest-status group is actually slightly ahead of the highest-status group in a language change. In this case it appears that the upper-middle class is slightly ahead of the upper class in the fronting of the allophone of /uw/ with noncoronal onsets. The lead of the higher-status social groups in the fronting of /uw/ provides confirmation for other studies (such as Hinton et al. 1987; Luthin 1987; Hagiwara 1997; Labov 2001), suggesting that the fronting of back upgliding vowels is led by the middle class, rather than the working class.

9.2. THE FRONTING OF /ow/

In some of the dialects of American English with /uw/ fronting, the long mid vowel /ow/, as in *go* and *sow*, is also shifting forward in a parallel movement (figure 9.1), always lagging behind /uw/ (Labov 1994, 208; Thomas 2001). Whereas for most dialects the nucleus of /uw/ is acoustically in front position, advanced fronting of /ow/ is found only in some of them. In those, the nucleus of /ow/ has so far moved to central position, with the most advanced speakers being slightly front of the normalized center line of 1550 Hz for the entire vowel system. *ANAE* (2006, chap. 12) reports that the fronting of /ow/ is the most advanced in the Mid-Atlantic region, in the Midland, and in the South. Advanced fronting of back upgliding vowels has also been reported for a number of dialects in the West (Hinton et al. 1987; Luthin 1987; Hagiwara 1997; Conn 2002; Ward 2003; Hall-Lew 2004, 2005). However, *ANAE* shows clearly that while /ow/ fronting is indeed fairly advanced in the West in comparison with the Inland North, for instance, it is overall less advanced there than it is in the Midland and the South (*ANAE* 2006, maps 10.28, 11.10, and 12.3).

There is allophonic conditioning in /ow/ fronting similar to that in /uw/ fronting (Fridland and Bartlett 2006), but the effect of a coronal onset is much smaller. One additional factor that plays a role in the extent of the forward movement of /ow/ is the position of the vowel in a word: /ow/ in free position, as in *go* and *sow*, is usually fronter than when it is in checked position, as in *goat* and *toast*.[3] This distinction will be used in the analyses to follow; /ow/ in checked position is labeled /owC/ in the vowel plots, and /ow/ in free position is labeled /owF/. As in the case of /uw/, /ow/ before /l/ does not participate in the fronting and remains at the back of the vowel space—the analyses to follow are for /ow/ not before /l/. In this respect Charleston differs from the rest of the South and is similar to most other dialects of American English (see Luthin 1987; Labov 2001; Thomas 2001; Conn 2002; Hall-Lew 2004). The South is an exceptional dialect in that it shows considerable fronting of /uw/ and /ow/ even before /l/ (*ANAE* 2006, figures 12.7 and 18.8). Charleston does not share this Southern characteristic: the two vowels before /l/ are firmly at the back of the vowel space.

The speech of the informants in this project shows that Charleston has undergone extensive fronting of /ow/, and it is now among the most advanced dialects in all of North America. This of course was not always the case, as in the traditional form of the dialect the back long mid vowel, as in *go*, *sow*, and *boat*, was monophthongal and often ingliding, with a nucleus which was high and back, as it was in the speech of William McTeer (figure 2.6) and as it still is in the speech of some of the oldest Charlestonians, such as Victoria G., 90, John E., 80, and Richard A., 77, in figures 9.16–9.18.

As figure 9.19 shows, however, there has been a dramatic change in the position of /ow/ in Charleston over the last few decades. Whereas the F2 of /owF/ for the oldest Charlestonians in the sample is as low as 1200 Hz, it rises to more than 1800 Hz for some Charlestonians around 20 years of age, indicating the most advanced fronting of /owF/ not only in the South, but also in the whole of North America.[4] Figure 9.20 below shows the vowels of Sally A., 55, a daughter of Richard A., 77, in figure 9.18, with /ow/ around the center of her vowel space, and figure 9.21 shows the vowels of Geena E., a 20-year-old Charlestonian, with /ow/ front of center.

A regression analysis of F2 of /owF/ shows that the fronting is a very vigorous change in apparent time, indicating that with every consecutive generation of 25 years, the F2 of /owF/ can be expected to increase by 157 Hz (table 9.6).

FIGURE 9.16

Victoria G., 90, Charleston, S.C., Upper-Middle Class: /ow/

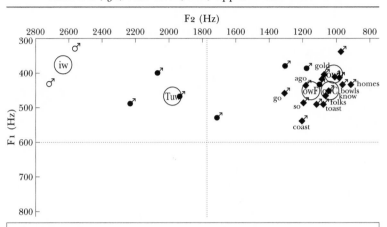

♂ /iw/, as in *dew*

✦ /uw/ after coronals (Tuw), as in *do*, and noncoronals (Kuw), as in *coon*

✦ /ow/ in free position (owF), as in *go*, and in checked position (owC), as in *coon*

FIGURE 9.17

John E., 80, Charleston, S.C., Middle Class: /ow/

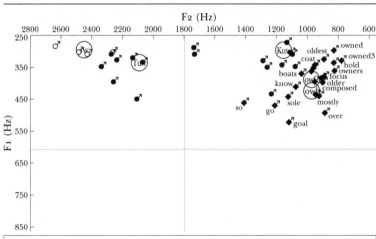

♂ /iw/, as in *dew*

✦ /uw/ after coronals (Tuw), as in *do*, and noncoronals (Kuw), as in *coon*

✦ /ow/ in free position (owF), as in *go*, and in checked position (owC), as in *coon*

FIGURE 9.18
Richard A., 77, Charleston, S.C.: /ow/

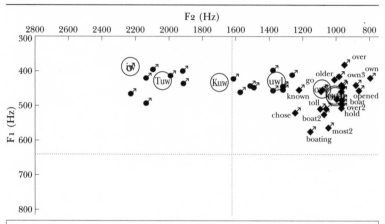

FIGURE 9.19
F2 of /ow/ in Free Position by Age

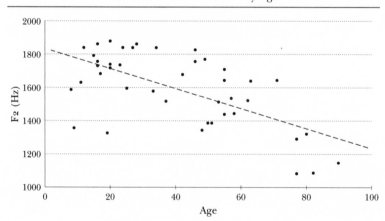

FIGURE 9.20

Sally A. (daughter of Richard A.), 55, Charleston, S.C., Upper Class: /ow/

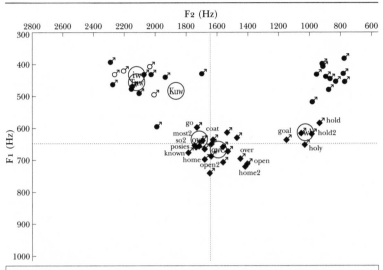

♂ /iw/, as in *dew*

🐦 /uw/ after coronals (Tuw), as in *do*, and noncoronals (Kuw), as in *coon*

◆ /ow/ in free position (owF), as in *go*, and in checked position (owC), as in *coon*

FIGURE 9.21

Geena E., 20, Charleston, S.C., Upper-Middle Class: /ow/

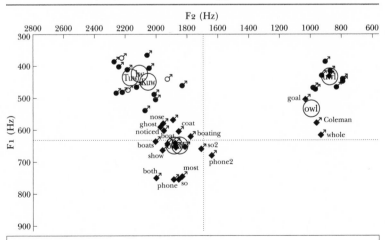

♂ /iw/, as in *dew*

🐦 /uw/ after coronals (Tuw), as in *do*, and noncoronals (Kuw), as in *coon*

◆ /ow/ in free position (owF), as in *go*, and in checked position (owC), as in *coon*

TABLE 9.6

Regression Analysis of F2 of /ow/ in Free Position

r^2 (adjusted) = 44.6%		
Variable	*Coefficient*	*Prob*
Constant	1720	< 0.0001
Social class	42	0.021
Age (in 25-year generations)	–157	< 0.0001

Figure 9.22 presents the expected values of F2 of /owF/ by decade, derived from adding the regression coefficient of each decade to the regression constant. The graph suggests that there was a rapid change in the fronting at the time represented by decades 8 to 6—corresponding to the change from the traditional system of long mid ingliding vowels to a system of upgliding vowels discussed above. It also shows a peak for young adults in their 20s and a relatively low value of F2 for children below age 10. This is likely not a reflection of the retreat of the fronting in apparent time but rather an indication that the fronting of /ow/ is led by teenagers and young adults. A similar peak in apparent time, representing a reorganization of the vernacular in late adolescence, has been found

FIGURE 9.22

Expected Values for Fronting of /uw/ in Free Position by Age in Decades

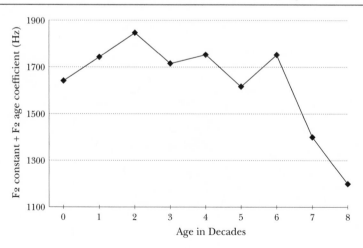

in other studies of sound change, for example, in the lenition of (ch) in Panama City (Cedergren 1973, 1984), in *l*-vocalization in Philadelphia (Ash 1982), and in changes of the Philadelphia vowel system (Labov 2001, chap.14).

There is a gender difference in the fronting of /owF/: women can be expected to be ahead of men by 69 Hz. Although this difference does not come out as significant in the regression analysis, it is in the same direction as in the fronting of /Kuw/, where women are expected to be ahead of men by 80 Hz. Therefore, we can follow Fisher (1925) to obtain the overall significance of the gender difference by adding the logs of each *p*-value. Minus twice the sum of the logs is equal to chi-square for the overall relationship with $n-1$ degrees of freedom. As shown in table 9.7, the probability of the gender difference in the fronting of /Kuw/ and /owF/ being due to chance is .007. This result, that is, that women lead in the fronting of the two back upgliding vowels, also found in other studies (e.g., Luthin 1987; Labov 2001; Ward 2003; Hall-Lew 2004), provides support for the generalization that women tend to lead linguistic change.

Social class also emerges as a significant factor—the value of the social class coefficient in table 9.6 is positive, indicating that the higher the social class, the more advanced the fronting of /owF/. Figure 9.23 is a graph of the mean F2 values of /owF/ for each of the five social classes represented in the sample for speakers up to age 65.[5]

The mean F2 values show that the fronting of /owF/ is being led by the highest-status social groups, the upper-middle and the

TABLE 9.7

Cumulative Significance of Gender Differences in the Fronting of /uw/ after Noncoronals and /ow/ in Free Position

	Women's Lead	Prob	Ln(prob)
F2 (Kuw)	80	0.222	−1.506
F2 (owF)	69	0.113	−2.180
SUM			−3.687
Chi-square (= −2×SUM)			7.374
Prob (1 df)			0.007

FIGURE 9.23
Mean F2 Values for /ow/ in Free Position by Social Class
for Speakers up to Age 65

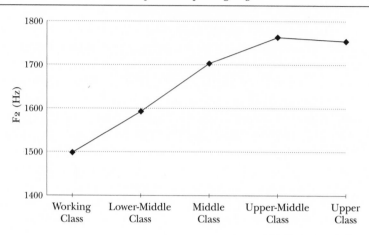

upper classes, with mean F2 at around 1750 Hz. The lower social classes show successively less fronting, indicated by the lower F2 values, with the working class being the lowest, at around 1500 Hz.

This is borne out by a regression analysis of the F2 of /owF/ for speakers up to age 65, with three social classes as separate factors: working class (working and lower-middle class combined) as the residual factor, middle class, and upper class (upper-middle and upper classes combined) (table 9.8). The middle class can be expected to be more advanced in the fronting of /owF/ by 163 Hz in comparison with the working class, whereas the difference increases to 219 Hz for the highest-status social group.

Although the social class coefficients for /ow/ are smaller than the ones for the fronting of /Kuw/ in table 9.4, the effect of social class is actually greater in the case of /ow/, as the available acoustic space for forward movement is smaller for /ow/, a mid vowel, than it is for /uw/, a high vowel. In other words, a smaller movement in terms of F2 values for /ow/ covers a greater proportion of the available space.

Furthermore, it turns out that the dynamics of the fronting of /owF/ are different for different social classes. Table 9.9 pres-

TABLE 9.8

Regression Analysis of F2 of /ow/ in Free Position
for Speakers up to Age 65

Variable	r^2 (adjusted) = 33.3%	
	Coefficient	*Prob*
Constant	1536	< 0.0001
Upper class	219	0.0002
Middle class	163	0.013
Working class	0	–

TABLE 9.9

Age Coefficients for F2 of /ow/ in Free Position for Three Social Classes

	Constant	*Age (in 25-year generations)*	*Prob*
Working class	1593	–43 Hz	0.3863
Middle class	1811	–133 Hz	0.0245
Upper class	2058	–239 Hz	< 0.0001

ents the age coefficients for three social classes separately: working, middle, and upper class. All three age coefficients are negative, indicating that for all three social classes the fronting of /owF/ can be expected to be more advanced for younger speakers, but also the higher the social class the higher the rate of change in apparent time, expressed by the increase in F2 with each successive generation of 25 years: 43 Hz for the working class, 133 Hz for the middle class, and 239 Hz for the upper class. This can be also seen in the different slopes of the regression lines in the graph in figure 9.24 showing the values of F2 of /owF/ versus age separately for each of the three social classes—it is the steepest for the upper class.

As a result of the high rate of change in the upper class, the youngest members of this social group lead in the fronting of /owF/ not only in Charleston itself, but also in the whole of North America, with F2 of /owF/ as high as 1850 Hz. Figure 9.25 presents the mean F2 of /owF/ for five social classes for speakers between ages 15 and 40, which underlines the direction of the change across the social spectrum, with the highest-status group showing the highest mean F2. It also shows that even for the lower social classes in this age range, the fronting of /owF/ is more advanced in Charleston

FIGURE 9.24

F2 of /ow/ in Free Position by Age and Social Class

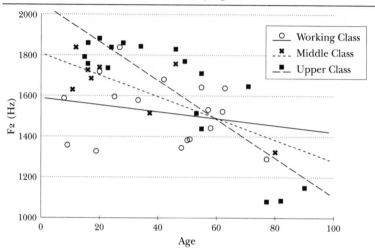

FIGURE 9.25

Mean F2 Values for /ow/ in Free Position by Social Class
for Speakers Ages 15–40

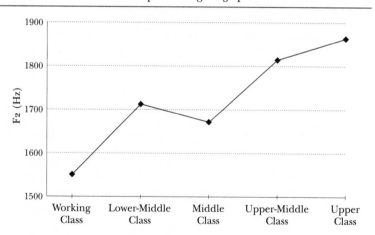

than it is in most other dialects of American English. Figures 9.26–9.30 present examples of speakers of different social classes in the youngest generation, showing differential fronting of /ow/.

The age coefficient for the working class in table 9.9 is not statistically significant. The only significant factor for this social class turns out to be gender: women can be expected to be ahead of men by 158 Hz in F2 of /owF/ (table 9.10). In fact, this is the only social class for which there is a significant gender effect. It is in the expected direction in that women are ahead of men, as they usually are in this type of sound change, that is, in vowel shifting (Labov 2001, chap. 8.3). It is quite possible, given what we know about the role of gender in linguistic change, that women initially led in the fronting of /owF/ in the higher social groups as well, but as the change progressed, men have caught up with women and are fronting the vowel just as much. As a consequence, upper-class

FIGURE 9.26
Catherine A., 25, Charleston, S.C., Working Class: /ow/

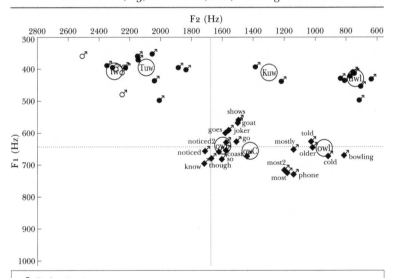

σ /iw/, as in *dew*

σ /uw/ after coronals (Tuw), as in *do*, and noncoronals (Kuw), as in *coon*

σ /ow/ in free position (owF), as in *go*, and in checked position (owC), as in *coon*

FIGURE 9.27

Jane Y., 16, Charleston, S.C., Middle Class: /ow/

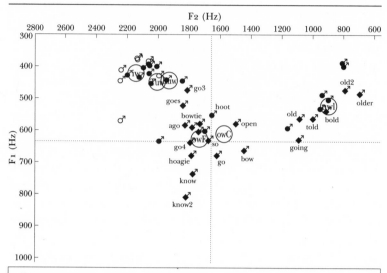

♂ /iw/, as in *dew*

♦ /uw/ after coronals (Tuw), as in *do*, and noncoronals (Kuw), as in *coon*

♦ /ow/ in free position (owF), as in *go*, and in checked position (owC), as in *coon*

FIGURE 9.28

Pam K., 16, Charleston, S.C., Upper Class: /ow/

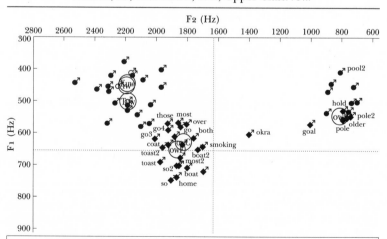

♂ /iw/, as in *dew*

♦ /uw/ after coronals (Tuw), as in *do*, and noncoronals (Kuw), as in *coon*

♦ /ow/ in free position (owF), as in *go*, and in checked position (owC), as in *coon*

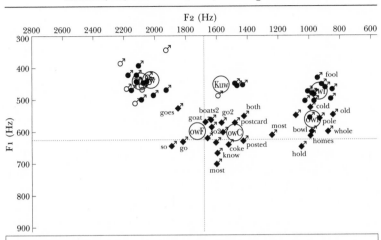

FIGURE 9.29

Kevin P., 20, Charleston, S.C., Working Class: /ow/

♂ /iw/, as in *dew*

✦ /uw/ after coronals (Tuw), as in *do*, and noncoronals (Kuw), as in *coon*

✦ /ow/ in free position (owF), as in *go*, and in checked position (owC), as in *coon*

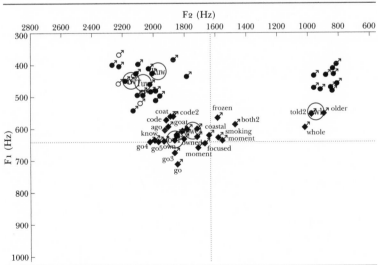

FIGURE 9.30

Jonathan C., 28, Charleston, S.C., Upper Class: /ow/

♂ /iw/, as in *dew*

✦ /uw/ after coronals (Tuw), as in *do*, and noncoronals (Kuw), as in *coon*

✦ /ow/ in free position (owF), as in *go*, and in checked position (owC), as in *coon*

TABLE 9.10
Regression Analysis of F2 of /ow/ in Free Position for Working Class

Variable	Coefficient	Prob
Constant	1438	< 0.0001
Women	158	0.034

men can be expected to be more advanced in the fronting of /owF/ than working-class women (and men). As the working class is the social group most resistant to the fronting—it is lagging behind the other groups—it is not surprising to see women ahead of men in that group.

The fronting of /ow/ in checked position (/owC/), as in *boat* and *goat*, is also very advanced in Charleston. As in all dialects of American English showing the fronting of /ow/, /owC/ is slightly behind /owF/, which is indicated by a lower F2. It is, however, an even more vigorous change than the fronting of /owF/, as indicated by the age coefficient in table 9.11: with each successive generation of 25 years, the F2 of /owC/ can be expected to increase by 179 Hz. This does not include /owC/ before /l/, as in *goal* and *pole*, which does not participate in the fronting, remaining at the back of the vowel space, as in the speech of any of the speakers in figures 9.26–9.30.

Again, for the oldest speakers, such as William McTeer (figure 2.6) or the oldest speakers in figures 9.16–9.18, /owC/ is a high back vowel, with a tense nucleus and a monophthongal or ingliding offglide. For those speakers, representing the sound system of the traditional Charleston dialect, there is no difference between /ow/ before a lateral, as in *goal*, and /ow/ before other consonants, as in *goat*—both allophones are at the back of the vowel space. Speakers for whom the long mid back vowel of *boat* and *goat* is upgliding,

TABLE 9.11
Regression Coefficients for F2 of /ow/ in Checked Position

r^2 (adjusted) = 49.1%		
Variable	Coefficient	Prob
Constant	1510	< 0.0001
Age (in 25-year generations)	−179	< 0.0001
Social class	63	0.003

on the other hand, show extensive fronting of the nucleus of /ow/, which increases in apparent time, as shown in the scatterplot in figure 9.31.

As in the case of /owF/, social class emerges as another significant parameter, with its positive value indicating that the F2 of /owC/, that is, the fronting of the nucleus, increases as one travels up the scale of social prestige accorded to different groups in the community. Table 9.12 includes the results of a regression analysis of the F2 of /owC/ for speakers up to age 65 which treats each of the five social classes as a separate parameter, with the lowest social class as the residual factor; figure 9.32 graphs the expected values of F2 for each of the five social classes before the effect of age.

These results show clearly that the fronting of /ow/ in Charleston is a change from above in the sense that it spreads downward across the social hierarchy—it is being led by the highest-status social group and is being resisted the most by the working class. The leading of the upper class is brought into sharper focus once we look at the youngest generation of speakers between the ages of 15 and 40: the mean F2 for the upper class is as high as 1782 Hz in that age group—it is considerably higher than in the other social classes (figure 9.33).

FIGURE 9.31
F2 of /ow/ in Checked Position by Age, Excluding /owl/

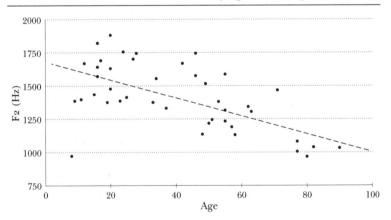

TABLE 9.12

Regression Analysis of F2 of /ow/ in Checked Position
for Speakers up to Age 65

r^2 (adjusted) = 37.4%

Variable	Coefficient	Prob
Constant	1371	< 0.0001
Upper class	322	0.001
Upper-middle class	302	0.002
Middle class	276	0.005
Lower-middle class	182	0.045
Working class	0	–
Age (in 25-year generations)	–3.145	0.086

FIGURE 9.32

Expected F2 Values for /ow/ in Checked Position by Social Class
for Speakers up to Age 65 (before the effect of age)

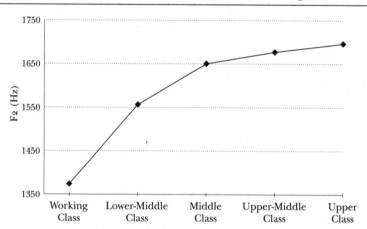

The difference between women and men in this age range is the smallest in the highest-status social group. Table 9.13 presents the mean F2 of /owC/ for three social classes of speakers between ages 15 and 40: working class (working class and lower-middle class), middle class, and upper class (upper-middle and upper class). There is virtually no difference between the two genders for the highest class, whereas women are clearly ahead of men in

FIGURE 9.33

Mean F2 Values for /ow/ in Checked Position by Social Class
for Speakers Ages 15–40

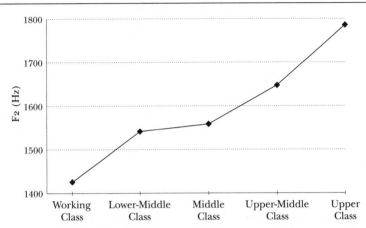

the fronting of /owC/ in the other social classes. The upper class is leading the change, and the youngest upper-class men have likely caught up with women at this advanced stage in the change. As the other social groups are less advanced in the fronting of the vowel, there is still a gender differential in the expected direction, women being ahead of men.

The fronting of the back upgliding vowels in Charleston, being led by the highest social class, seems to be a counterexample to the curvilinear hypothesis, whereby linguistic changes from below are led by an intermediately located social group, rather than the lowest or the highest one (Labov 2001). Labov's Project on Linguistic Change and Variation in Philadelphia provided support for the hypothesis, adding to the evidence from Norwich (Trudgill 1974), Panama City (Cedergren 1973), and New York City (Labov 1966). Figure 9.34 presents the F2 coefficients for six Philadelphia vowels involved in fronting for six social classes. Each point on the graph represents the size of the effect of a given social class on the fronting of the vowel. A clear pattern emerges in that an intermediately located social group, in this case the upper-working class, has the

TABLE 9.13

Mean F2 of /ow/ in Checked Position for Three Social Classes
for Speakers Ages 15–40

	Working Class	Middle Class	Upper Class
Women	1497 Hz	1600 Hz	1683 Hz
Men	1426 Hz	1511 Hz	1685 Hz

highest F2 coefficient for almost all the changes, indicating that
this social group is leading in almost all of them.

Interestingly, /owC/ does not show a curvilinear pattern as
clearly as other sound changes in Philadelphia. Although the lower-middle class seems to be slightly ahead, the other middle classes
are following closely behind, with the working classes being the

FIGURE 9.34

Philadelphia Sound Change
(after Labov 2001, fig. 5.7)

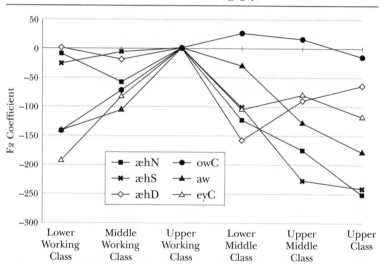

NOTE: The notations in the key are those used by Labov to describe sound
changes in Philadelphia. The /h/ after /æ/ indicated ingliding. The capital letters indicate classes of phones or position: /_N/ 'before nasals'; /_S/
'before front voiceless fricatives'; /_D/ in mad, bad, and glad; and /_C/ 'in
checked position'.

least advanced. Labov concludes that "by one means or another, this characteristic feature of the Southern Shift has escaped stigmatization and become associated with middle class norms" (Labov 2001, 187) and adds that the fronting of /uw/ and /ow/ seems to follow "a different social pattern from the raising and fronting of the front vowels" (169, n. 13).

The fronting of /uw/ and /ow/ in Charleston provides strong support for this observation, as the changes clearly do not show a curvilinear pattern—the fronting expressed by the F2 of the nucleus is a monotonic function of social class, with the highest-status social group leading and the internal social classes following behind it.

While the fronting of /ow/ in Charleston is being led by the highest-status social group, it is not clear whether it is a change from above or below the level of social awareness. If it were a change from above the level of awareness, it would show style-shifting in the direction of more fronting in more formal styles. If it were a change from below, there might be style-shifting away from the fronting in more formal styles as the change neared completion.

However, the evidence from style-shifting displayed by the speakers in the sample is inconclusive. The two styles compared are spontaneous speech—the bulk of the interview—and the reading of a word list. There is no consistent shift in F2 toward the front or the back of the vowel space between the two styles for the speakers whose speech has been analyzed acoustically. The mean F2 of /ow/ is greater in the word list than it is in spontaneous speech for 15 speakers, whereas it is smaller for 22 speakers. In other words, while 15 speakers show more fronting in a more formal style, 22 speakers show some retraction of the vowel with an increase of the amount of attention paid to speech. A regression analysis of the difference in F2 between the two styles, which considered age, gender, and social class, did not reveal any significant effects.

Although this study has not found any significant style shifting, we cannot rule out the possibility that the fronting of the back upgliding vowels in Charleston is indeed a change from above the level of social consciousness and, as such, is a borrowing introduced into the dialect by the highest-status social group. We do not necessarily expect to see style-shifting at an early stage of a change from above, when the new form is being introduced by one social group, while others have not yet developed sensitivity to it. If it is an early stage and the change is just crossing the threshold of so-cial awareness, it can only be tested with perception experiments. Such experiments have been conducted for the fronting of /ow/ in the South, and the results of the studies by Fridland, Bartlett, and Kreuz (2004) and Torbert (2004) suggest that the fronting of /ow/ is indeed just above the level of awareness, at least for some speak-ers in the South. If the fronting of the back upgliding vowels in Charleston is then a change from above the level of awareness, led by the highest-status social group, it is only an apparent counter-example to the curvilinear principle, which is a generalization on changes from below. This point will be returned to in the conclud-ing chapter of this book.

As far as Charleston's relation to other dialects of American English is concerned, the advanced fronting of /uw/ and /ow/ puts it in a rather special position. For speakers up to age 65, Charles-ton is ahead of the rest of the South. Furthermore, for the young-est generation, it is ahead of all of North America, including the most advanced Midland cities, such as Kansas City and Columbus, Ohio, which have been found to show the most advanced front-ing of the back upgliding vowels among all dialects of American English (*ANAE* 2006, chap. 12). Figure 9.35 presents a typology of American dialects based on the extent of /Tuw/ and /ow/ fronting—it shows the Southeastern region, the Midland, and the South to be at the forefront of this change. Superimposed on it is Charleston for speakers up to age 65 (/ow/ $F_2 = 1557$ Hz; /Tuw/ $F_2 = 2068$ Hz) and speakers between ages 15 and 45 (/ow/ $F_2 = 1651$ Hz; /Tuw/ $F_2 = 2094$ Hz), showing Charleston to be leading American English in both /uw/ and /ow/ fronting.

Finally, Charleston with its advanced fronting of /uw/ and /ow/ provides strong evidence for the lack of a structural relation between the Southern Shift—as defined by the chain shifting of the front vowels—and the fronting of the back upgliding vowels. Charleston is a dialect which is resisting the Southern Shift, though

FIGURE 9.35

The Fronting of /uw/ after Coronals and /ow/ by Dialect

(adapted from *ANAE*, fig. 12.6)

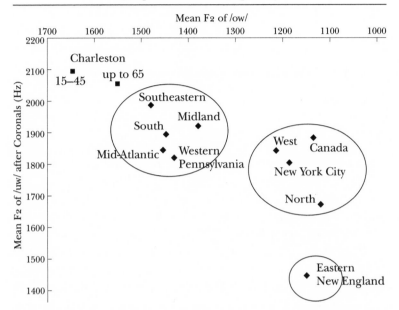

it is in close contact with dialects affected by it, and yet it is showing very advanced fronting of /uw/ and /ow/. Furthermore, while the highest-status social group is leading in the fronting of the back upgliding vowels, it lags behind the rest of the community in the chain-shifting of the front upgliding vowels, which is in turn most advanced in the lowest social class. This provides support for treating the two processes as separate phenomena (*ANAE* 2006).

10. THE DEVELOPMENT
OF NASAL SYSTEMS
FOR /æ/ AND /aw/

10.1. DEVELOPMENT OF A NASAL SYSTEM
FOR SHORT-*A*

In the traditional dialect short-*a*, as in *pat* and *sack*, occupied a low-front position and did not show an allophonic distinction between /æ/ followed by nasal and oral consonants. *PEAS* transcribed the vowel of *aunt* as [æˑ] and [æˑə] and the vowel of *half, glass,* and *bag* as [æˑ] and [æᵛə] (Synopses 135–36). The lack of allophonic differentiation is confirmed by the acoustic analysis of the speech of William McTeer, presented in chapter 2. Figure 2.9, repeated here as figure 10.1, shows both allophones in low position, slightly front of center, which is in fact more retracted than the position suggested by the phonetic symbol [æ].

The speech of the informants in this project indicates that there has been a major change in the short-*a* system as compared with the speech of William McTeer, representing the dialect at the turn of the twentieth century: there is now a clear allophonic distinction between short-*a* before oral consonants and before nasals; the latter, as in *pants* or *man*, is raised and fronted, while the former remains firmly in low front-central position. There is considerable phonetic separation between the two allophones for the majority of the speakers in the sample—it is a nasal rather than a continuous short-*a* system (*ANAE*, 13.2). Although there is considerable overlap between the two allophones for the oldest speakers, the nasal tokens tend to be slightly fronter and higher, as in the speech of Sarah E., 80, Charles C., 71, Elizabeth O., 82, and Richard A., 77, marking the beginning of a nasal system for short-*a* in apparent time (figures 10.2–10.5, resp.).

FIGURE 10.1
William McTeer (1965), Beaufort, S.C., Middle Class: /æ/

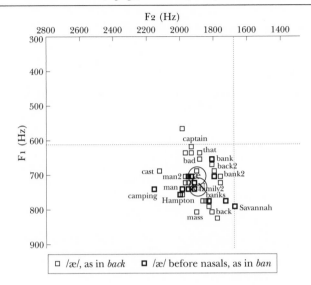

□ /æ/, as in *back*   ◼ /æ/ before nasals, as in *ban*

FIGURE 10.2
Sarah E., 80, Charleston, S.C., Middle Class: /æ/

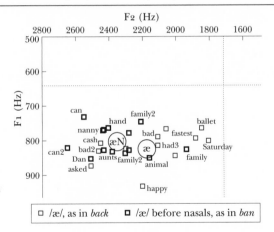

□ /æ/, as in *back*   ◼ /æ/ before nasals, as in *ban*

FIGURE 10.3

Elizabeth O., 82, Charleston, S.C., Upper Class: /æ/

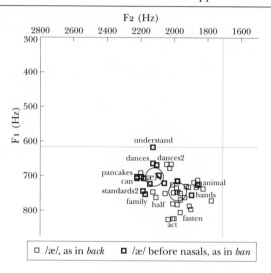

FIGURE 10.4

Richard A., 77, Charleston, S.C., Upper Class: /æ/

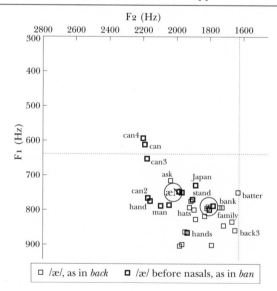

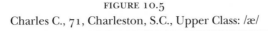

FIGURE 10.5
Charles C., 71, Charleston, S.C., Upper Class: /æ/

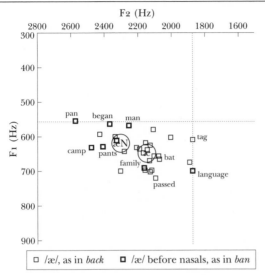

□ /æ/, as in *back*   ■ /æ/ before nasals, as in *ban*

For the vast majority of speakers below 70, however, the overlap between the two allophones is much smaller, and they are usually clearly separated from each other in phonetic space, the allophone before a nasal being much higher and fronter, as in the speech of Sally A., 55, Richard A.'s daughter; Peter O., 15, Elizabeth O.'s grandson; or Heather G., 19 (figures 10.6–10.8, resp.).

The progress of the fronting of short-*a* before nasals in apparent time is presented in figure 10.9. Whereas for the oldest speakers /æN/ is at around 2200 Hz in the F2 dimension, the vowel becomes front for the younger generations, reaching around 2400 Hz.

A regression analysis of the F2 value of /æN/ reveals that the vowel can be expected to front by 59 Hz with each successive generation of 25 years (table 10.1). In addition, it also shows social class to be a significant factor in the fronting: the middle class appears to be leading the change, while the upper class (combined with upper middle) lags behind it by 109 Hz. The result conforms to Labov's finding known as the curvilinear hypothesis, whereby linguistic change is led by an intermediately located social group (Labov 2001).

FIGURE 10.6

Sally A., 55, Charleston, S.C., Upper Class: /æ/

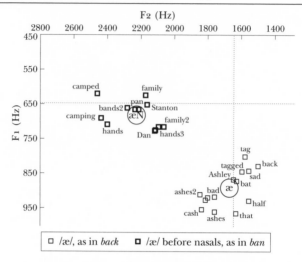

FIGURE 10.7

Peter O., 15, Charleston, S.C., Upper Class: /æ/

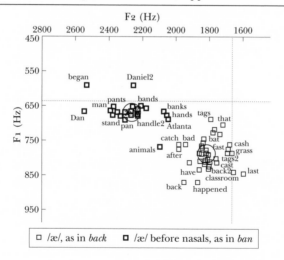

FIGURE 10.8

Heather G., 19, Charleston, S.C., Working Class: /æ/

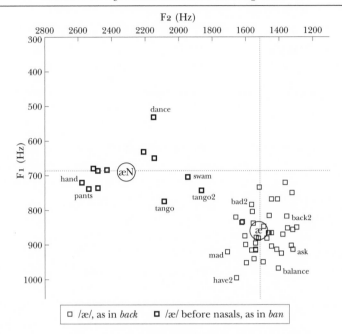

□ /æ/, as in *back*   ◘ /æ/ before nasals, as in *ban*

FIGURE 10.9

Fronting of /æ/ before Nasals by Age

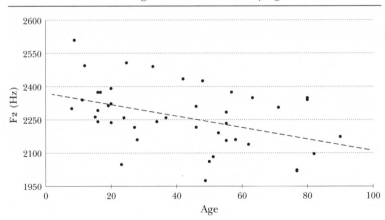

TABLE 10.1

Regression Analysis of F2 of /æ/ before Nasals

Variable	Coefficient	Prob
r^2 (adjusted) = 23.7%		
Constant	2306	≤ 0.0001
Age (in 25-year generations)	–59	0.007
Working class	85	0.053
Middle class	109	0.042
Upper class	0	–

As suggested by the vowel plots in figures 10.6–10.8, the nasal allophone of /æ/ is not only fronted, but it is also becoming raised. While the mean F1 of /æN/ for 80-year-olds is 773 Hz, it is 630 Hz for teenagers. Age turns out to be the only significant social factor: each successive generation of 25 years can be expected to raise the vowel by 51 Hz (table 10.2).

There seems to be little, if any, social evaluation of the raised and fronted /æ/ before nasals, as there is little evidence of style-shifting. For the majority of speakers whose speech has been analyzed acoustically, there is no significant difference between the mean of /æN/ produced in spontaneous speech and the mean of the word-list tokens—the tokens produced in the more formal style, the word list, do not tend to be less front or less raised. However, there are four speakers for whom there is a difference: their /æN/ produced in word-list style is less front or less raised than the one produced in spontaneous speech; figures 10.10–10.12 show the vowel in the two styles for three of the speakers.

However, in three of these cases, the word-list tokens are actually more peripheral—they are fronter, though they are lower than the spontaneous speech tokens. This may be an undershoot effect

TABLE 10.2

Regression Analysis of F1 of /æ/ before Nasals

Variable	Coefficient	Prob
r^2 (adjusted) = 39.2%		
Constant	580	≤ 0.0001
Age (in 25-year generations)	51	≤ 0.0001

FIGURE 10.10

Sherry D., 63, Charleston, S.C., Lower-Middle Class: /æ/ before Nasals

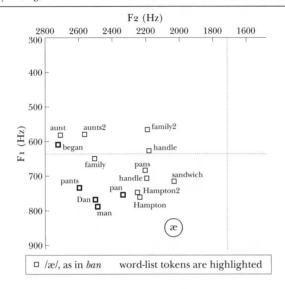

□ /æ/, as in *ban*   word-list tokens are highlighted

FIGURE 10.11

Margaret C., 46, Charleston, S.C., Middle Class: /æ/ before Nasals

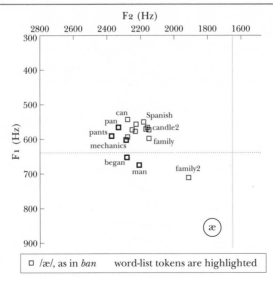

□ /æ/, as in *ban*   word-list tokens are highlighted

FIGURE 10.12

Vincent J., 33, Charleston, S.C., Lower-Middle Class: /æ/ before Nasals

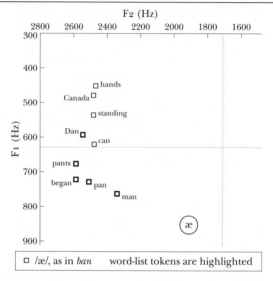

for the spontaneous-speech tokens: the word-list tokens carry more stress and have longer durations—the words tend to be shorter, resulting in longer vowel durations—which allows them to approximate their targets more closely. It is should be emphasized that these four cases are exceptions in the sense that for the majority of speakers there is no difference in the position of tokens produced in the two different styles, spontaneous speech and the word list, as shown in the examples in figures 10.13 and 10.14. This suggests little social evaluation, as indicated by style-shifting, of short-*a* before nasals in Charleston, as opposed to a dialect such as New York City's (Labov 1966).

Furthermore, for 9 out of the 43 speakers analyzed acoustically, the tokens of /æN/ produced in the more formal style of word-list reading are in fact more advanced in that they tend to be more raised and fronted than /æN/ produced in spontaneous speech. Figures 10.15–10.17 show examples of 3 such speakers. This result does confirm the lack of negative evaluation of the raising and fronting of the vowel, but it is also likely to have been affected by the choice of words for the word list, which are shorter than many

FIGURE 10.13

Claire S., 16, Charleston, S.C., Upper-Middle Class: /æ/ before Nasals

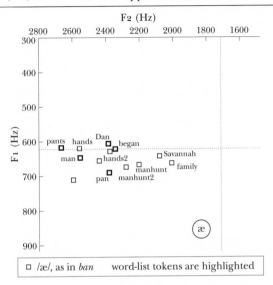

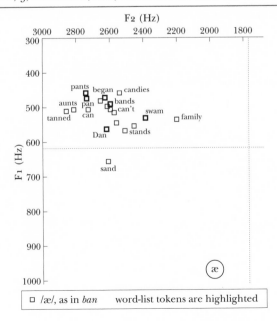

FIGURE 10.14

Mark T., 9, Charleston, S.C., Lower-Middle Class: /æ/ before Nasals

FIGURE 10.15

Emily C., 20, Charleston, S.C., Middle Class: /æ/ before Nasals

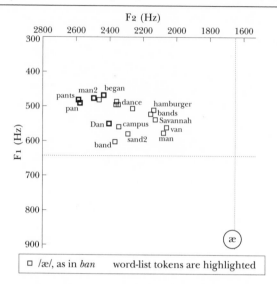

FIGURE 10.16

Kevin P., 20, Charleston, S.C., Working Class: /æ/ before Nasals

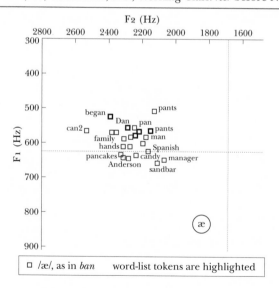

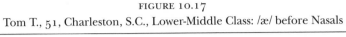

FIGURE 10.17

Tom T., 51, Charleston, S.C., Lower-Middle Class: /æ/ before Nasals

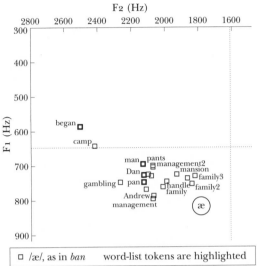

of the words produced spontaneously during the interview and, as such, are not affected by polysyllabic shortening found in a stress-timed language such as English.

At the same time, the allophone of /æ/ before oral consonants, as in *bad* or *bag*, has been retracting at the rate of 67 Hz for each successive generation of 25 years (table 10.3). For the youngest speakers it is now in central position, and for the most advanced speakers, it is slightly back of center, as in the speech of Jane Y., 16, in figure 10.18. Regression analysis reveals that those most advanced speakers are women, who can be expected to be ahead of men by 108 Hz.

The women's lead in the backing of /æ/, not unexpected in a change such as the fronting or backing of vowels, is seen more clearly in figure 10.19, where the women's regression line is lower and steeper than the men's. A regression analysis conducted separately for women reveals that they can be expected to retract the vowel by as much as 93 Hz with each successive generation of 25 years (table 10.4). The expected change for men, on the other

TABLE 10.3
Regression Analysis for F2 of /æ/ before Oral Consonants

r^2 (adjusted) = 34.2%		
Variable	Coefficient	Prob
Constant	1786	≤ 0.0001
Age (in 25-year generations)	67	0.0008
Women	−108	0.003

FIGURE 10.18
Jane Y., 16, Charleston, S.C., Middle Class: /æ/ before Nasals

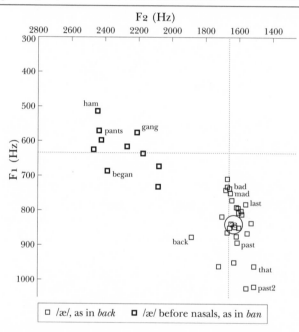

hand, is at the rate of 31 Hz for each successive generation, though it does not reach statistical significance. In addition, the amount of variation explained, as expressed by the r^2 value, rises from 34% to 40% when women are considered separately from men.

In addition to backing, /æ/ has been lowering in phonetic space, as expressed by an increase in the value of F1. The increase has been moderate, yet significant: for each successive generation

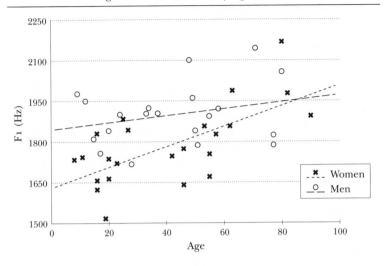

FIGURE 10.19
Backing of /æ/ before Nasals by Age and Gender

TABLE 10.4
Regression Analysis of F2 of /æ/ before Oral Consonants for Women

r^2 (adjusted) = 39.8%		
Variable	*Coefficient*	*Prob*
Constant	1635	≤ 0.0001
Age (in 25-year generations)	93	0.0007

of 25 years, short-*a* before an oral consonant can be expected to lower by 26 Hz (table 10.5). As in the case of the retraction of the vowel, the lowering is also led by women, who can be expected to be ahead of men by 33 Hz. This is not surprising, as the two processes, backing and lowering, are part of the same change, the movement of the vowel along a diagonal.

A measure that combines the fronting and raising of /æN/ and the backing and lowering of the nonnasal allophone, which can thus express the growing allophonic differentiation more accurately, is the Cartesian distance in Hertz between the nuclei of the two allophones. The increase of the distance in apparent time is presented in figure 10.20. The mean distance between the two

TABLE 10.5

Regression Coefficients for F1 of /æ/ before Oral Consonants

r^2 (adjusted) = 21.2%		
Variable	Coefficient	Prob
Constant	870	≤ 0.0001
Women	33	0.05
Age (in 25-year generations)	−26	0.005

FIGURE 10.20

Cartesian Distance between /æ/ before Nasal and Oral Consonants
by Age and Gender

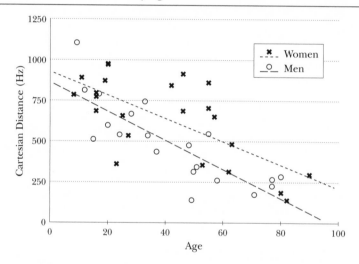

allophones rises from 200 Hz for 80-year-olds to 690 Hz for teenagers, indicating a rather vigorous change. A regression analysis
reveals that the distance can be expected to increase by 198 Hz
with each successive generation of 25 years, and that women are
ahead of men by 137 Hz (table 10.6), though the rates of change
are close for women and men, as indicated by the roughly parallel
regression lines in figure 10.20.

Given the differentiation between the two allophones, the
short-*a* system in Charleston can be categorized as a nasal system,
"in which /æ/ is raised and fronted before any nasal consonant in
a separate distribution from other /æ/" (*ANAE*, 181). As such it is

TABLE 10.6

Regression Coefficients for Cartesian Distance between /æ/
before Nasal and Oral Consonants

r^2 (adjusted) = 57.3%		
Variable	*Coefficient*	*Prob*
Constant	824	≤ 0.0001
Women	137	0.0122
Age (in 25-year generations)	−198	≤ 0.0001

similar to other dialect areas, such as New England and the large
Midland cities of Pittsburgh, Columbus, and Indianapolis, though
it is different from most of the South, characterized by Southern
breaking (*ANAE*, map 13.5).

Another similarity with the Midland is the size of the distance
between the two allophones, as expressed by the difference between the F1 of /æ/ and the F1 of /æN/, a measure used in map
13.3 of *ANAE*. For two Telsur speakers from Charleston, the difference falls between 200 and 300 Hz, and for the third one it is
between 100 and 200 Hz—a similar pattern is present in the Midland (*ANAE*, map 13.3). This finding, based on only three Telsur

FIGURE 10.21

Difference in Heights between /æ/ before Nasal and Oral Consonants
by Age in Decades

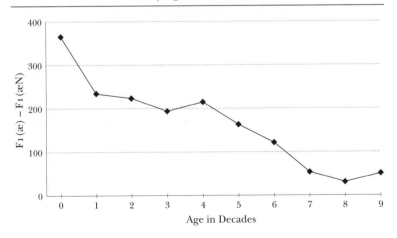

informants from Charleston, is confirmed by the present study. As figure 10.21 shows, for the majority of speakers under age 50, the F1 difference between the two allophones of short-*a* is above 200 Hz, with a mean difference of 243 Hz for that age range.

10.2. DEVELOPMENT OF A NASAL SYSTEM FOR /aw/

Another phoneme which has developed a distinct nasal allophone is /aw/, as in *down* or *sound*. There is no allophonic differentiation in the traditional system: the nucleus of /aw/ before a nasal consonant occupied the same low position as /aw/ before other voiced consonants or in free position. The vowel in the word *down* was transcribed by *PEAS* as [aʊ] and [ɑʊ] (Synopses 135–36).

However, the beginning of the allophonic distinction is already seen in the speech of William McTeer, representing the dialect at the turn of the twentieth century. Figure 10.22 presents tokens of /aw/ before voiced consonants and in free position, with the tokens before nasals in bold. Although there is no difference in height between the two allophones, /awN/ is significantly more front than /aw/ before other voiced consonants and in free position—the mean F2 of the nasal allophone is greater by 103 Hz.

This difference in F2 is found in the speech of all the speakers in the sample: /aw/ before nasal stops is always fronter than /aw/ before other consonants and in free position, and as such it constitutes a distinct allophone of /aw/. There has then been a change from the traditional system with no allophonic differentiation to the present state with two distinct allophones of /aw/, as exemplified by the speech of Claire S., 16, in figure 10.23.

It is less clear, however, whether the change is still in progress, that is, whether the nasal allophone is continuing to front. Linear regression does not yield any significant results for any of the three social factors: age, gender, or social class, suggesting, among other things, that the fronting of /awN/ in apparent time does not change. However, a look at the formant values of the vowel reveals that the relationship between F2 and age in apparent time is not linear—in fact there seem to be two distinct stages in the apparent time history of this variable: fronting for speakers age 90 to around

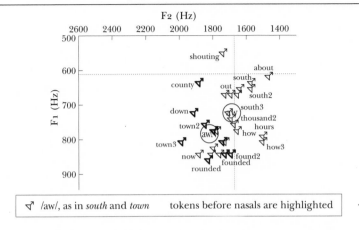

FIGURE 10.22

William McTeer (1965), Beaufort, S.C., Middle Class: /aw/

⊽ /aw/, as in *south* and *town*   tokens before nasals are highlighted

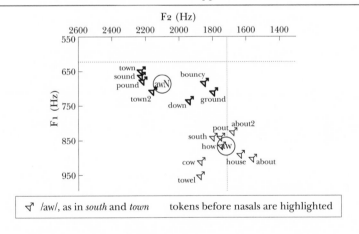

FIGURE 10.23

Claire S., 16, Charleston, S.C., Upper-Middle Class: /aw/

⊽ /aw/, as in *south* and *town*   tokens before nasals are highlighted

40, followed by a retrograde movement for speakers under age 40 (figure 10.24). The apparent reversal of the change can also be seen in figure 10.25 below, presenting changes in the Cartesian distance in Hertz between the nuclei of the two allophones in apparent time by decade.

FIGURE 10.24

Mean F2 of /aw/ before Nasals by Age in Decades

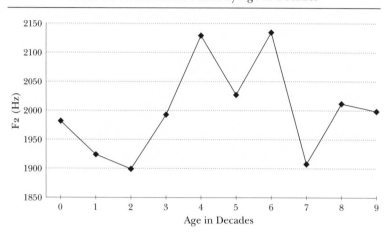

FIGURE 10.25

Cartesian Distance between /aw/ before Nasal and Oral Consonants
by Age in Decades

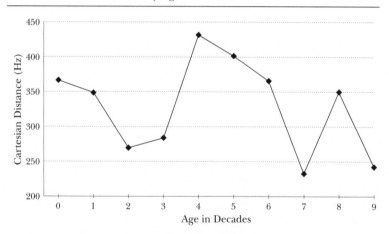

In addition to fronting, the nasal allophone has also become more raised in comparison with the traditional dialect, but, again, it appears that the raising has stopped or perhaps even reverted, as seen in figure 10.26, showing the distance between the two allophones in F1 against age in decades. It may seem that the raising expressed by the difference in the height of the two nuclei may be an artifact of the lowering of /aw/ before voiceless consonants with the retreat of Canadian Raising. However, essentially the same picture emerges when we look at the F1 of /awN/ by itself, as shown in figure 10.27: the nasal allophone of /aw/ was gradually raised (indicated by decreasing F1) in apparent time for speakers between ages 90 and 40, at which point the raising stopped advancing and began a retrograde movement.

Accordingly, if we divide the apparent-time period into two separate phases, up to age 49 and above age 40, regression analyses yield significant results indicating change in apparent time at exactly the same rate, albeit in opposite directions: raising of /awN/ for speakers age 90 to 40, and then lowering for speakers younger than age 49 (tables 10.7 and 10.8). Figures 10.28 and 10.29 include scatterplots showing the change graphically.

In summary, /aw/ in Charleston has a distinct nasal allophone, which is fronter and higher than /aw/ before oral consonants and in free position. It appears that the differentiation began around the turn of the twentieth century with /awN/ becoming fronter and

FIGURE 10.26

Difference between /aw/ before Nasal and Oral Consonants
by Age in Decades

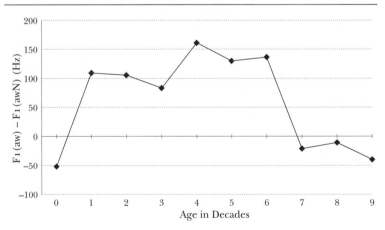

FIGURE 10.27

Mean F1 of /aw/ before Nasals by Age in Decades

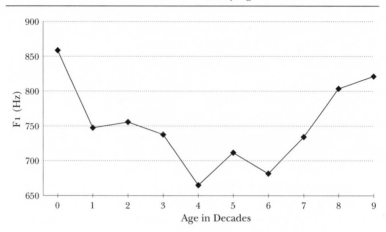

TABLE 10.7

Regression Analysis of F1 of /aw/ before Nasals for Speakers up to Age 49

r^2 (adjusted) = 15.1%		
Variable	*Coefficient*	*Prob*
Constant	820	≤ 0.0001
Age (in 25-year generations)	–79	0.028

TABLE 10.8

Regression Analysis of F1 of /aw/ before Nasals
for Speakers Age 40 and Older

r^2 (adjusted) = 43.5%		
Variable	*Coefficient*	*Prob*
Constant	523	≤ 0.0001
Age (in 25-year generations)	79	0.0005

higher. The nucleus of the nasal allophone of /aw/ is the highest and most peripheral for speakers in their 40s. Apparent time data suggest that the fronting and raising of /awN/ was halted around the time that generation was acquiring the dialect and may have now been reversed. While the evidence for the initial stage of the

FIGURE 10.28
F1 of /aw/ before Nasals for Speakers up to Age 49

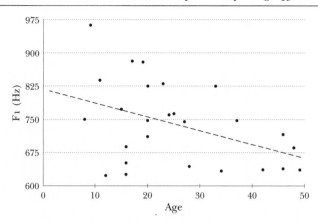

FIGURE 10.29
F1 of /aw/ before Nasals for Speakers Age 40 and Older

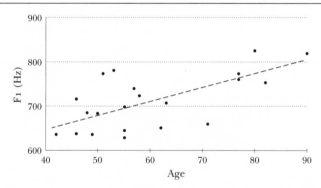

change, the fronting and raising of /awN/, is fairly strong for the generations between ages 90 and 40, as indicated by the relatively high value of r^2 (43.5%), there has been a considerable amount of variation in the last few decades, represented by the speech of speakers up to age 40, which remains largely unexplained (r^2 at 15.1%). Further research is needed to confirm the preliminary hypothesis that /awN/ may now be reverting to a lower and less peripheral position.

11. CHARLESTON
AND ITS PEOPLE

THIS CHAPTER PRESENTS a few representatives of the city and its dialect in extensive quotations from the interviews. Although the 100 Charlestonians interviewed for this project span a few generations and come from vastly different social backgrounds, they all seem to share a pride in the historical heritage of the city and the special position that it therefore enjoys and, at the same time, show an awareness of the vast economic and, consequently, social changes that the city has undergone in the last few decades as a result of the gentrification of the historic downtown section. Many of them feel that Charleston is distinct in a number of ways (including linguistic) from other parts of the South or even the rest of the state and identify it as being part of the Low Country. Many of them note that Charleston has changed linguistically in the last few decades in that the traditional Charleston accent is no longer heard in the youngest generations. They generally acknowledge the close connection between the white community and the Gullah culture of the African American slaves—the vast majority have had African American maids or nannies at some point in their lives, though not all of those spoke Gullah—and some suggest that Gullah has had a linguistic influence on the speech of the white community.

ELIZABETH O., 82, UPPER CLASS

Elizabeth O. is an 82-year-old upper-class Charlestonian, whose family arrived in Charleston right after the city was founded in 1670; one of the streets in Charleston is named after her ancestors. She lives in a house in the historic downtown section of Charleston, which is where three generations of her family were interviewed: her husband, three of her daughters, and her grandson.

She takes pride in the historical heritage of the city:

It's very definitely a Southern city– We're proud to be Southerners. We take a lot of pride in it. Well, they say about Charlestonians: they're like the Chinese, they worship their ancestors and they worship rice. [laughter] Rice is one of our big dishes here. We're proud of our heritage and proud to be Southerners.... More old historic buildings I think than any other city. And of course this is where the first shot of the War of Northern Aggression took place, right in Charleston Harbor. But we Southerners call it the War of Northern Aggression, not the Civil War. Couldn't be a civil war! We had uh abdicated from the state, from the union. Civil war is within a country, and we had abdicated, left by that time. But, as I said, the first shot was fired from here and– We are not a RECONSTRUCTED city, we are a city that has its old buildings.

She is one of the few speakers in the sample with most of the distinctive phonological features of the traditional dialect—her husband is another one, though her daughters have none of those features and neither does her grandson. When asked if there are any differences in the way different generations of Charlestonians talk, she notes:

Definitely. I'm one of the few left with an accent. But even my children, growing up around me—I have more of an accent than my husband does—they don't speak with a Charleston accent anymore. I think it's because—and my grandchildren certainly don't, and my great grandchildren, of course don't—but I think it's because when my children were young was when television came in. And they got so used to hearing that type of voice, you know, that they don't speak with the Charleston accent anymore. There's very little of it left around.

She is sometimes identified as a Charlestonian when she travels in the rest of the state. This is reported by some of the oldest speakers in the sample who have the traditional phonology, though not by anyone without those features, that is, not by anyone younger than 60. Elizabeth O. is aware of the distinctiveness of the traditional dialect and offers the following story about her brother:

He was– flew bombers in the Pacific, during World War II. He was the main pilot, the captain. And they were all given a code to telephone in to the airfield that when they were coming back from a mission and were landing, they were given a code, so that the ground forces would realize it was one of their planes coming in and not an enemy plane. And my brother's code was 88—and *eight* is one of the words that Charlestonians really say differently than anybody else—and he was flying and approaching the field he said "This is captain from eighty-eight, eighty-eight!" And the ground forces sounded the alarm and said "Undercover! There's a Jap in the crowd!" [laughter] They closed the airbase, couldn't understand his Charleston accent. And that really happened, that was written up in the papers several times, which I think is an interesting story on our Charleston accent.

Finally, like most of the speakers of her generation, she distinguishes between *pin* and *pen* in both production and perception but realizes that her dialect is distinct from other Southern cities in this regard:

pin and *pen* [pronounced differently]; I think they sound differently and that's one of the first words that I can remember hearing in college that I didn't know what somebody from Greenville was asking for. They came in and said, "You got a pen?" and I said, "A what?!" and they said, "a pin," and "Do you want a pin or a pen?!" So, that I think I definitely pronounce differently and people in Greenville don't [laughter].

JOHN M., 75, UPPER CLASS

John M. is another upper-class Charlestonian, a lawyer, living in downtown Charleston, whose ancestors arrived in the area around 1790. He has some of the traditional features of the dialect, such as the lack of distinction between /ihr/ and /ehr/, as in *beer* and *bear*. Here he comments on his awareness of this merger and of the PIN-PEN merger:

Beer, as much as *pen*, I was teased about, still am but not as much. When I was in the Navy, I would say I want a brew, in order to avoid the usual laughter and good-natured teasing I got about the way that I pronounced the word, and I tried to learn to say BEER [high vowel].

Pin-pen [pronounced as close]; now here are the two I've had so much trouble with. And when I say I'm teased about it. I was a young boy, I guess I resented it and was embarrassed by it but after that it's been a source of amusement. *Pin* and *pen*, I hear the difference and other people tell me there's no difference the way I pronounce them.

As was the case with Elizabeth O., John M. is aware of the distinctiveness of the traditional Charleston dialect from the rest of the South:

When I was a small boy, 10 years old, and first went out of Charleston to summer camp, boys from other parts of the state and the other parts of Carolina and Georgia took great delight in asking us to say the same little ditty that involved several of your words. And it was like "get up at eight, and read *The State*, and go to the Battery, and throw bricks at the battleships" and that little recitation uh, older people do it, young people don't fool with this as much, but every once in a while when I go away from Charleston but I'm still in the South, I will be asked by an old-timer to repeat those words.

He further offers the following story:

Let me tell you one other funny story. When I was in the Navy, I was on an aircraft carrier, and a commander came aboard our ship to watch air-ops. I did not know him, I'd never met him, but I was standing next to him in the island of the ship watching the operations, and I overheard him talking to other people. And I thought to myself, "I've been teased all my life about my Charleston accent, and I don't usually hear it in myself or other people but that man seems to be talking the way they tell me I talk," so I turned to him and said, "Commander, where are you from?" and he looked at me and smiled and said, "I'm from Hampton Park. Where are you from, the Battery?" In other words, he immediately recognized that we were both from Charleston and he asked me, told me where he had been raised in Charleston and asked me where I had been raised.

ROBERT B., 49, UPPER CLASS

Robert B., age 49, is another upper-class Charlestonian, a lawyer, who was raised and now lives in the downtown section below Broad Street. His family has lived in Charleston for 250 years. He was interviewed together with his 79-year-old father, Christopher B. Robert B. notes that his experience of growing up in the downtown section south of Broad Street was fairly typical for children of this social milieu.

In the summer, the thing that really sort of defined a Charleston youth, I think, summer was sail. Certainly as a child, the harbor was my babysitter. When I was 5 years old, my father built a boat for us, which was my first boat, and that we used that on the lake, but then when I was 9, he built a larger boat, and from the time I was 9 until about 16, I sailed practically every day in the summer. I would, you know, put a sail on my shoulder and walk down to the local club, where we kept our boat, and just head out and sail for hours and hours on end. And we had lots of races and I think [to father] you grew up sailing all the time. I think that very much defined Charleston summer for many of us.... I think I had, growing up, I had a very traditional Charleston summer as a child, which consisted of three things: sailing, Sullivan's Island, and the mountains. That was really quite the traditional Charleston summer. We were very fortunate to have a family house in Sullivan's Island, which we would spend, you know, a number of weeks over there. We had a very small place up in western North Carolina, and we would spend perhaps two weeks up there, and then the rest of the time I was sailing. And that, I think you would find that if you interviewed, you know, 50 people who grew up in this area, quite a lot would have some variation of that thing.... [Sullivan's Island] was the closest of the beaches. It was the beach that tended to have people from downtown Charleston, from peninsula Charleston. There's another close beach, which is Folly Beach, but Folly had smaller lots, it didn't tend to have people from downtown Charleston, and had a very very different character, and today it has quite a different character. You can go over to Sullivan's Island today and walk down the beach and– I feel very comfortable there because in the summer I know, I mean, I can't walk 200 feet without running into people that I know, even though it's a beach which serves an area of a half a million people, we still know many many of the owners of the houses there. Our house over there we've had for 75 years.

His family has always had strong connections with Virginia, and in his opinion this is the case for a lot of Charlestonians. This might provide an explanation for one of the traditional Charleston features, Canadian Raising, which is not found much in the rest of South Carolina or Georgia, but is a prominent feature in Virginia. Robert B. has Canadian Raising for /aw/ and is the youngest speaker with this feature in the sample.

I think one of the things that you found 50 or 100 years ago was that oddly enough there was not a great deal of mix with North Carolina but there was quite a lot of mix with Virginia. There are a lot of families in Charleston which intermarried with families from Richmond and other areas; one of the reasons, I guess, being that for many years Charleston people would go to school at the University of Virginia.... But I think that was quite the case for a lot of Charlestonians that if there was mixture, it tended to be with Virginia. For example, growing up I knew far more people from Virginia than I did from Savannah, far more people from Virginia than I did from North Carolina, even though both North Carolina and Savannah were closer.

Both Robert B. and his father Christopher B. suggest that the impact of the recent changes in Charleston is best seen in the context of the relative isolation of Charleston until World War II, which marked the beginning of the influx of outsiders into that city which has increased considerably in the last few decades.

CHRISTOPHER B.: First of all, Charleston was a relatively small city. I think in 1935, 1940, all 50, 60 thousand in the metropolitan area. So it was not a big city. There was very little exchange outside of the city. It was not until the Second World War that we had outside influences. In the First World War it was relatively short. The men were off to fight, came back within about a year to a year and a half, and settled back in Charleston. Charleston was still in effectively an economic depression that had been going on since 1865. And it wasn't until the Second World War that things began to pick up.

ROBERT B.: We had fairly substantial military presence here, starting in the late '30s– But starting with World War II, it started building and then after the war it was quite significant, and that brought in a lot of influx from elsewhere in the country.

In commenting on the recent economic changes in Charleston, the revitalization of the downtown section and the growth of tourism, Robert B. points out the fact, stressed by many other informants in this study, that the new prosperity has had the unfortunate effect of driving prices up and forcing people to move out of the peninsula. At the same time, he sees the positive aspects of the changes and views change itself as inevitable:

Charleston has seen a huge amount of turnover in property, starting in the mid-'70s, and then the Spoleto, and what I call the marketing of Charleston. Although Joe Riley is a good mayor, he's changed the character of Charleston dramatically. And it has its good and bad to it. I mean it's good in that there's quite an influx of intelligent attractive people. It's bad in that by marketing Charleston and bringing in lots of people, the prices have run up so much that locals can't afford to stay. Most of the neighborhoods in downtown Charleston are no longer local people. If you go to Legare Street or East Battery, South Battery, very few of the houses are in the same hands.

The changes in Charleston really are– They present the traditional love-hate relationship, you know, they– We've had a lot of marvelous people come in to the city as a result of these changes—they are well educated, they're attractive, they make for very vibrant society, yet at the same time, they change the society.… The people that I grew up with, most of them can't afford to stay on the peninsula. It is so much traffic, so many people here that the life of children on their bicycles—I mean, we, you know, lived all around downtown on bicycles and running around and things like that—has simply vanished. There are very few children who ride bikes around now. It's, you know– the world changes, and if you try to resist that, you're sort of silly. I mean, I, we are, of any family, we are the last ones to complain about outside influences, because we can go back seven or eight generations in Charleston and no B. male has ever married a Charleston girl.

For Robert B., as for many other informants, Charleston is very much part of the South, though at the same time it is in some ways distinct from the rest of the region and even from the rest of the state:

South Carolina is made up of three different regions. There is South Carolina. There is New Jersey, which is also known as Myrtle Beach. And then there is the Low Country, which is sort of Georgetown down to Savannah, stopping before you get to Hilton Head, by the way. Hilton Head, of course, is a region that has come from all over, as is Kiawah, but Beaufort, Charleston, Georgetown are what we perceive as the Low Country. The area of Myrtle Beach and, that area has lost almost all of its character as, you know, a South Carolina region, because of the incredible influx of people from all over, retirees, and so you know, when you cut the coast off, then you've got the rest of South Carolina, which I feel is more homogenous without us than with us. I think Charleston is perceived by most of the state as being, you know, a different area. And, you know, I think we all have to acknowledge that one of the strongest attributes of Charlestonians is a hideous sense of arrogance. You know, Charlestonians think they're better than everybody else and everybody, you know, in the rest of the state seems to resent Charlestonians.... Are we Southern? Yes, we're Southern. Are we different from the South? Absolutely. What brings about that dichotomy? I'm not sure. I think that probably we have some of the similar values that the rest of the South has, but I think the difference is that we were for so long, two things, we were a leader and we were isolated.

Robert B. is aware that Charleston sounds different from other parts of the South, and just like many other informants, he is usually not identified as a Southerner when he travels to other parts of the country:

Is Charleston Southern? It's very interesting, because you know, you look at the South, and certainly Charleston, as I see it, is rather different than an awful lot of the South, in outlook, in linguistic attributes. [Is Charleston different from the rest of the South?] Grossly so! Certainly, the Southern drawl, as it were, I mean, to the New York mind, to the New York ear, we're all a bunch of hicks. You know, depending on what part of the South you're from, maybe if you're a 23-year-old female, you sound sweet and attractive, but if you're anyone else, you're a redneck or a hick, you know, in the view of so many in the North. Charleston, as– you know the story: one does not perceive one's own accent, and so I don't really know what I sound like, but when I go elsewhere, people always say to me, "Where are you from?" They don't pigeonhole me as being from the South, unless they know Charleston, in which case they say, "Oh yes, you're from Charleston." ... Because of my schooling and my bride and my business, I tend to travel more than my father does, in the last 15 years I have, and so I'm in various parts quite frequently. And I find very frequently, people say, you know, "Are you from England? Are you from–? " They have no idea where I'm from.

The issue of the linguistic distinctiveness of Charleston comes up again in the discussion of Gullah, which Robert B. acknowledges as in important influence on Charleston. He also confirms other informants' reports on the virtual disappearance of Gullah from the city:

You've really got two very very distinct influences, which cross on some, in some areas, which of course is the Gullah, which is not at all the Charleston accent, but it becomes a heavy component of what we all, you know, speak and are exposed to, meaning the Charleston accent, which is, I think, a somewhat unique accent in that it does not have the traditional Southern, "Ah! He's from Alabama. Ah, he's from Georgia," the Southern drawl. It's a little bit peculiar, I'm not quite sure what it is.... My experience growing up is that as children we really learned almost to speak two completely different dialects—you learned, you know, the Charleston brogue, or whatever, but then you also learned really to be comfortable speaking in a Gullah dialect, and as children we could sort of switch back and forth. I can't do that now, because ... you have to be around people to sort of practice your tongue, and you lose it after some years. And the ability to speak the Gullah dialect, really, there's very little Gullah left now, and I can remember as a child, I think we, and [to father] you I'm sure the same thing, you could switch into it quite comfortably and talk with people in Gullah and then switch out of it, but it's probably been thirty years since I've had people with whom I could do that, so I've lost that.... [Gullah] was something we were all around, something we were all used to, yet we had very distinct influences at home as to the pronunciation of words and things like that. It was clear that we were taught, you know, not to speak the Gullah, yet we also learned it with our interactions, and it wasn't just the black maids but, you know, people that you would encounter all over. And, of course, the Gullah influences in the city of Charleston really started disappearing in the 1950s and 1960s. By the early '70s there was almost no Gullah found in the city; you could still find it on the islands but–

STEVE M., 24, UPPER-MIDDLE CLASS

Steve M. was raised in downtown Charleston below Broad Street, where he now lives; he went to the same Episcopal-affiliated private elementary school as many of his upper-class friends did; he had African American nannies; and his parents were successful business entrepreneurs, but, importantly, he does not come from an old Charleston family. In fact, his parents were not raised in Charleston—his father is from Ohio—and he refers to them as transplants into the area, which is something he seems to be very aware of. His language throughout the interview is rather formal, which is reflected in the overly complex syntax and choice of vocabulary. This, along with the hypercorrect use of *whom* for *who* five times during the interview, as in the excerpt below, indicates a fair amount of linguistic insecurity.[1]

... and moved back here to that address, that street, to begin the College of Charleston, and had taken up an apartment and uh, in speaking with my father, whom had not been in Charleston for about four years, really...

We were mostly surfing at the Isle of Palms, Sullivan's Island, and Folly, which are all common places to go surfing now. Before [Hurricane] Hugo there was a different pattern of sandbar systems that facilitated actual waves out on Sullivan's Island and the Isle of Palms and a much more regular period through the warmer months of the year, whereas now you tend to only to find it surfable the majority of time during the wintertime...

He offers very perceptive comments on the role of Gullah in the upper-class community—which he is not a part of, due to a lack of the requisite heritage—suggesting that Gullah-speaking maids were actually sought out in the nearby islands where Gullah could still be found:

For some folks, there were a number of families at the time whom, I think a lot of people would refer to as sort of your old Charleston families, who were, even though we lived amongst them, my parents were what I would call sort of transplants to the area, who would own properties aside from the peninsula and other places, say around the Edisto, and their maids a lot of time tended, or Johns Island for instance, when they owned property there, tended to have been selected from groups of African Americans that spoke a language that's generally referred to as Gullah. And the interesting thing about it is that you find some individuals, young ones, but mostly men and women between the ages of 35 and say 60, I would say, that picked up on the uniqueness of that language that was spoken by their maids, and especially, I think, a lot of times when the maids would get together with other maids, when say, get together with their friends and various maids would show up, and they would use that language between one another ... and I think that a lot of people really picked up on it and it was a lot more of a prized subject then than it is now.... As far as those languages go, on the peninsula of Charleston you had a little bit of influence from Gullah traditions in language, but it wasn't as prevalent with people whom simply just lived on the peninsula and found maids, who also lived on the peninsula as it was with people that sourced their housekeepers, maids, whatever you want to refer to them as, from the Johns Island and the Edisto areas.... There are some people whom were very influenced by it...

Like many other informants, he notes that the traditional Charleston accent is disappearing and offers some more perceptive comments:

I think that the Charlestonian accent, the Charleston accent is something that really has shown itself to be a dying accent over the past uh probably three generations. There are women, especially women, that you'll find that still speak it; and I say women because a lot of the men with the migration of interests businesswise from the North into this area have sort of disregarded it, so as to better fit in with a more national business structure, when need be. And a lot of the women that you find that still speak it, that carry that accent or almost a language, really, just the way that it's spoken, are women that tend to be mothers that have stayed home for most of their life, that have never been put in the position to have to interact on a business capacity with folks from outside of the region.... The Charleston vernacular itself, the one that I'm referring to, you generally don't find many people that actually naturally speak it. You will find people that will imitate it in my peer group, simply because of the way their parents speak, and oftentimes just sort of in a casually mocking manner.... But I would say that most of the people that actually survive that speak it are above the age of fifty.

SARAH E., 80, MIDDLE CLASS

Sarah E. was interviewed together with her husband, a retired journalist, John E, 85. They now live in West Ashley, the area northwest of the historic peninsula city across the Ashley River, though they both grew up on the peninsula and both attended the College of Charleston. Their ancestors arrived in the area in the late 1700s. Sarah E. points out the traditionally strong affinity between Charlestonians and England, noted by McDavid (1948):[2]

We're a proud people and we're more English, I think, than anything. Because this was an English settlement, really. And everywhere you look, if you've been to England, it reminds you of England. Our customs, tea at 4 o'clock in the afternoon, washing down the marble steps every day, shining the brass [laughter], just little English things. When we go to England, we feel very much at home.

While both Sarah E. and her husband John E. have the distinctive features of the traditional Charleston system, she notes that the younger generations do not sound distinctly Charlestonian anymore:

The way we speak, the words we use now, they're not doing this anymore. I mean, I think it's because people travel and different people are coming into the community, and television, I think, that uh… Our accents have disappeared, by and large. My granddaughter doesn't speak like she's coming from Charleston; neither does my son.

She is one of the few speakers in the sample who are sometimes identified as Charlestonians when they travel outside of the area— all of them are speakers over 65 who have the traditional phonological system:

I walked into an antique shop in St. Michael's, Maryland, Chesapeake Bay, and I asked for something, and the lady looked me dead in the eye and she said, "You're from Charleston, South Carolina!" and I said, "Is it that obvious?" and she said, "Yes, it truly is." She said, "My husband was from Charleston and I know a Charlestonian wherever they are."

SHERRY D., 63, LOWER-MIDDLE CLASS

Sherry D. is a registered nurse, who is now retired and works part-time in a grocery store. She is gregarious and outgoing, as seen in the excerpt below, and her interview resulted in four more interviews with three generations of her family.

In grammar school the boys would chase the girls and they'd kiss 'em. And then if you got to the tree before you got caught, you didn't get kissed. A lot of girls didn't like getting caught– but I *loved* getting caught. And then we had monkey bars, what we called monkey bars, or swings, and I can remember one time I was on the swing and I had my lunch money, I had a quarter. Swallowed it– Well, Aunt Elizabeth then gave me a lot of, told me to eat a lot of bread. And I cried 'cause I'd lost my quarter. And they said, "Don't worry about it! We'll give you lunch!" And she did. They gave me my lunch that day.

Having African American maids or nannies in the home was fairly common in Charleston, and was not at all limited to the highest social classes, though admittedly not all Charlestonians had help in the household, and relatively few had live-in maids in the home. Sherry D. points out that the African American maids were often treated almost like part of the family:

We called the black people that worked for my aunt, we called them Miss Sally. We didn't– We respected our elders regardless of color. [Were they maids?] They were more than maids. They were almost like family. Miss Irene had 10 children and my Aunt Elizabeth was uh, she took, kind of took care of them when they had needs. I'm an RN, a registered nurse, and I worked at this black hospital, was uh called McClellan-Banks [McClennan-Banks]. And I didn't get to see her but one of the black women that was from Ravenel where she was from was in the hospital, and my Aunt Elizabeth visited her and brought her a gown and some bedroom slippers. And those were the kind of things she did.

We had maids. We had, we had, one was Bess and then we had Miss Margaret. That's only two that I remember their names. But they would plait our hair, and tell us things– And when our doll babies turned brown—we had left them out in the sun—so when she went home, we gave her our doll babies 'cause they matched her color– And then when my momma and daddy, when they would go down to the Barbadian, oh, she had a big time. She'd paint us all up, we'd have lipstick all over us and eye makeup. I mean, she would do all kind of stuff to us [laughter], 'cause she was only 4 or 5 years older than us.

She comments on the negative impact of the recent economic boom in Charleston, resulting in skyrocketing property prices and an influx of outsiders, and notes that although people may be more affluent, they tend to be less family-oriented than her generation was:

[Has Charleston changed in the last few decades?] Oh yes, dramatically, dramatically! I would say 75 percent of the old homes that are in Charleston are no longer owned by the older families. I think they've been bought up by Northerners, or even foreigners, people who have a lot more money. I mean when you could sell your home that you paid $30,000 for for a million, I mean, you know, I think, they did it. I think that people are a lot more materialistic than they were in my day. However, we were poorer yesterday than we are today, but we didn't know that we were poor because everybody else was. And the other thing is people have become more affluent but they– they're more affluent, but they– They're more affluent, more educated but there's a certain group of people that are very child oriented—they want their children to do extremely well and are very involved in their lives. And then you've got this other group that are not involved at all. Even though our parents, our mothers had to work in a cigar factory or somewhere outside the home, and we had serv– our maids, they were still very much part of our lives. We all went on vacations together. And we helped momma, because she was so tired when she'd get home from the cigar factory. My daddy, actually, before we went to school, I know my mom and daddy would sit up and have a cup of coffee at around five o'clock in the morning, and they'd have their, you know, as an example to us, I mean I remember watching them really communicate with one another. You know, it was a feeling of security, and I could see, you know, daddy kissing momma goodbye, and then my daddy would actually cook us breakfast and would wash the dishes, and we would make beds, and we helped momma with ironing clothes and stuff like that, and when she went to the cigar factory. And now when she got home, we would cook my daddy supper, and we would drive to the drugstore and take him his supper. You know, we knew everybody in the drugstore. And, I don't know, it was, everybody knew everybody.

CHRISTINE D., 57, WORKING CLASS

Christine D. was born and first lived on the peninsula but the family moved to James Island when she was a few years old, where she has lived since. She did not have nannies when she was growing up, but two African American women would come and help with the ironing every Wednesday:

On Wednesdays was my mother's day off, and this is when Miss Sally and this other lady would come, and they would just iron clothes; that's all they did, that was their job.... I remember, we had a very small house—my parents rented this house. And it had a little kitchen off of the back end. And those houses downtown, you didn't have built-in anything! It had a stove and she had a little cabinet in there that she put her dishes and on that cabinet there was a little stand there. And so my mother would always cook dinner on Wednesdays. I mean she cooked every day but Wednesdays, you'd only gotten home from school, she'd have dinner ready. And so we were sitting at the table and my mom said, "Sally, come on in here and sit down eat," and she said, "No, I'll have my food in here, Miss Lilly," which was in the kitchen. And she said "No, no, you can come sit at the table with us," and she said "No, no, no, no, can't do that" [laughter]. So she, you know, I didn't know why at that time, it never occurred to me why, but now I understand why. But the other lady now, she would come in and sit down with us, and you know, it was years later and different circumstances.

Spending time on the beach has always been a big part of growing up and living in Charleston, and although sharks are known to infest the coastal waters of South Carolina, they are not perceived to be a particularly serious threat. However, their proximity came to Christine D. as a surprise one day:

Sharks? We eat shark [laughter]. It's the best food; it's really great. I'll tell you an incident that happened to us one time when our children were teenagers. I guess our daughter was probably 17, our son was 13 at the time, and we rented a house down there. And my husband and the other couple that we went with, they put what they call a seine net out. That's what they catch shrimp with, which is *il-le-gal* [laughter]. But anyhow, they put it out along the stretch when you walk down onto the sand and to the water, just to see if they could catch anything in there. And sure enough, several hours later, they pull the net in and they had, I don't know, 20 sharks about so long. Now this is water that's ankle deep. So we were standing there, and I was just amazed at what was in the net that was that close. And so this guy that was standing there that was a friend of the family, he was standing there, and I looked at him, and I said, "God, I can't believe that these sharks are this close and here you are wading out into the water, you know!" And he said, "Well, you see those people right out there in the water?" and they were, you know, good ways out, but they were out wading in the water and playing, and I said, "Yeah," and he said, "That's where I caught my biggest tiger shark." And I looked at him and said, "Those are our children, out in that water! [laughter] Get in here!" [laughter] But that frightened me, 'cause I didn't realize they would come this close, but as far as attacks and stuff like that, I don't know of any. I mean, I'm sure they've had 'em, you know scares and stuff like that, but I don't know of any.

When discussing the question of whether Charleston is distinct from the rest of the South and the rest of the state, she offers the following story:

We had Hurricane Hugo in 1989 here, and there was a lot of damage and, you've probably heard all of that, and my husband's friend from Missouri came to Charleston. He was an insurance adjustor for State Farm. And so when he got into town—he stayed out on Johns Island, Kiawah, or some place—and he called us, and he said, "You know, I'm in town and would like to see you all" and so– Anyhow, we set up a time, which wo– 'Cause he was very busy at that time, so he kind of had to fit us in, you know, where he could fit us in, so, he had been in town probably for about two weeks when we finally saw him the first time. And he came over and sat down and, and so we were talkin'. This was his first time in Charleston, and of course this was not the best of time to be here, and uh– He said, uh, "So what is all this about whenever you go into somebody's home"—'cause he was doing a lot of the adjusting on the Battery and places—he said, "The first thing everybody from Charleston asks you is 'Where are you from?! And how long are you stayin'?!'" [laughter] I said, "You're kiddin' me." He said "No! You would not believe the people that– you walk in the door, you say 'I'm so and so with State Farm and I'm here as your adjustor,' and the first thing they say is 'Where are *you* from?! And how long are you stayin' here?!'" [laughter] I said, "Well, I don't know," but you do find yourself doing that. You do.

12. CONCLUSIONS

Many of the changes described above, both the traditional features retreating from the dialect and the new developments, show a high degree of correlation with one another (table 12.1), indicating that the changes are not a series of unrelated independent developments, but rather, being part of the same linguistic system, changes in one element have consequences for the rest of the system. The correlations presented in table 12.1 and a comparison of the apparent-time chronology of the linguistic variables point to parallel developments in the changes representing the retreat of the traditional features, suggesting that they may have arisen as a result of a common triggering event.

While correlation in itself is not an indicator of causality, it is possible that the introduction of constricted /r/ in postvocalic position contributed to the emergence of the contrast between /ihr/ and /ehr/ (figures 12.1 and 12.2), as a lack of distinction between front vowels before (underlying) tautosyllabic /r/ tends to be more common (though is not exclusive) in nonrhotic dialects of English, such as New Zealand, various English dialects (Wells 1982), and, in certain contexts, New York City (Labov 1966).

The introduction of rhoticity and a distinction between /ihr/ and /ehr/ is paralleled by the retreat of two other distinctive features of the traditional dialect: the monophthongal and ingliding long mid vowels /e:/ and /o:/, as in *gate* and *goat*, and Canadian Raising for /aw/ and /ay/, as in *house* and *rice*. The traditional features turn out to be highly correlated with each other, with the *r* value in the region of 0.7 or higher (table 12.1), indicating that a decrease in the rate of one is accompanied by a corresponding decrease in the rate of the others. Figure 12.3 shows that all four features follow the same path in apparent time, pointing to the time of the language acquisition of the 70- and 80-year olds as the beginning of the retreat of the traditional features, which appears to have been completed by the time current 50-year-olds were born. The similarity between the four variables is confirmed numerically in figure 12.4, including the logistic transforms of the data in figure 12.3,

FIGURE 12.1

Acquisition of /ihr/-/ehr/ Contrast and Retreat of *r*-lessness
in Apparent Time

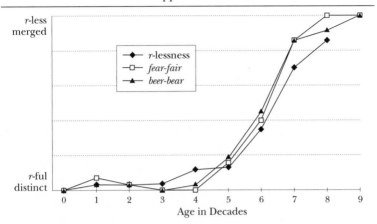

FIGURE 12.2

Logistic Transform of /ihr/-/ehr/ Contrast and *r*-lessness
in Apparent Time

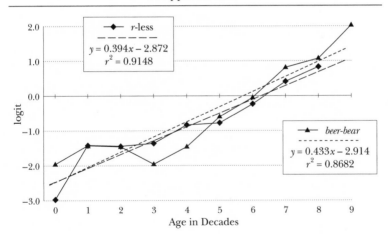

TABLE 12.1

Pearson Product-Moment Correlation between Charleston Variables
(cells with absolute r values ≥ .6 are highlighted)

	Ingliding /e:, o:/	/aw0/	/ay0/	%r	beer-bear	here-hair	fear-fair	pin-pen	horse-hoarse	cot-caught	merry-Mary	merry-marry	owF2
Ingliding /e:, o:/	1												
/aw0/	0.751	1											
/ay0/	0.718	0.786	1										
%r	−0.777	−0.742	−0.552	1									
beer-bear	−0.789	−0.685	−0.639	0.706	1								
here-hair	−0.726	−0.659	−0.571	0.789	0.88	1							
fear-fair	−0.701	−0.707	−0.591	0.714	0.851	0.848	1						
pin-pen	0.448	0.544	0.553	−0.407	−0.392	−0.335	−0.368	1					
horse-hoarse	0.766	0.715	0.676	−0.707	−0.633	−0.559	−0.663	0.567	1				
cot-caught	0.232	0.286	0.232	−0.318	−0.301	−0.247	−0.18	0.437	0.238	1			
merry-Mary	0.776	0.633	0.615	−0.634	−0.733	−0.648	−0.702	0.471	0.8	0.308	1		
merry-marry	0.357	0.403	0.372	−0.45	−0.474	−0.458	−0.409	0.487	0.382	0.687	0.442	1	
owF2	−0.682	−0.588	−0.657	0.647	0.665	0.6	0.583	−0.25	−0.605	−0.153	−0.558	−0.453	1

FIGURE 12.3
Retreat of Traditional Features in Apparent Time

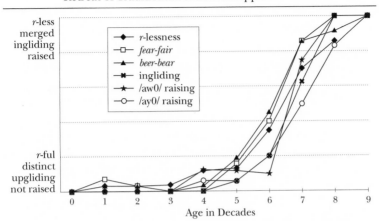

FIGURE 12.4
Logistic Transform of Traditional Features in Apparent Time

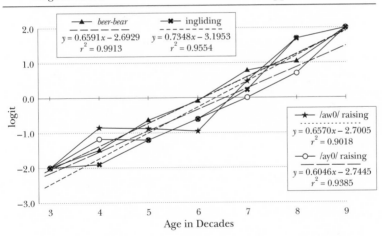

with very close slope and intercept values for the four features for decades 3–9.

Figure 12.3 indicates that speakers in their 70s (decade 7) were the first generation to show a movement away from the traditional features, marking the beginning of their retreat. Importantly, the change of all the traditional variables appears to have been initiated at around the same time, in the late 1920s and early 1930s, when the speakers currently in their 70s were acquiring their first language. This suggests that all of these changes are due to a common triggering event, which was strong enough to initiate a major reorganization of the dialect's sound system. World War II is known to have been an important triggering factor in the history of a number of languages and dialects, as in New York City, effecting a change in the evaluation of *r*-lessness and the introduction of rhoticity into the city's dialect (Labov 1966).

The apparent-time data in figure 12.3, however, suggest that the changes had begun before World War II—they point to the late 1920s and early 1930s. This is the time when Charleston began opening itself to the outside world after decades of relative isolation, as reported by Charleston historians (Fraser 1989; Rosen 1992; see chapter 1) and as suggested by Christopher B., 79, and his son Robert B., 49, upper-class Charlestonians quoted in chapter 11. The opening of the navy yard in 1901 started the trickling of outsiders into the Charleston metropolitan area, with World War I marking the first substantial wave of migrant workers from outside. Their numbers rose dramatically again during World War II and continued to rise as a result of the creation and rapid growth of the military industrial complex centered around the U.S. Naval Base, resulting in an influx of both military personnel and migrant workers from outside Charleston and the Low Country.[1] World War II was then a watershed in the history of Charleston, in that it marks the beginning of large-scale exchange of people and accents between Charleston and the rest of the South and beyond, which may have accelerated the retreat of the traditional features. As shown in figure 12.3, it also marks the beginning of a new chapter in the linguistic history of Charleston, in that speakers younger than 60, that is, those born after World War II, have the modern system, largely without the traditional features, which can still be found in the speech of speakers born before World War II.

The retreat of one of the traditional features, the ingliding of the mid long back vowel /oː/, as in *goat*, appears to be related to the development of a new feature of the dialect, the extreme fronting of /ow/. The two features are highly correlated ($r = -.682$), indicating that the lower the level of ingliding, the more advanced the fronting of /ow/, as expressed by the value of F2. In fact, there are no speakers with ingliding /oː/ and advanced fronting of /ow/. For those speakers who show monophthongal and ingliding /oː/, the nucleus of the vowel is mid-high and back, with no difference between lateral and nonlateral codas (chapter 9). Ingliding /oː/ is incompatible with the fronting of /ow/, which is a back upgliding vowel, as opposed to an ingliding vowel, and the fronting of the back vowels is a process involving back upgliding vowels, beginning with /uw/, followed by the parallel fronting of /ow/. While we see variable fronting of /uw/ after coronals for all speakers in the sample, the fronting of /ow/ is seen only for those for whom the long back vowel of *goat* has a back upglide.

The close link between the development of a back upglide and the fronting of /ow/ is seen in the parallel development of the two features in apparent time, presented in figure 12.5. The data points for /ow/ are based on the regression coefficients of /ow/ F2 for each decade (chapter 9), mapped onto the 0–2 scale used for the other variables. The greatest change in /ow/ is seen between decades 8 and 6, paralleling the loss of ingliding and the retreat of the other traditional features.

In addition to the retreat of the distinctive Charleston features, the dialect has lost a number of vocalic distinctions which have now also disappeared in most other dialects of English. Their development in apparent time is essentially identical to the loss of the traditional features in that the mergers of *dew-do, horse-hoarse,* and *merry-Mary* appear to have been completed by the time speakers currently in their 50s began their acquisition of the Charleston dialect (figure 12.6).

As figure 12.7 shows, the introduction of one Southern phonological feature into the dialect, the PIN-PEN merger, follows the

FIGURE 12.5

Retreat of Traditional Features and Fronting of /ow/ in Apparent Time

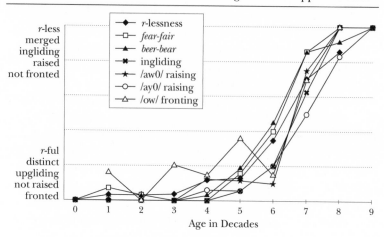

FIGURE 12.6

Retreat of Traditional Features in Apparent Time

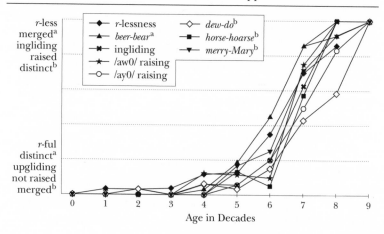

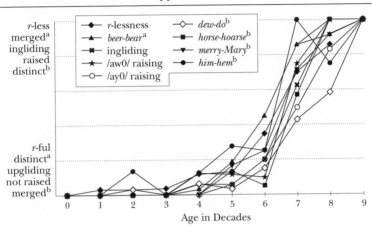

FIGURE 12.7

Retreat of Traditional Features and the PIN/PEN Merger
in Apparent Time

same course in apparent time as the other nearly completed mergers and the traditional features of the dialect. Admittedly, it does
not follow an S-shaped curve as neatly as the other features: some
speakers over the age of 80 display the merger, whereas speakers
in their 70s usually have a distinction. There is also social class
stratification (chap. 7), with the upper class lagging behind the
other social groups in the acquisition of the merger. In addition, a
number of speakers under the age of 60 still display a distinction
between the two vowels. Nevertheless, there is an abrupt change
toward a merger between the period represented by speakers over
70 and those in their 60s and younger, who are largely merged,
and in that the development of the change follows the retreat of
the traditional features discussed above. If, as suggested above, the
retreat of the traditional features was triggered by the opening of
Charleston to the outside world in the 1920s and 1930s, including
the rest of the South, after decades of relative isolation, then it is
not surprising that with the retreat of the distinctive local features,
some features found throughout the region, such as the PIN-PEN
merger, had found their way into Charleston's sound system.

Two other mergers which are found to be entering the dialect, the *merry-marry* merger and the low-back merger, show a different path of development. They are more recent: they are first seen for some speakers in their 50s and are far from completed at this point. The apparent-time data presented in figure 12.8 suggest that these two new mergers are a post–World War II phenomenon, and as such are not related to the retreat of the traditional features, which seems to have been initiated in the 1930s. Their distinctiveness from the other changes is confirmed visually and numerically as the different slopes and intercept points of the trend lines in figure 12.9.

The changes which Charleston has been undergoing can be thought of as part of the process called regionalization, found to be operating across North American English, whereby small local dialects are disappearing and becoming part of the larger regions.[2] Interestingly, the region into which Charleston is being integrated is not the South, as it is defined phonologically. Charleston was never part of the South as far as its sound system is concerned: it had its traditional features, which made it distinct not only from

FIGURE 12.8
Charleston Features in Apparent Time

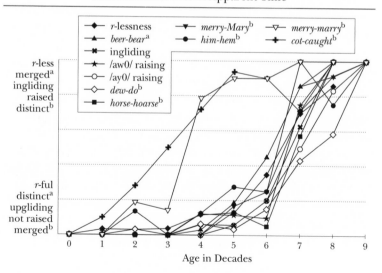

FIGURE 12.9

Logistic Transform of Charleston Features in Apparent Time

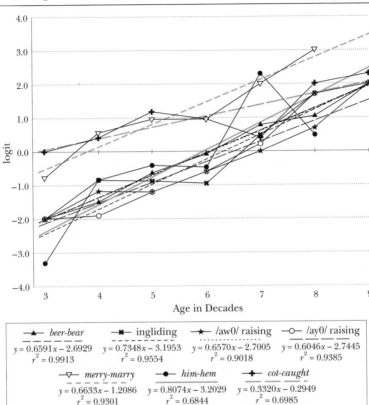

▲ *beer-bear*	✳ ingliding	★ /awO/ raising	○ /ayO/ raising
$y = 0.6591x - 2.6929$	$y = 0.7348x - 3.1953$	$y = 0.6570x - 2.7005$	$y = 0.6046x - 2.7445$
$r^2 = 0.9913$	$r^2 = 0.9554$	$r^2 = 0.9018$	$r^2 = 0.9385$
▽ *merry-marry*	● *him-hem*	✦ *cot-caught*	
$y = 0.6633x - 1.2086$	$y = 0.8074x - 3.2029$	$y = 0.3320x - 0.2949$	
$r^2 = 0.9301$	$r^2 = 0.6844$	$r^2 = 0.6985$	

most Northern dialects but also from the rest of the South. Even with the disappearance of those distinctive features, the dialect of Charleston is still not very Southern in its phonology. It now has one feature found in the rest of the South, the PIN-PEN merger, but it lacks the defining characteristic of the South as a dialect region, the Southern Shift with /ay/ monophthongization as its most salient element, and as such, it remains a marginal Southern dialect.

Instead, Charleston has now become part of the super-region called the Southeastern, extending from the Midland in the north to southern Texas and Florida in the south (*ANAE* 2006, map

11.11). It is defined by the lack of marked Southern features, such as /ay/ monophthongization before obstruents, by advanced fronting of the back upgliding vowels, and by variable low-back merger of *cot* and *caught* (*ANAE* 2006, chap. 11). As a result, Charleston's sound system in its modern form is closer to such Midland cities as Kansas City or Columbus, Ohio, located hundreds of miles away, than to, for instance, Greenville, South Carolina. This is confirmed perceptually by many speakers in this study, such as Robert B., 49, quoted in chapter 11, who are not identified as Southerners when they travel outside of the region. The core areas of the South may one day become more similar to the outer regions, as the *ANAE* as well as other studies, such as Fridland (1999, 2001) and Thomas (2001), suggest that the defining characteristic of the region, the Southern Shift, is receding in apparent time.

Throughout the discussion of the changes operating in Charleston, the upper class emerges as a social group playing a singularly important role in the shaping of the city's dialect. Historically it is perhaps not very surprising given that Charleston was initially an upper-class city, inhabited by plantation owners, with no middle class to speak of. At present this social group remains linguistically distinct, as it seems to have held on to the disappearing traditional features the longest. This is evidenced by some of the results discussed in the previous chapters, and it has been suggested by some of the informants in this study, such as Steve M., 24, an upper-middle class Charlestonian, quoted in chapter 11.

It is the seemingly paradoxical linguistic behavior of the upper class that is most intriguing. On the one hand, this group appears to be more conservative in some features, for example, in the adoption of the PIN-PEN merger (chapter 7); on the other hand, it is leading Charleston, and the rest of American English, in the fronting of the back upgliding vowels /uw/ and /ow/ (chapter 9). Its leading in the fronting of the back vowels provides an apparent counterexample to the curvilinear hypothesis, whereby linguistic changes from below are led by an intermediately located social group, rather than the lowest or the highest one (Labov 2001). There may be two interpretations of this finding: either the fronting of the back upgliding vowels does not follow the usual social pattern associated with vowel shifts, as suggested by Labov (2001,

169), or the fronting of the back upgliding vowels in Charleston is not really a change from below, but rather a change from above, a form introduced into the dialect from outside by the highest-status social group.

There is some indication that the answer may lie in the fact that different changes seem to be at different levels of awareness in the speech community, and that within that speech community, certain groups may be linguistically more sensitive than others. As shown in chapter 6, the PIN-PEN merger is on its way to completion in Charleston, with the exception of the highest-status social group, who lag behind the rest. At the same time, the upper class is undergoing the low-back merger at the same rate as everybody else. Therefore, its more conservative behavior does not seem to be motivated by the need to preserve contrasts which are reflected in the spelling. It is not clear why one merger should show social class differentiation while others do not, unless perhaps it is at a higher level of social awareness. The PIN-PEN merger, as opposed to most other mergers, may be above the level of awareness, at least for some speakers, as evidenced by the overt comments quoted in chapters 6 and 11. As a feature found throughout the South, it may be associated with other, marked features of the South, and as such may be resisted more than a feature such as the low-back merger, which is not associated with any particular region or social group.

The question of possible resistance to features of Southern phonology is related to Charlestonians' sense of distinctiveness and separateness from the rest of the South, or more precisely, a distinction between the Low Country along the coast of South Carolina, including Charleston and Beaufort, and the Upcountry. The division goes back to the original settlement patterns, with the Upcountry settled from the Midland, with a considerable Scotch-Irish component, as opposed to the tidewater area, settled from the coast predominantly by Southern British speakers (McDavid 1948). From the beginning there were socioeconomic differences between the two regions: the Low Country, with its plantation caste concentrated in Charleston, dominated South Carolina economically and culturally, enjoying a disproportionate amount of social prestige resented by the rest of the state (O'Cain 1972; see chapter 1).

Consequently, the speech patterns of the two regions were evaluated differently from the very beginning, as with prestigious *r*-lessness of the Low Country versus negatively viewed constriction of /r/ by poor whites in the rest of the state. McDavid (1948) reports a student of his saying: "The reason we Southerners resent the way the Yankees roll their /-r/ is that it reminds us of the way the crackers talk." McDavid goes on to explain that

in South Carolina the term *crackers* is used (though less than formerly) by the townspeople, the plantation caste, and the plantation-reared Negroes as a derogatory designation for the poor whites—nonslaveholders, or descendants of nonslaveholders—in areas where large slaveholdings once prevailed. [142]

That sense of the distinctiveness of Charleston, both culturally and linguistically, from the rest of the South and the rest of the state in the sense of the Upcountry, is seen in the comments made by the informants during the interviews quoted in chapter 11, such as the one made by Robert B., 49, an upper-class Charlestonian, quoted here one more time:

I think we all have to acknowledge that one of the strongest attributes of Charlestonians is a hideous sense of arrogance. You know, Charlestonians think they're better than everybody else and everybody, you know, in the rest of the state seems to resent Charlestonians.... Are we Southern? Yes, we're Southern. Are we different from the South? Absolutely. What brings about that dichotomy? I'm not sure. I think that probably we have some of the similar values that the rest of the South has, but I think the difference is that we were for so long, two things, we were a leader and we were isolated.

It is possible that the PIN-PEN merger is associated by some speakers with other marked features of the South, that is, with the speech patterns of the Upcountry, from which Charlestonians have always felt distinct. This association does not seem to be very strong, however, and it may require a greater than usual linguistic sensitivity—a sensitivity that the upper class in Charleston may have developed.[3]

While the fronting of the back vowels may be at a lower level of social consciousness than the PIN-PEN merger, insofar as it does not usually elicit any overt comments or show any marked style-shifting, it nevertheless seems to be just above the level of awareness, at least for some speakers, as indicated by the results of the studies by Fridland, Bartlett, and Kreuz (2004) and Torbert (2004). Interestingly, the only overt comment about the mid long vowel /ow/ in this study comes from 16-year-old Pam K., an upper-class Charlestonian, who comments on her Charleston accent by saying, "My sister went to Yale and everybody like an– I could not tell she has the Southern accent at all. She has it even less than I do, 'cause I do say certain words, like I guess *boat* [fronted /ow/], or different things, more so than others, but uh…" She thus associates the fronting of /ow/ with the South and makes an explicit comment about it, which is rare in the sense that /ow/ fronting is not generally known for being the subject of overt comments or stereotyping. As the fronting of the back upgliding vowels is most advanced in the Midland and in the South (*ANAE* 2006), it may be crossing the threshold of public awareness and may come to be associated with the Southeastern super-region (*ANAE* 2006, map 11.11). Upper-class speakers in Charleston may be more sensitive to this newly emerging pattern, which does not seem to be associated with other marked Southern features, and may be taking it even further.

Where does this heightened linguistic sensitivity of the upper class come from? It may come from Charlestonians' traditionally high exposure to speech patterns outside of the region. Charleston's upper class is known to have maintained stronger contacts with the other cultural centers on the East Coast, namely Boston, New York, and Richmond, and with England, than with the rest of the South. Even today, due to their education and professional contacts outside of the South, many upper-class Charlestonians, such as lawyers, operate on a national rather than local level. Finally, they tend to travel beyond Myrtle Beach or Greenville, South Carolina, as suggested by Robert B. in chapter 11—some of them travel to Europe, including England, with which they seem to have had a special connection, both in the past (McDavid 1948) and at present, as reported by Sarah E., 80, quoted in chapter 11, or

Elizabeth O., 82, whose family has spent a few years in England and considers it their second home.[4] This exposure and contact with speakers of dialects outside of the region may have led to a heightened linguistic sensitivity and awareness of newly emerging speech patterns.

It seems then that the fronting of the back upgliding vowels in Charleston is not a change from below, but rather a change from above the level of awareness at an early stage. It is then a borrowing, introduced into the dialect by the highest-status social group, not unlike the adoption of rhoticity in the dialect of New York City led by the upper-middle class (Labov 1966), and as such it is only an apparent counterexample to the curvilinear principle, which is a generalization on changes from below.

APPENDIX:
CHARLESTON WORD LIST

take	pay	go	goat	so
sore	door	morning	mourning	hoarse
horse	fear	fair	dear	dare
tie	might	my	born	spice
Dan	began	barn	cash	bear
last	cast	man	pan	rice
beer	merry	married	Mary	day
feel	fill	pull	pool	dull
dead	sad	bad	force	bought
towel	deer	here	there	porch
garden	cow	car	cart	do
dew	Tuesday	new	dude	could
should	shoe	tea	pea	sea
did	pet	bed	sit	set
gate	book	hook	sight	house
put	boot	mad	hoot	get
bit	bet	bat	pill	peel
joy	toy	south	pout	card
cord	pin	pen	him	hem
Don	dawn	sound	pound	Down
palm	calm	sort	taller	dollar
town	two	how	on	off
farm	corn	guard	pants	sight
time	full	cold	told	shirt
term	sport	fool	tide	tight
side	hurt	police	about	gull
sock	talk	cut	gut	hut
bother	which	third	father	whale

NOTES

CHAPTER 2

1. Jespersen (1949) argues that the merger was caused by the diphthongization of the monophthong, with a diphthong as a resulting vowel, but the consensus today seems to be that the merger occurred as presented here.
2. Not all tokens depicted in the vowel charts were used to calculate the means. Tokens before /l/, after glides, or after obstruent-liquid clusters were excluded, because these allophones are usually skewed considerably from the word class as a whole.

CHAPTER 3

1. For the best and most accessible introduction to acoustic analysis, the reader is advised to consult chapter 8, "Acoustic Phonetics," of Ladefoged (2006). A more in-depth and technical, yet still very accessible, introduction to acoustic phonetics is Johnson (2003).

CHAPTER 4

1. Chapter 9 discusses the fronting of /ow/ in detail.
2. /aw/, as in *house*, glides toward the upper back region of the vowel space, that is, it is realized as a back upgliding vowel.
3. In addition, there are only 43 speakers analyzed acoustically, as opposed to 100 speakers analyzed impressionistically.
4. The term *Geechee* comes from the name of the Ogeechee River in Georgia. Robert B. and his father, Christopher B., point out during their interview that it was not used in Charleston until recently, though it refers to the same language: *Geechee* was simply a term used in Georgia, and *Gullah* was the term used in Charleston. However, it is clear that both are now commonly used in Charleston.

5. Thomas (2001) supports a language contact explanation for the quality of the long mid vowels in the Low Country; Feagin (1997) suggests a similar substrate mechanism for r-lessness in the South.

6. Steve M., 24, is quoted more extensively in chapter 11.

CHAPTER 6

1. There are no results for speakers over 70 in the lowest-status group; there is one working-class speaker over 70 in the sample, but he was not able to perform the minimal-pair test.

2. The distance between two points on the F1/F2 grid is determined using the following equation:

$$CD = \sqrt{(2 \times (F1^a - F1^b))^2 + (F2^a - F2^b)^2}$$

3. O'Cain (1972) found similar lexical variation in the two vowels.

CHAPTER 7

1. There was a weak gender effect in the same direction detected in the minimal-pair test for *cot-caught*, but it was not statistically significant.

2. It is also a feature of African American English across the United States.

3. On the other hand, it may be that the PIN-PEN merger does draw more attention to itself because the correspondence between the phonology and the spelling is simple and unambiguous, as opposed to the low-back merger, where spelling has been found to offer little help in distinguishing the two vowels for one-vowel region speakers.

4. The Mid-Atlantic region of New York City and Philadelphia still retains a three-way distinction.

CHAPTER 8

1. *PEAS* reports the raising of the nucleus of /ay/ in eastern New England and upstate New York before both voiceless and voiced consonants.

2. He was interviewed in Charleston but is not part of the 100-speaker sample.

CHAPTER 9

1. The cause of the allophonic differentiation between /uw/ after coronals and after noncoronals seems to be physiological: as the tongue tip or blade makes contact with or approximates the coronal region in the production of the coronal onset, there is not enough time for the body of the tongue to return to its resting position before the beginning of the vowel, which is pronounced more toward the front of the mouth than when the tongue body remains low during the production of a labial or dorsal onset. This hypothesis is supported by the fact that the fronting is usually blocked by an /l/ in the coda, even when the onset is coronal, as in *tool*, which is then just as retracted as with noncoronal onset, as in *pool* or *school*. The lateral consonant is generally dark, that is, velarized, in American English, particularly so before another consonant or word-finally—as the back of the tongue is raised in anticipation of the /l/ and the tip of the tongue touches the apical region for the production of the onset, the body of the tongue is lowered in relation to the position it occupies when no /l/ follows the vowel, as in *too*. In consequence, the vowel is produced further back in the mouth.

2. Gender also plays a role: women can be expected to be ahead of men by 80 Hz for speakers up to 65 years of age, though the difference does not come out as significant in the regression analysis. Its statistical significance is discussed together with the female lead for /ow/ below.

3. This factor is minimized for /uw/ because words in which the vowel occurs in free position mostly have coronal onset—words like *two*, *too*, and *do* are common, whereas words like *coo, boo, goo*, and *poo* are rare.

4. Both /ow/ and /uw/ generally glide toward the back of the vowel space from the nucleus, rather then the front, as seen in some Southern dialects, though the glide is often very short, ending in the center or even in front of the center of the vowel space.

5. The means for speakers of all ages would not present an accurate picture, as the oldest speakers represent a very different phonological system with ingliding, rather than upgliding, mid long vowels, with tense and peripheral nuclei. As such, they should not be analyzed together with the rest of the sample.

CHAPTER 11

1. He seems much more formal in his speech than the other informants; the hypercorrect use of *whom* does not occur in the speech of any other speakers in the sample. There are further quotes from Steve M. showing two more examples of hypercorrect *whom* in chapter 3.

2. McDavid (1948, 141) comments, "The tidewater planters and merchants kept up their ties with England after the American Revolution, and a fair number of their sons were educated in England. Even today the socially elite in Charleston and Savannah tend toward uncritical admiration of things English, at least of the practices of the English upper classes."

CHAPTER 12

1. McDavid (1948, 140) notes the importance of the influx of military personnel from outside of South Carolina for the spread of constricted /r/: "The presence in local military posts of many Northern and Western servicemen, with strong constriction of their /-r/, as well as a different and more sophisticated line of conversation, has led many Southern girls to the conclusion that a person with constriction can be acceptable as a date for the daughter of generations of plantation owners, or even possibly as a husband."

2. This is similar to DIALECT LEVELING found in a number of European languages, including British English, but it is different from the usual process in that the major dialect regions of American English are diverging from each other, rather than leveling to a national pattern.

3. On the other hand, it is possible that the PIN-PEN merger is more salient because the correspondence between the spelling and the quality of the vowels is more transparent than it is in the low-back merger, and as upper-class speakers tend to be more educated, they may pay more attention to the contrasts maintained in spelling.

4. One wonders if the fronting of /ow/ associated with the British prestige pattern may have had an influence on the social perception of this feature in the United States, as suggested by Eckert (2004). There is no concrete evidence for this at present, and as such it must be considered to be a rather remote possibility.

REFERENCES

ANAE. The Atlas of North American English: Phonetics, Phonology, and Sound Change. 2006. By William Labov, Sharon Ash, and Charles Boberg. Berlin: Mouton de Gruyter.

Anderson, Bridget, Lesley Milroy, and Jennifer Nyguyen. 2002. "Fronting of /u/ and /ʊ/ in Detroit AAE: Evidence from Real and Apparent Time." Paper presented at the 31st Annual Conference on New Ways of Analyzing Variation in English (NWAV 31), Stanford, Calif., Oct. 10–13.

Ash, Sharon. 1982. "The Vocalization of /l/ in Philadelphia." Ph.D. diss., Univ. of Pennsylvania.

Bailey, Charles-James N. 1973. *Variation and Linguistic Theory.* Arlington, Va.: Center for Applied Linguistics.

Bailey, Guy. 2004. "Digging Up the Roots of Southern American English: On Michael Montgomery and Connie Eble's 'Historical Perspectives on the *pen/pin* Merger in Southern American English.'" In *Studies in the History of the English Language II: Unfolding Conversations,* ed. Anne Curzan and Kimberly Emmons, 433–44. Berlin: Mouton de Gruyter.

Bernstein, Cynthia, Elizabeth Gregory, and Guy Bailey. 1993. "The Status of Glide-Shortened /ai/ as a Marker of Southern Identity." Paper presented at the 22nd Annual Conference on New Ways of Analyzing Variation in English (NWAVE 22), Ottawa, Oct. 14–17.

Boersma, Paul, and David Weenink. 2004. Praat 4.2: Doing Phonetics by Computer. Software. http://www.praat.org.

Brown, Vivian R. 1991. "Evolution of the Merger of /ɪ/ and /ɛ/ before Nasals in Tennessee." *American Speech* 66: 303–15.

Cedergren, Henrietta. 1973. "The Interplay of Social and Linguistic Factors in Panama." Ph.D. diss., Cornell Univ.

———. 1984. "Panama Revisted: Sound Change in Real Time." Paper presented at the 13th Annual Conference on New Ways of Analyzing Variation in English (NWAVE 13), Philadelphia, Oct. 25–27.

Chambers, J. K. 1973. "Canadian Raising." *Canadian Journal of Linguistics* 18: 113–35.

————. 1989. "Canadian Raising: Blocking, Fronting, Etc." *American Speech* 64: 75–88.

————. 1992. "Dialect Acquisition." *Language* 68: 673–705.

Conn, Jeffrey. 2002. "It's Not All Rain and Coffee: An Investigation into the Dialect of Portland, Oregon." Paper presented at the 31st Annual Conference on New Ways of Analyzing Variation (NWAV 31), Stanford, Calif., Oct. 10–13.

————. 2005. "Of 'Moice' and Men: The Evolution of a Male-Led Sound Change." Ph.D. diss., Univ. of Pennsylvania.

Crane, L. Benjamin. 1973. "Social Stratification of English among White Speakers in Tuscaloosa, Alabama." Ph.D. diss., Univ. of Massachusetts.

Di Paolo, Marianna, and Alice Faber. 1990. "Phonation Differences and the Phonetic Content of the Tense-Lax Contrast in Utah English." *Language Variation and Change* 2: 155–204.

Eckert, Penelope. 2004. "A Brush with Particularism: Style, Persona, and the Emergence of a Preadolescent Social Order." Plenary address at the 33rd Annual Conference on New Ways of Analyzing Variation (NWAV 33), Ann Arbor, Mich., Sept. 30–Oct. 3.

Feagin, Crawford. 1990. "The Dynamics of a Sound Change in Southern States English: From *r*-less to *r*-ful in Three Generations." In *Development and Diversity: Linguistic Variation across Time and Space*, ed. Jerold A. Edmondson, Crawford Feagin, and Peter Mühlhäusler, 129–45. Dallas, Tex.: Summer Institute of Linguistics.

————. 1994. "'Long *i*' as a Microcosm of Southern States Speech." Paper presented at the 23rd Annual Conference on New Ways of Analyzing Variation (NWAV 23), Stanford, Calif., Oct. 20–23.

————. 1997. "The African Contribution to Southern States English." In *Language Variety in the South Revisited*, ed. Cynthia Bernstein, Thomas Nunnally, and Robin Sabino, 123–39. Tuscaloosa: Univ. of Alabama Press.

————. 2003. "Vowel Shifting in the Southern States." In *English in the Southern United States*, ed. Stephen J. Nagle and Sara L. Sanders, 126–40. Cambridge: Cambridge Univ. Press.

Fisher, R. A. 1925. *Statistical Methods for Research Workers*. Edinburgh: Oliver and Boyd.

Fraser, Walter J., Jr. 1989. *Charleston! Charleston! The History of a Southern City*. Columbia: Univ. of South Carolina Press.

Fridland, Valerie. 1999. "The Southern Shift in Memphis, Tennessee." *Language Variation and Change* 11: 267–85.

————. 2001. "The Social Dimension of the Southern Vowel Shift: Gender, Age and Class." *Journal of Sociolinguistics* 5: 233–53.

Fridland, Valerie, and Kathryn Bartlett. 2006. "The Social and Linguistic Conditioning of Back Vowel Fronting across Ethnic Groups in Memphis, Tennessee." *English Language and Linguistics* 10: 1–22.

Fridland, Valerie, Kathryn Bartlett, and Roger Kreuz. 2004. "Do You Hear What I Hear? Experimental Measurement of the Perceptual Salience of Acoustically Manipulated Vowel Variants by Southern Speakers in Memphis, TN." *Language Variation and Change* 16: 1–16.

Garde, Paul. 1961. "Réflexions sur les différences phonétiques entre les langues slaves." *Word* 17: 34–62.

Gordon, Elizabeth, Lyle Campbell, Jennifer Hay, Margaret Maclagan, Andrea Sudbury, and Peter Trudgill. 2004. *New Zealand English: Its Origins and Evolution*. Cambridge: Cambridge Univ. Press.

Gordon, Elizabeth, and Margaret A. Maclagan. 1989. "Beer and Bear, Cheer and Chair: A Longitudinal Study of the Ear/Air Contrast in New Zealand English." *Australian Journal of Linguistics* 9: 203–20.

————. 2001. "Capturing a Sound Change: A Real Time Study over 15 Years of the NEAR/SQUARE Diphthong Merger in New Zealand English." *Australian Journal of Linguistics* 21: 215–38.

Hagiwara, Robert. 1997. "Dialect Variation and Formant Frequency: The American English Vowels Revisited." *Journal of the Acoustical Society of America* 102: 655–58.

Hall-Lew, Lauren. 2004. "The Western Vowel Shift in Northern Arizona." First qualifying paper, Stanford Univ. http://www.stanford.edu/~dialect/Hall-Lew%20QP1.pdf.

————. 2005. "One Shift, Two Groups: When Fronting Alone Is Not Enough." In *Selected Papers from NWAVE 32*, ed. Maciej Baranowski, Uri Horesh, Keelan Evans, and Giang Nguyen, 105–16. *University of Pennsylvania Working Papers in Linguistics* 10.2.

Hay, Jennifer, Paul Warren, and Katie Drager. 2006. "Factors Influencng Speech Perception in the Context of a Merger-in-Progress." *Journal of Phonetics* 34: 458–84.

Herold, Ruth. 1990. "Mechanisms of Merger: The Implementation and Distribution of the Low Back Merger in Eastern Pennsylvania." Ph.D. diss., Univ. of Pennsylvania.

Hinton, Leanne, Birch Moonwomon, Sue Bremmer, Herb Luthin, Mary van Clay, Jean Learner, and Hazel Corcoran. 1987. "It's Not Just the Valley Girls: A Study of California English." In *Proceedings of the Thirteenth Annual Meeting of the Berkeley Linguistics Society*, ed. Jon Aske, Natasha Beery, Laura Michaels, and Hana Filip, 117–28. Berkeley, Calif.: Berkeley Linguistics Society.

Holmes, Janet, and Allan Bell. 1992. "On Shear Markets and Sharing Sheep: The Merger of EAR and AIR Diphthongs in New Zealand English." *Language Variation and Change* 4: 251–73.

Jespersen, Otto. 1949. *A Modern English Grammar on Historical Principles.* Vol. 1, *Sounds and Spellings.* London: Allen and Unwin.

Johnson, Keith. 2003. *Acoustic and Auditory Phonetics.* 2nd ed. Malden, Mass.: Blackwell.

Joos, Martin. 1942. "A Phonological Dilemma in Canadian English." *Language* 18: 141–44.

Kenyon, John Samuel. 1994. *American Pronunciation.* Ed. Donald M. Lance and Stewart A. Kingsbury. 12th ed. Ann Arbor, Mich.: Wahr.

Kenyon, John Samuel, and Thomas Albert Knott. 1953. *A Pronouncing Dictionary of American English.* Springfield, Mass.: Merriam.

Keyser, Samuel J. 1963. Review of *PEAS* (1961). *Language* 39: 303–16.

Kroch, Anthony. 1989. "Reflexes of Grammar in Patterns of Language Change." *Language Variation and Change* 1: 199–244.

———. 1996. "Dialect and Style in the Speech of Upper Class Philadelphia." In *Towards a Social Science of Language: Papers in Honor of William Labov,* vol. 1, *Variation and Change in Language and Society,* ed. Gregory R. Guy, Crawford Feagin, Deborah Schiffrin, and John Baugh, 23–45. Amsterdam: Benjamins.

Labov, William. 1963. "The Social Motivation of a Sound Change." *Word* 19: 273–309.

———. 1966. *The Social Stratification of English in New York City.* Washington, D.C.: Center for Applied Linguistics.

———. 1994. *Principles of Linguistic Change.* Vol. 1, *Internal Factors.* Oxford: Blackwell.

———. 2001. *Principles of Linguistic Change.* Vol. 2, *Social Factors.* Oxford: Blackwell.

———. 2006. Plotnik 08. Software. http://www.ling.upenn.edu/~wlabov/Plotnik.html.

Labov, William, Maciej Baranowski, and Aaron Dinkin. 2006. "The Effects of Outliers on the Perception of Sound Change." Paper presented at the 35th Annual Conference on New Ways of Analyzing Variation (NWAV 35), Columbus, Ohio, Nov. 9–12.

Labov, William, Mark Karen, and Corey Miller. 1991. "Near Mergers and the Suspension of Phonemic Contrast." *Language Variation and Change* 3: 33–74.

Labov, William, Malcah Yaeger, and Richard Steiner. 1972. *A Quantitative Study of Sound Change in Progress.* Vol. 1. Report on National Science Foundation Contract NSF-GS-3287. Philadelphia, U.S. Regional Survey.

Ladefoged, Peter. 2006. *A Course in Phonetics.* 5th ed. Boston: Thomson Wadsworth.

Luthin, Herbert W. 1987. "The Story of California /ow/: The Coming-of-Age of English in California." In *Variation in Language: NWAV-XV at Stanford; Proceedings of the Fifteenth Annual Conference on New Ways of Analyzing Variation,* ed. Keith M. Denning, Sharon Inkelas, Faye C. Mc-Nair-Knox, and John R. Rickford, 312–24. Stanford, Calif.: Dept. of Linguistics, Stanford Univ.

Maclagan, Margaret A., and Elizabeth Gordon. 1996. "Out of the AIR and into the EAR: Another View of the New Zealand Diphthong Merger." *Language Variation and Change* 8: 125–47.

McDavid, Raven I., Jr. 1948. "Postvocalic /-r/ in South Carolina: A Social Analysis." *American Speech* 23: 194–203. Repr. in *Dialects in Culture: Essays in General Dialectology,* ed. William A. Kretzschmae, Jr., 136–42. University: Univ. of Alabama Press, 1979.

———. 1955. "The Position of the Charleston Dialect." *Publication of the American Dialect Society* 23: 35–49. Repr. in *Dialects in Culture: Essays in General Dialectology,* by Raven I. McDavid, Jr., ed. William A. Kretzschmar, Jr., 272–81. University: Univ. of Alabama Press.

Montgomery, Michael, and Connie Eble. 2004. "Historical Perspectives on the *pen/pin* Merger in Southern American English." In *Studies in the History of the English Language II: Unfolding Conversations,* ed. Anne Curzan and Kimberly Emmons, 415–34, 444–46. Berlin: Mouton de Gruyter.

Nearey, Terence M. 1977. "Phonetic Feature Systems for Vowels." Ph.D. diss., Univ. of Connecticut.

O'Cain, Raymond K. 1972. "A Social Dialect Survey of Charleston, South Carolina." Ph.D. diss., Univ. of Chicago.

Paddock, Harold. 1981. *A Dialect Survey of Carbonear, Newfoundland.* Publication of the American Dialect Society 68. University: Univ. of Alabama Press.

PEAS. The Pronunciation of English in the Atlantic States: Based upon the Collections of the Linguistic Atlas of the Eastern United States. 1961. By Hans Kurath and Raven I. McDavid, Jr. Ann Arbor: Univ. of Michigan Press.

Peterson, Gordon E., and Harold L. Barney. 1952. "Control Methods Used in a Study of the Vowels." *Journal of the Acoustical Society of America* 24: 175–84.

Phillips, Betty S. 1981. "Lexical Diffusion and Southern *tune, duke, news.*" *American Speech* 56: 72–78.

———. 1994. "Southern English Glide Deletion Revisited." *American Speech* 69: 115–27.

Pitts, Ann. 1986. "Flip-Flop Prestige in American *tune, duke, news.*" *American Speech* 61: 130–38.

Primer, Sylvester. 1888. "Charleston Provincialisms." *American Journal of Philology* 9: 198–213.

Reed, John Shelton. 1982. *One South: An Ethnic Approach to Regional Culture.* Baton Rouge: Louisiana State Univ. Press.

Rogers, George C., Jr. 1969. *Charleston in the Age of the Pinckneys.* Norman: Univ. of Oklahoma Press.

Rosen, Robert N. 1992. *A Short History of Charleston.* 2nd ed. Charleston: Peninsula Press.

Thomas, Erik R. 2001. *An Acoustic Analysis of Vowel Variation in New World English.* Publication of the American Dialect Society 85. Durham, N.C.: Duke Univ. Press.

Torbert, Benjamin. 2004. "Southern Vowels and the Social Construction of Salience." Ph.D. diss., Duke Univ.

Trudgill, Peter. 1974. *The Social Differentiation of English in Norwich.* Cambridge: Cambridge Univ. Press.

———. 2004. *New-Dialect Formation: The Inevitability of Colonial Englishes.* New York: Oxford Univ. Press.

Turner, Lorenzo D. 1945. "Notes on the Sounds and Vocabulary of Gullah." *Publication of the American Dialect Society* 3: 13–28. Repr. in *A Various Language: Perspectives on American Dialects,* ed. Juanita V. Williamson and Virginia M. Burke, 121–35. New York: Holt, Rinehart, and Winston, 1971.

Vance, Timothy J. 1987. "'Canadian Raising' in Some Dialects of the Northern United States." *American Speech* 62: 195–210.

Ward, Michael. 2003. "Portland Dialect Study: The Fronting of /ow, o, uw/ in Portland, Oregon." M.A. thesis, Portland State Univ.

Weinreich, Uriel, William Labov, and Marvin Herzog. 1968. "Empirical Foundations for a Theory of Language Change." In *Directions for Historical Linguistics: A Symposium,* ed. W. P. Lehmann and Yakov Malkiel, 95–188. Austin: Univ. of Texas Press.

Weldon, Tracey L. 2004. "Gullah: Phonology." In *A Handbook of Varieties of English,* vol. 1, *Phonology,* part 2, "The Americas and the Caribbean," ed. Edgar W. Schneider, 393–406. Berlin: Mouton de Gruyter.

Wells, J. C. 1982. *Accents of English.* 3 vols. Cambridge: Cambridge Univ. Press.